D1476636

75+
Templates
Included

THE EXECUTIVE COACHING PLAYBOOK

How to Launch, Run, and Grow Your Business

NADINE GREINER, PHD & BECKY DAVIS, MA

FOREWORD BY MARSHALL GOLDSMITH

atd
PRESS
Alexandria, VA

Portions of chapter 10 are adapted from *Stress-Less Leadership: How to Lead in Business and in Life* by Nadine Greiner (2019) and are reprinted with permission from Entrepreneur Media DBA Entrepreneur Press.

ATD Press is an internationally renowned source of insightful and practical information on talent development, training, and professional development.

ATD Press
1640 King Street
Alexandria, VA 22314 USA

Ordering information: Books published by ATD Press can be purchased by visiting ATD's website at td.org/books or by calling 800.628.2783 or 703.683.8100.

Library of Congress Control Number: 2023943637

ISBN-10: 1-953946-82-8
ISBN-13: 978-1-953946-82-9
e-ISBN: 978-1-953946-94-2

ATD Press Editorial Staff
Director: Sarah Halgas
Manager: Melissa Jones
Content Manager, Senior Leaders and Executives: Ann Parker
Developmental Editor: Alexandra Andrzejewski
Production Editor: Katy Wiley Stewts
Text Designer: Shirley E.M. Raybuck
Cover Designer: Rose Richey

Printed by BR Printers, San Jose, CA

To all executive coaches who are
determined to shape the actions of leaders.

"Hope doesn't come from words.
Hope only comes from actions."
—Greta Thunberg

Contents

Foreword

For more than four decades, I have had the privilege of working with leaders across every industry and geography, helping them become the best versions of themselves. It has been a rewarding and humbling experience to see the power and impact of coaching first-hand. But as any experienced executive coach will tell you, building a robust repertoire of insights, tools, and interventions takes time and effort.

That's why I am thrilled to endorse *The Executive Coaching Playbook*, a book that presents a proven methodology, grounded in psychological theory and research. Whether you're a beginner or a seasoned coach, this book provides a wealth of insights, tools, and templates to help you upskill your coaching practice and meet the diverse and complex challenges executives face.

Dr. Nadine's four-step executive coaching process is a proven model that any coach can use to build or refine their practice. The real-life examples and templates curated from a long career in coaching will help you build or scale your coaching practice. With more than 75 templates to use in client-facing communication, coaching interventions, client practices, and building and managing your business, this book will arm you with the tools you need to make a real difference. The focus on relationship skills throughout the book highlights the crucial importance of building, maintaining, and cultivating relationships with your clients. This is the key to building a lasting coaching practice and what defines truly great coaches!

In many ways, *The Executive Coaching Playbook* is the resource the industry has been needing. It will become your best guide and reference, and applying the insights and methods from this book will help set you apart in a very competitive environment.

I highly recommend this book to anyone looking to enhance their coaching practice and make a meaningful impact in their clients' lives. It is my great pleasure to welcome you to the tremendous world of executive coaching, and I urge you to keep reading and start applying the four-step model today!

—Marshall Goldsmith, Thinkers50 #1 Executive Coach
  New York Times bestselling author, *The Earned Life*, *Triggers*, and *What Got You Here Won't Get You There*

Preface

As a follow-up to my 2018 book, *The Art of Executive Coaching*, I'm back to offer you a powerful companion: *The Executive Coaching Playbook*. It's the only book that offers a proven four-step coaching model tied to more than 75 immediately usable templates for your coaching business, along with a process for building your business, key considerations for you as an entrepreneur, and methods for taking care of yourself along the way. Real client stories throughout bring to life the model and templates. The methods and aids are together a turnkey resource inspired by my 30 years of experience as an executive coach and a C-level entrepreneur. Consider this your "coaching in a box" companion proven to accelerate and deepen your coaching clients' successes.

The Art of Executive Coaching was a story-format case-study piece designed to put you in the shoes of an experienced executive coach—bringing to life coaching conversations, pain points, and victories—to give you a sense of the creativity and finesse required to successfully transform an executive. Now in the playbook, I give you what you need to bring your practice of coaching to life. You don't need to read the first book for this one to benefit you, but I stand behind the idea that executive coaching is *both* an art and a science. So if you would like to see executive coaching come to life, then *The Art of Executive Coaching* is well worth the read.

Many coaching books offer helpful insights about the *what* and *why* of executive coaching, and so this book chooses not to focus solely on coaching theory—although it does contain a solid and unique theoretical backdrop. Instead, the playbook helps you sort out the *how* with sensible advice and a blueprint for results to help you achieve success with your dream clients. I have mentored and developed aspiring new coaches with these best practices, enabling them to move with confidence into the executive coaching world. In fact, each of those mentees went on to experience success in their first year of business. That is why I wanted to write this book: to package these best practices for those looking to enter coaching and entrepreneurship.

If you're a newly minted executive coach or if you have begun a coaching practice that doesn't seem to be gaining much momentum, then this book is for you. If you have a drive for continuous learning and seek ways to become a better coach, this book is for you. If you happen to be coaching executives internal to your organization, the model and coaching processes will give you a proven method for engaging with senior leaders and supporting their individual development.

For this book, I also introduce a writing partner, Becky Davis, who did a spectacular job helping me distill what felt like mountains of experience and resources into something navigable and helpful. She sprinkles in examples and wisdom from her own coaching experience throughout, giving you an even broader perspective.

I am thrilled you are saying *yes* to your dreams of being an executive coach, and it's my deepest desire that this book become an essential companion to your journey.

—Nadine Greiner

Introduction

Coaching is deeply personal and deeply rewarding. It's an opportunity to develop a dedicated relationship with your client, helping them unlock their potential while working through the day-to-day joys, challenges, and impacts of leading in the 21st century. It's rewarding, creative, and dynamic work to support another leader in achieving their goals, deepening their strengths, and addressing obstacles that may be holding them back from advancing or reaching their professional aspirations. Coaching helps the leader change in the ways they want to change, and sometimes change in the ways essential for their effectiveness as an executive. It helps guide clients and deepen their capacity to take in feedback from various sources to build an individual development plan. Welcome to the playbook, where I present a faster, deeper, better way of coaching your clients and running your business.

To illustrate, I'll share the story of Eric, a client with whom I developed a dynamic coaching relationship that led to his rewarding transformation. Eric sought out coaching because he was not getting promoted, despite strong performance. He heard about me through word of mouth and engaged me as his executive coach, which speaks to what can happen when you manage your business with as much focus and enthusiasm as you use to conduct your coaching services. It all comes down to the power of relationships.

Eric made a lateral job move to a large healthcare provider after many years at another "big brand" healthcare provider. Part of this move was motivated by his belief that he could grow to the next level. He was eager to prove himself and earn his VP stripes. He did all the right things: performed at a high level, managed his team to deliver, and joined a leadership academy program to grow the desired VP leadership skills. Still, no promotion.

I worked with Eric on three key competencies: authenticity, managing up and out, and ambition. I learned in the assessment interview that people had a hard time getting to know Eric. He seemed aloof and not very personable. I worked with him on being more open and authentic at work. This involved simple things like bringing a couple of photos into his office to help people find common ground on a personal level. And he did deeper work around learning to connect with others and be vulnerable to share more of himself.

> **COMPETENCIES**
>
> Throughout the book, we'll highlight the language of competencies by naming those that our clients have worked on. Competencies are the currency of coaching, and by keeping this context front of mind, you're on your way to thinking like a successful executive coach. The coaching model you will learn about in this book is grounded in competency development, which I'll cover in detail later.

Regarding managing up and out: Although Eric had many opportunities to be in front of the executive team and board, he still wasn't perceived as VP material. I worked with him on his executive presence and focused on these presentation moments as a time to show his executive gravitas. This included a small change that had a big impact: When presenting business metrics, instead of jumping into the details, Eric gave a high-level message relevant to the audience (such as "all good news this quarter") and a few bullet points to support the message. Think of it as an executive summary in presentation mode, which helped elevate others' perception of him.

Lastly, we worked on ambition. You may be surprised to see ambition as a competency for Eric to develop, given his clear goal of upward mobility. However, Eric had not told anyone—including his boss—of his goal. I worked with Eric to develop a conversation plan to communicate his interests with his boss and identify areas to focus on to get him VP-ready before the next promotion cycle. Eric finally enlisted his boss's support. And guess what—he got promoted!

Eric is just one of the dozens of executives I've invested in over my career who have brought deep satisfaction to my work. Becky and I offer many client stories throughout the book to bring concepts to life, as a peek behind the curtain of this unique relationship called executive coaching. To preserve confidentiality, we have changed the names of our clients and their businesses and industries.

The Whys

Every great coach strives to make a positive difference in and with their clients. This is your big why (we'll get into that later)—the reason you got into this profession. Whereas you're here to make a positive difference, your client seeks support for an opportunity or a goal. You can help them!

There are several reasons someone is sponsored into coaching:

- They want to prepare for the next promotion faster.
- An undeveloped key leadership expectation is holding them back.

- They are being "sent" to coaching to fix a troubling behavior or set of behaviors, sometimes with a tone of "last-ditch effort."

In addition, they may seek ongoing development and a trusted confidant. As they say, it's lonely at the top, and executives need a skilled partner to guide them as they express frustrations, experiment and fail, and learn and grow their executive competencies. That is the field and privilege of coaching.

Other reasons a client may seek coaching include:

- Identify a career or job that fits.
- Accelerate a career path.
- Find immediate success in a new job.
- Build relationships with colleagues.
- Enhance their reputation.
- Improve their ability to lead change in a fast-paced environment.
- Find more balance with the demands of work and life.

These are just a few examples of why clients seek support from you, and over your career you'll uncover many more. You have the privilege to enable, guide, and witness these life-changing moments. This affords you the fulfilling and joyful feeling of helping another person achieve something meaningful. You get the satisfaction of seeing real, significant change that lasts. That is what my way of coaching is all about.

As coaches, we are brokers of hope to entice a leader to see their opportunities for growth; recognize that despite their tremendous success, there is more to do; and ultimately help them become even more effective in their executive roles and careers. This work can have a spillover effect in clients' lives, which is also incredibly rewarding; for example, to help a partnership get back on track or to mend a wounded friendship.

The Landscape

The good news for you is that executive coaching is a booming business and can have significant financial rewards. Once a service kept mostly secret and offered to only an elite few at a company, executive coaching is now an investment offered to a much wider band of leaders and future leaders.

The coaching industry is one of the fastest-growing sectors in the world. The estimated global total revenue from coaching in 2019 was $2.849 billion, a 21 percent increase over the 2015 estimate (ICF 2020). It just keeps growing, which might explain why you picked up this book!

Coaching is growing in popularity because it works. According to the Institute for Professional Excellence in Coaching (iPEC), 99 percent of those coached were "satisfied or very satisfied," and 96 percent said that "they'd repeat the process" (Hudson 2016). A third of all Fortune 500 companies include executive coaching in their standard leadership development for their elite executives and talented up-and-comers (iPEC Coaching n.d.), and that figure is growing. Using the coaching model and business practices in this book will help you become more skillful in your work and stand out with professional skills and proven concepts, contributing meaningfully to that growing market.

What Is Executive Coaching?

I get this question all the time, especially from clients and coaches who are new to coaching and want to understand what to expect from a coaching program. Coaching offers a formal, tailored method of working with a client in a series of one-on-one meetings. The meetings are designed to establish and achieve defined competencies in a few areas relevant to the client's leadership position, level, and scope of work. The client builds competency through focused skill development and personalized development plans. Coaching is focused on the present—what the leader in front of you needs to become even more effective *now*. Executive coaching is an exciting, fulfilling, intimate, and transformative journey like no other.

For this book, an executive is anyone in a leadership capacity or with administrative authority in their company. It's up to you to further refine the type of client you're interested in working with. For example, you could focus on established C-suite leaders, vice president and director-level leaders, or leaders looking to make a professional change. That's just three client examples in this broad category of "executive," and in chapter 7, we'll consider more ways for you to specialize as you home in on your ideal client.

Ultimately, the core belief of coaching is that individuals are capable of change. It's grounded in the idea that while an individual may have the answers to their own problems and challenges, they need support finding or learning those answers in a more efficient way. Additionally, the client may need support in identifying and taking steps to improve themselves or their situation.

CLIENT SPOTLIGHT
Basking in Another's Success

The joy of coaching can continue beyond the coaching engagement. Recently, I was in the waiting room of a local medical office. I was awash in pride and happiness to see a former coaching client prominently featured on the company's mission poster, having earned another promotion since I had last seen her. I took a moment to reflect on Maria and how we worked to increase her already substantial leadership capability to position her for advancement. And look, she'd been promoted to the top job and was literally the poster child for the company's mission and values. I sat with the success of this individual and felt deep gratitude for the small part I got to play in helping her succeed. Moments like that remind me of why I became a coach: to help others achieve their dreams.

Competencies
Executive presence, strategic agility, communication skills

Sometimes the client does not have the answers. But as a coach, you have or can find the answers, because you have been an executive yourself and have both a deep understanding of human motivation and a clear, transparent method.

CLIENT SPOTLIGHT
Managing the Moment

Becky worked with Susan, an HR leader of a large manufacturing company. Susan was struggling with the demands of the work and her deeply rooted work ethic, which made it difficult for her to prioritize or say no when new requests came rolling in. Susan just worked harder, drove her team harder, and wound up feeling burned out. The coaching program helped Susan learn where her pattern of herculean effort stemmed from, which helped her manage this old pattern differently. She also learned that she was the keeper of the pressure valve and could modulate it as needed when other priorities were piling up. Lastly, Susan needed to learn how to have honest, direct conversations with her leader about how to prioritize in a dynamic environment. These conversations helped her build trust with her leader and allowed her to better manage the demands of her job. Susan's story shows how coaching influences a client's present to have real and immediately realized effects.

Competencies
Prioritization, crucial conversations, balance

Other Forms of Support That Aren't Coaching

It's important to differentiate among the many support modalities leaders and managers have at their disposal to clarify where you fit into the mix as a coach. Clients sometimes explore mentoring and counseling early in a coaching engagement as they seek to understand the differences and what to expect (Table I-1; Clutterbuck and Schneider 1998). Let's review some of the similarities and differences between coaching, mentoring, and counseling, which offer useful collaboration and insight as you work with your executives.

Table I-1. Different Learning Methods

	Coaching	Mentoring	Counseling
Question	How?	What?	Why?
Focus	Present	Future	Past
Aim	Improve skills	Develop learning goals	Overcome psychological barriers
Objective	Raise competence	Open horizons	Build self-understanding and heal past wounds

There are other means that might support a leader in their career journey. Many of these partnerships are quite specific, so they're touched on here lightly to offer some differentiation from coaching and ideas for where your client may benefit from another support structure.

Mentoring

Mentoring is like coaching in that it's an agreement between two people to help someone learn or develop on an accelerated path. A mentoring relationship usually focuses on the future, career development, and broadening an individual's horizons. Mentors can be assigned or chosen by the individual. Many workplace mentorship programs are aimed at building business acumen and expanding an individual's network within the company.

Counseling

Counseling is a powerful therapeutic intervention and can be a productive counterpart to coaching. It's done with a credentialed physician or therapist. Counseling often focuses on the past, helping the individual overcome barriers and issues rooted in their family, upbringing, and personal history. Coaching can sometimes do the same—for example, by helping a client unlearn the negative impact of a manager—but it does not explore the same depths with the same purpose.

Sponsor or Advocate

Sponsorship is essential in career progression. A sponsor can be thought of as someone who will speak on the client's behalf, especially when they're out of the room. They're the door openers who network for the client. They believe in the client and their potential. They're willing to spend some of their political capital and reputational currency to advocate for them. This might mean speaking on the client's behalf when new programs are discussed: "Monique would be a terrific program manager. In my experience, she is highly organized, able to build a high-performing team, and knows how to execute a complex project on time, on budget, and above expectations." That is a pretty terrific sponsor.

Advisor

An advisor is someone the client may call upon for specific input or guidance. This could range from business advice to troubleshooting a particularly difficult organizational situation. An advisor tends to be someone who has a strong relationship with the client, but the relationship is more transactional in nature, focused on problem solving.

For example, the client may be new to a business area and need to learn a novel technology. It's wise for this client to seek out the technical experts in the business group to learn quickly about the product and what is on the horizon from a development perspective. There will likely be a few meetings of intense learning so they can gain a working knowledge of the new technology.

Another example is board experience. Often executives have the opportunity to present to the company's board of directors. For a new leader, this can feel like being on a trapeze without a net! An advisor is that net, working alongside the new executive to help them understand the audience, what works and doesn't in this situation, and how to prepare for and practice a board presentation.

HR Business Partner

The HR business partner can be a key, well, partner for leaders. They know the organizational culture and values. They're experts on HR programs and leadership expectations. They support leaders in a broad suite of talent programs, like succession planning and annual reviews. They can be a powerful ally for a leader and a helpful input for the coaching process.

Guides

Another support structure for executives is a newer concept called a "guide" or "navigator." Internally, the guide is very helpful when an executive is new to a company (as part of onboarding) or new to a level or role (as part of the transition plan). This person, often assigned to a new executive, helps show the executive the ropes of the company. The guide has walked the path ahead of this person and figured out a few helpful things to jump-start learning and assimilation. Additionally, there are associations such as SCORE that offer business mentors who are similar to a guide as described in this section.

Requirements of a Good Executive Coach

Wherever you may be in this journey—an emerging coach who just finished coaching school and is seeking your first paying client, or an extremely experienced coach who has worked with hundreds of people over many years—those who do the best, including financially, are the ones who have a deep passion for the work itself, high emotional intelligence (EQ), and the ability to truly care for and connect with their clients. Coaching requires honesty, rigor, skill, motivation, and commitment from both the coach and the client.

After mentoring aspiring coaches and entrepreneurs for many years, I have observed that many coaching schools seem to certify new coaches without proven models that can be leveraged as they begin coaching, and very few offer practical advice for starting a coaching practice. This might leave you wondering which credentials are really necessary to be successful, and whether you really need a dual PhD (no, you don't). The main requirements for being a great executive coach are:

1. **Experience as an executive or a senior leader.** Experience is the best teacher, so it's necessary to have operated at or near the level of your clients. This helps you gain a true sense of their challenges and their world. Having worked as an executive or a leader gives you credibility and confidence to operate as an effective executive coach. It gives you the ability to translate your own experiences into competencies—what it takes to be highly effective at this level—and to use those competencies to help your client grow. Unlike some other methods of support, in coaching I encourage you to offer your expertise to support a client in their growth. Why let your client spin and waste time if you have experience in an area?

2. **Deep understanding of human motivation.** An essential role of a coach is to keep your client engaged in making significant changes through the coaching process. Knowing how to identify and stimulate their motivation is key as you work together

to create an individual development plan (IDP) and engage in experiments, observations, and reflection to tie coaching work to the outcomes that motivate your client. Having and honing your ability to identify levers to motivate your client, keep them engaged, and offer meaningful rewards that keep them in the game is a core competency. Your client may be motivated by prestige, approval (even your approval!), enhancing their public image, mastery of their role or a skill, competition and winning, rewards and recognition, accomplishing something important, or belonging in a team, organization, or community. The list is almost endless—we are all unique in our experiences and approach to our work. During the initial chemistry meeting with your client, and then throughout the coaching engagement, tune into what your client says about what motivates them. Use these insights to keep them motivated to do the work of the coaching program. If you don't have a psychology degree (or perhaps you do, but you forgot the motivation classes!), consider taking a class or module in human motivation.

3. **A clear and transparent methodology.** You're in the unique and privileged position of working with a human being on important goals for their work and life. You should not enter this dynamic without a proven methodology. That is the focus of the first half of this book: providing a proven method to have a powerful, productive coaching engagement that is fulfilling and reaches the client's goals. Develop your capability and confidence with this method, and then hone your capability as you work with each client.

If you meet these requirements, you do not need to go through a coaching certification program to be successful. If you do want to go through a certification program, make sure to vet it thoroughly. I also recommend that you have a coach yourself—one who has successfully built a coaching business. The support from your own coach will help ensure the coaching you provide is free of your own biases. You could also join a forum for coaches to compare notes and share trials.

Executive coaches must create a safe, structured, and trusting environment. The coaching relationship is creative and dynamic with a goal to maximize the leader's professional potential. The best coaches inspire their clients to build leadership competencies, experiment with new skills, reflect on the outcomes and impacts, and set goals to continue to improve. Executives do great things and achieve monumental goals thanks, in part, to an effective coach.

To build on the previous three facets of your strong foundation, the following key skills are crucial to have and develop throughout your coaching career:

1. **Listening.** It may be obvious, but listening is a forgotten art in leadership. Being able to listen to what is being said and not said is an essential skill. Learn to hear how something is being shared, and use those cues as opportunities to explore the message further. Pay attention to tone, word choice, and body language as cues for important information and areas to further explore.

2. **Asking skillful questions.** Knowing when and how to post provocative questions is the science and art of coaching. This is learning to tune into your instinct about what is being shared and ask the question that needs to be asked to deepen your client's learning and development. For example, you might have a client who is skilled at throwing blame and refusing to take ownership of issues. Reflecting this tendency back to your client can open up a meaningful dialogue about this pattern. You'll find many skillful questions in chapter 4.

3. **Courage.** Coaches must have the courage say the thing that needs to be said, even if that's not what you would say in "polite conversation." You are the client's champion and, in some ways, also their challenger. It's your job to help them stay focused on growth, take risks to try new things, and learn from what actions they take (or don't take).

4. **Building rapport.** This is a unique relationship, and knowing how to build rapport quickly and maintain trust is essential. For example, making eye contact, asking clarifying questions, and restating what your client says can be powerful ways to develop rapport, elicit honesty, and uncover truths, especially with clients who are less than enthusiastic about plumbing the depths of the issues you were hired to explore.

5. **Emotional intelligence (EQ).** This is your ability to perceive, use, understand, and manage emotions in real time in a coaching conversation. Learning to recognize your own emotions and those of others will help you create a safe space for your client to practice new competencies, whether that be effective delegation or delivering a strategic plan to the company's board of directors. It also helps you tune into what is happening with them in each session to ensure the appropriate climate for development.

6. **Focus.** It can be enticing to get caught up in the story or crisis of the day. These are meaningful things happening in your client's life. However, your job is to hold

the thread of development throughout the coaching journey, from conversation to conversation and in between. Stay focused on the IDP, the actions and experiments, and client observations in each session. Don't let your client stay too long in their stories; bring them back to their development of competencies.

7. **Identifying executive competencies.** Building on your experience as an executive, you have an ability to identify competencies that another leader may need to develop. By pulling from your own experience and leveraging the resources in this book, your ability to quickly and succinctly identify relevant executive competencies to deepen or develop will be key to your success as a coach.

8. **Summary and reflection.** It's helpful to know how to summarize key points, share those with your client, and offer reflection on what has been shared. This can help your client see things from another perspective, understand more thematically what may be happening, and take further action on their development areas.

What Makes a Good Entrepreneur?

In addition to the core capabilities to be an amazing executive coach, you also need the chops to run your own business. This is covered at length in the second half of this book, including several assessments to help you identify your strengths and where you might need to further develop your entrepreneurial skills.

To foreshadow, think about the breadth of responsibilities you will carry as an entrepreneur and how you'll plan for excellence in each key area (Figure I-2).

Figure I-2. The Buckets of Entrepreneurship

Do the Work
- Coach
- Consult
- Continuous development
- Collaborate

Business Operations
- Budget
- Invoicing
- IT
- Goal setting

Build the Pipeline
- Client meetings
- Proposals
- Networking
- Follow-ups

You are likely highly skilled in several areas and can ground your start as an entrepreneur in these strengths. There are probably also areas where you are not as strong because you haven't had the exposure, education, or experience to deepen those skills. No problem; loads of resources are available to help you round out your entrepreneurial skill set.

The Power of Relationship

I discuss the intentional client-coach relationship throughout this book, so I thought it might be helpful to foreshadow what this means in the context of a coaching relationship, which I expound on in chapter 1. Research shows that the strength and quality of the coach-client relationship are the best predictors of positive outcomes (DeAngelis 2019). That's why I focus deeply and with some urgency on this topic. I cannot overstate the importance of having and always strengthening relationship skills. A caring, trustworthy, and skilled executive coach builds a strong, positive relationship to support their clients in achieving their dreams and becoming the desired future versions of themselves.

You may have many kinds of relationships in your life. Some are temporary or transactional; others are deep and enjoyed over many years or even decades. The effective coaching relationship is both profound and temporary, which is one of the reasons it is unique and powerful for both your client and you.

Another, perhaps more important, reason this relationship is unique is the nature of the work you manage together. You are on the inside of a successful executive's world, where they have ascended to a high level in a company and an industry, lead large teams, manage huge budgets, navigate constantly changing landscapes in their industry, and work with hundreds of people week in and week out. Most leaders are not prone to showing weakness or sharing lofty goals with just anyone. You are their broker of hope, the person engaged with them to help them achieve their goals and grow their capabilities—often beyond what they had envisaged. This is a highly vulnerable engagement that demands trust and support from both parties. You are of service to your client in a unique and transformative way.

Because of this unique relationship, it's crucial that you engage with a particular focus, skill, and intention. You need to continuously develop mutual trust and respect throughout the entire coaching program and keep communication lines open and customer focused at all times. Your ability to build and maintain a transformative relationship with your client becomes the calling card for your entire business. Coaches who struggle with relationship skills will certainly struggle to be effective executive coaches. These competencies are fundamental—the essence of coaching. Without them, great coaching is not possible.

There are five superpowers when it comes to relationship skills in coaching: beacon of hope, customer focus, monitoring and building the relationship, integrity and trust, and perspective. These are covered in detail in chapter 1 and called forward throughout the first half of the book to highlight the most critical relationship skills at each step of the coaching process.

In This Book

As an executive coach with the opportunity to transform leaders, you have a powerful influence on the success of your leader's company and its people. Because you have that responsibility, I want to thoroughly equip you for the job.

Part 1 of the playbook is focused on the four-step coaching process and the tools and templates I have used in each phase of executive coaching. You'll learn everything you need to know about beginning, assessing, setting goals for, implementing, and closing out a coaching engagement. I offer you a proven methodology with numerous client examples to illustrate key points. Downloadable documents and templates make the application of my method truly turnkey, saving you time and effort every step of the way. Creative prompts and checklists help you think through solutions to your most pressing problems.

Check Out the Templates!

More than 75 templates are offered for your use, in whole or in part, to help you put these tools to work immediately. Put them in your own words, make them your own, and choose the ones most useful for you and your coaching business. Remember to put your business logo and information on them to begin to build your brand! The templates are all downloadable online at www.td.org/book/the-executive-coaching-playbook.

Part 2 is about you—the entrepreneur—and your business. I explore what it means to be an entrepreneur: the good, the bad, and the ugly. I offer guidance on defining your business and setting yourself up for success with the right business structures to start or grow your practice. Start-up ventures can be challenging; these business insights and templates will help stack the odds in your favor. I also talk about how to take care of yourself in this thrilling and challenging world of entrepreneurship. You are, after all, the heartbeat of your company, and if you don't take good care of your mental, emotional, physical, social, and spiritual needs, your business will suffer.

I will know I have succeeded in helping you as a coach and an entrepreneur when you are thriving in your practice and your work is helping shape and improve the work of the executives you coach. These individual improvements extend to their teams and companies, changing how they perform and increasing their chance to make a positive impact in their industry and on the world. While you may think about coaching as a one-on-one engagement with a local impact, I like to think about the aggregate impact of all coaches and how making one small change or improvement with one leader can have a global impact. That is the hope and inspiration for the work all coaches do.

Becky and I want to see this book beside you at a coffee shop, with writing in the margins and important pages turned down for quick reference, a statement of your joyous consumption of the content and key learning. Read it, make notes, put stars next to important topics, and underline key points you want to remember. And take advantage of the vast library of templates and tools prepared for your coaching practice, adapting them to your needs.

Becky and I wish you great success, a thriving business, and deep professional and personal fulfillment in this noble profession!

PART 1

The Coaching Method

Chapter 1
Begin Your Coaching Engagement

"Coaching is unlocking a person's potential to maximize their growth."
—John Whitmore

"The ability to learn is the most important quality a leader can have."
—Padmasree Warrior

"I absolutely believe that people, unless coached, never reach their maximum capabilities." —Bob Nardelli

In this chapter, I cover:

- An overview of the four-step executive coaching process: assessment, goal setting, implementation, and review and wrap-up.

- Establishing your client: Learn how to build authentic and memorable rapport while taking care of the business side of coaching efficiently and effectively.

- Identifying client personas: Explore how your client may fit the mold of some classic profiles, and use that as your springboard for considering how coaching will benefit them.

- Managing the sponsor: Many of your clients will be sponsored in a coaching engagement. Make a plan for how you will care for this important relationship.

- The power of relationship: Take an in-depth look at how the relationship fuels a coaching engagement and the relational competencies you'll need to nourish.

- Uncoachable clients: Examine what this might look like and how you can react constructively.

My model of coaching yields fast and deep results for your coaching clients—and makes for a smooth ride for you, the coach. I have built and honed this method over 30 years, using a unique blend of experience:

- **Executive leadership.** I led my first company as a CEO at 38.
- **Psychology education.** I have a PhD in clinical psychology.
- **Adult learning expertise.** I have a PhD in organization development.

This trifecta of key ingredients makes up the model you'll learn in this book. When I founded my practice, I called it "personal consulting" because the term *executive coach* didn't exist yet. Now, in a business world that's more attuned to the benefits of executive development, you will learn to employ the process with transparency and confidence.

As we begin the four-step model, let's assume that you have a client (yay!) and that the groundwork needs to be set for a successful coaching engagement. In the second half of the book, I discuss more about how to land clients, with a whole chapter dedicated to business development and client acquisition.

The Four-Step Coaching Process

The coaching process I outline in the coming chapters is divided into four steps:

- Assessment
- Goal setting
- Implementation
- Review and wrap-up

You'll want to make sure that the client, the sponsor, and anyone involved in the client's development understands the purpose of each step. "Overview of the Coaching Process" (Template 1-1) lays out the components of each step as a visual checklist, so you can pull it out as an aid whenever you're talking to someone about the process.

In a multimonth coaching program, the time invested in each stage varies. In general, the assessment and goal-setting steps are about 25 percent of your time, implementation is about 70 percent of your time, and review and wrap-up is the final 5 percent. You mostly spend your time on implementation with your clients, which is built upon the previous two steps; exquisite work in assessment and goal setting supports a more meaningful implementation.

Looking ahead to the overall coaching program, the approach, frequency, and duration can vary widely. A six-month program is a common approach, with coaching sessions held every other week. Another approach is more intensive workshops with a client, spending multiple hours on-site with them, then meeting again several weeks or months later. The approach you use is designed with and for the client, to meet their needs while ensuring a frequency that keeps them in the process throughout the program.

At times, you may have a client who wants to continue the coaching engagement past the initial coaching program design. Perhaps they secured the new job, got the promotion, changed companies, or have a more persistent development goal that needs a bit more time to refine. You can manage this request by securing another coaching contract and continuing the coaching program, perhaps revisiting the individual development plan (IDP) given the updated circumstances. Your client may simply want the option to "phone a friend" to get them through a transition or tough circumstance; in that case, you can sort out your pricing and agreements for this more just-in-time coaching support. Be prepared for this request, which occasionally comes up toward the end of your initial coaching engagement.

Template for Success

> Template 1-1. Overview of the Coaching Process
> An overview of the four-step executive coaching process for you to share with your potential client, 360 interviewees, sponsors, and so on. You can also use it as a marketing piece.

Assessment

The assessment process is crucial because it sets the stage for the entire coaching journey. In this step, you begin to build rapport and a relationship with your client focused on supporting their development. You start collecting information and data from your client and their key stakeholders and putting together patterns and ideas about competencies that could be appropriate for the client.

The initial assessments are meant to help you have a full and true picture of your client: their strengths and areas for growth, and even behaviors they may be unaware of. These assessments allow you to uncover the opportunities that coaching is uniquely positioned to support, and quickly and objectively align with your client and key partners on the priorities for the coaching program and their role in the development journey. This is like an X-ray of your client: no secrets, no surprises.

The assessment step includes these processes, which are mapped out in detail in the next chapter:

- **Self-assessment.** This reveals the executive's perception of their strengths and areas for development.

- **360 feedback.** This helps uncover how the executive is perceived by four to six close leaders, peers, and direct reports. You get important insight about what the client needs to do more of, do less of, start, or stop. You also hear the priorities from each of these individuals about the top things this leader can do to improve the team or organization.
- **Psychological profiles.** Conduct personality, psychological, and performance assessments, each of which has unique value and insight. Together, they uncover important themes for your leader.
- **Other inputs.** These could include business plans, performance reviews, employee engagement data, or customer feedback.

Goal Setting

The next step is to define goals with your client. Together, you review all the inputs received in the assessment process and align on the top competencies for the coaching program. I recommend three to five focus areas to improve the likelihood of making gains in these critical areas. In this stage, I extensively use the book *FYI: For Your Improvement* by Michael Lombardo, and recommend that both you and your client have this critical tool handy. You will also lean on it heavily during implementation.

In defining goals, your client creates (with your guidance) the IDP, which is the bedrock of the coaching engagement. You agree on competencies, skills, behaviors, and measures of success. You discuss the timeline and processes by which the program will be implemented. And, you help your client identify resources available to them to support their growth.

You also discuss obstacles and challenges, and plan for ways to overcome them. Encourage them to review the IDP with their manager and colleagues so they can begin to feel the support structure available to them as they start the coaching journey.

Implementation

Now the work begins in earnest! The implementation step is where the bulk of the coaching journey happens, with a sequence of coaching sessions over several months. You implement actions and experiments that are aligned to the competencies identified in the IDP. These are new behaviors or ways of leading that your client is motivated to develop or improve. Often homework is assigned to help your client deepen their understanding of a topic or apply the learning in a new way. Your client brings in observations about those experiments, what they learned, and what they will try next time. You and the client review how these actions and experiments are or are not moving them toward their identified goals.

There is rich discussion and feedback in each session, aligned to the competencies your client seeks to improve, such as decision making, planning, time management, or political savvy. You uncover barriers and tackle them immediately with helpful interventions. You continue to shape their motivation and keep them engaged in their development. The templates in the implementation chapter will help you consider interventions and experiments aligned to targeted competency development.

Your client is working hard to practice a new way of thinking, behaving, and being. This is tough work, but it's essential to ingraining new executive competencies. During this step, you will both lean on the power of your coach-client relationship to progress toward executive competencies. This will motivate your client and help them feel safe to try new things, and it should be part of the undercurrent of every coaching meeting.

Review and Wrap-Up

When you're about three-quarters through the implementation step, you should begin wrapping up with your client. Conduct a post-360 process to collect feedback from the initial input group to determine if your client has achieved the desired changes in competencies, skills, behaviors, and measures of success. This gives you powerful feedback to focus the final 25 percent of the coaching program on ensuring that the key stakeholder group is experiencing shifts in your client. You also have an opportunity to advocate for your client with these key individuals, seeking their support of your client and the hard work your client is pursuing.

In this step, you document and celebrate wins with your client. You provide an updated assessment, include recommendations for continued work, and encourage your client to share this information with their leader. When there are only a few coaching sessions left, remind your client that the end of the coaching engagement is coming; ask what they want to focus on in the remaining time you have together, perhaps informed by the updated 360; and begin to prepare them for separation from their trusted partner—you! Let them know you'll want to reflect on the coaching journey and share feedback with each other in the final coaching session so they can prepare with intention and forethought.

Finally, it's time to part ways, for now. The final sessions are a time for your client to reflect on the journey, share what they've learned, and offer any feedback to you as a coach to support your continued growth. You secure agreements about continued contact and separate thoughtfully. This is a time to wrap up this one-of-a-kind relationship and create a reflective, supportive, thoughtful goodbye.

Establishing Your Client: The First Meeting

Congratulations—you booked your client! Clients come to you in various ways: through your own business development or networking, through referrals from colleagues or other coaches, or by word of mouth from prior clients, just to name a few. It's important to get started with the client as soon as possible.

You have probably already met the client and their sponsor (if they have one) during a chemistry meeting (covered in chapter 9). However, there is still helpful context to be set as you begin a client engagement. All the up-front work to prepare yourself for a successful coaching engagement is just as important as the engagement itself. In fact, without a little homework and preparation, you might not secure that client after all. You may have already gathered some of the following information when you first met the client or their sponsor, so try to be as efficient as possible in these meetings by avoiding redundant questions or asking the leader to do more intake work than you truly need.

A corporate client (often an executive leader or the head of HR) might contact you about a particular employee they'd like you to coach. We'll call this person the "sponsor" throughout the book—the person who is engaging you if it's not the executive themselves. Although the person who pays you may or may not be this executive leader, your true client and your focus is the person you're working with in the coaching program. That is whom I will refer to throughout the book as your "client."

An individual client may seek out coaching services directly, perhaps learning about you through a colleague or friend. Because this person is paying out of pocket to secure your services, not as part of a corporate contract, it signals high motivation for what coaching has to offer.

It's helpful to remember that regardless of how the relationship came about, everything you do from this point forward should be in conjunction with building and maintaining rapport. Relationship building is the result of your thoughtfulness in the questions you ask and the way you ask them.

Getting Started With a Sponsor

If your client has a sponsor, request a meeting with both of them as soon as you can. If your client's company is sponsoring coaching as part of a program, it's important to include the program manager in the intake and evaluation process. Include them in the interview process as well: Ask them about the leadership requirements in the program, and clarify what this leader (your client) is expected to master. Template 1-2 offers an email template for the sponsor outreach.

Do a little homework before this meeting, but remain open to what gets revealed in the initial conversations with your sponsor. Learn about the company and industry, especially if they are new to you. Come prepared with thoughtful questions for the sponsor about the purpose of the coaching program, why this executive is being selected at this time, and the leadership model and expectations for this leader. Template 1-3 gives you a good framework for this conversation with the sponsor, but tailor it to your situation so you can maximize time. You might even want to share these questions with the sponsor in advance so they're prepared.

This first sponsor meeting is meaningful and instructive. It's crucial that you understand their expectations, how they have been working with or coaching your client on the topics of interest, and how they will stay engaged throughout the process. You will find out who your coaching client is and take care of the business side of contracting your services.

If you're hired for an in-house leadership development academy or acceleration program, the coaches (there are often more than one to cover the needs of the cohort) meet with the sponsor first to understand the goals and outcomes of the program, the rules of engagement, the purpose of the program's coaching piece, and the program's curriculum and timeline. A group kickoff will likely cover this foundational information, and then you'll be matched with your clients.

For a closely managed engagement like those described in the book, it would be more common to meet with your client and sponsor together at the beginning to set expectations, in the middle to check progress and make any adjustments, and again at the end to review progress and outcomes. Although you will get some information about *who, what, why,* and *why now* from the hiring executive, the real insights and purpose will emerge in a conversation with your client, so be sure to schedule that as soon after the initial sponsor briefing as possible.

Templates for Success

> **Template 1-2. Sponsor Outreach Email**
> An email to arrange a meeting with your client's direct leader and the leadership program manager
> before the coaching engagement begins. You'll use this meeting to ensure that the sponsors are engaged
> in the coaching process and that you understand their goals for sending their employee to coaching as
> part of the leadership development program. Your client should also be present at the meeting.
>
> **Template 1-3. Sponsor Interview**
> When someone other than your client has hired you, this is a starting interview format to collect
> initial information about your client, the company, and leadership expectations.

Getting Started With the Coaching Client

When coaching is sponsored, it's still important to meet the coaching client early and determine if you have good chemistry for the development partnership. You'll want to understand if your client knows why coaching is being offered to them, especially if the sponsor has a "fix this behavior" tone. You'll also want to assess if the client appears open to coaching and development. Do they respond to your initial questions with an open posture and interest in learning more? Or do they seem defensive or overly tied to their title, position, or authority? Conversely, be aware of how you are coming across. Your goal is to be warm, authentic, articulate, prepared, respectful of their time, organized, and confident about your clear method (all good coaching competencies to hone throughout your career).

Your client is a busy executive who will want to know what they're getting into. They will begin deciding right away "if the juice is worth the squeeze." Your job is to help them see the tremendous investment being provided and why it's in their best interest to engage in this development opportunity fully and openly. You can use the worksheet in Template 7-3 to help your own thinking about the return on investment (ROI) of your coaching offering and maybe share it or its concepts with the sponsor.

During this meeting, ask the client, "Why coaching now?" Perhaps they have just taken a new job and could use some focused support for the first 90 days. Or they may be on a succession plan for the top job. Or maybe they have a few key competencies to develop, such as executive presence, public speaking, and strategic planning. Coaching can accelerate this development and prepare them to be succession-ready much sooner than if they were on their own. You can use Template 1-4 as a guide for the conversation.

ON THAT NOTE
Meeting Location

A coaching engagement involves lots of meetings, so it's important to discuss where to meet. Virtual coaching over a videoconferencing platform has become the norm, and the good news is that these tools allow executives and their coaches to continue with their programs regardless of work location. The downside is that a lot is missed when meeting only virtually. I highly recommend that at least a few of your coaching sessions are in person, to bring back more of the deep learning and relationship building that is available only in person. Although this is more time-consuming and might narrow your client base to those geographically closer to you, in-person coaching yields better results.

If you can meet in person, be sure the setting is appropriate and private. You should also build in observation time to see your client in action with their team or key customers. Sometimes, weather and time permitting, it's nice to get out of the office and change up the scenery for your coaching session. Go on a walk or find a quiet spot in a nearby park. Shifting location can be a powerful lever for learning new things about your client. Of course, build into your contract the time and cost of travel.

Underscore with your client the difficulty of doing new things and learning new skills. Help them understand that what is difficult is not impossible. You are there to support them in their journey and help them learn competencies like executive presence, collaboration across organizational boundaries, or listening and communication skills to achieve their goal of a promotion, increased job scope, or creating a productive and positive team climate. As you can see, a lot happens in this initial meet and greet!

In subsequent meetings, you will share the purpose of coaching and the overall timeline for the coaching program. You will review the four steps of the executive coaching process (Template 1-1). I recommend also sharing your executive coaching bio, which we'll review in chapter 9 (Template 9-2). Helping your client understand what coaching is, why it's being offered, and what to expect is essential.

At the end of this first meeting, or even before the meeting, ask your client to complete a self-assessment (more on this in the next chapter), which provides an essential tuning fork for their self-awareness and growth path. It's helpful to learn in this initial conversation the individual's goals for coaching. This engages them right at the start with thinking about their goals and how executive coaching can help. In advance of the first meeting, if you think this will be perceived positively and not as a time burden, you might request the client fill out and return a client intake form (Template 1-5) for basic information, as well as a coaching history form (Template 1-6) if they have worked with a coach in the past.

ON THAT NOTE

Paperwork

Many organizations and prospective clients do not like to do paperwork, especially of a personal nature. If your process is to obtain notes from the client, consider pre-filling as many fields as you can. This reduces the burden for them. If your client is not able or doesn't want to spend time on an intake form, you can use it as a template for your initial calls with them to guide your own thinking and initial exploration. Then keep these completed forms for your reference throughout the coaching engagement. Some clients may be concerned about privacy, so develop a clear guideline for how you store these materials and your document retention and removal timelines.

Your contractual terms and other initial documents are helpful to get organized and be prepared to present to your prospective client. Template 1-7 outlines the expectations I set with clients about our coaching agreement. If you'd like to move forward, you can give this to your client or at least review the expectations in conversation. If your client agrees to the expectations and your way of working, share an accountability form (Template 1-8), which they can use to select ways they'd prefer you to hold them accountable. For example, if they're not prepared for a meeting, does the client want you to reschedule with no questions asked, or would the client prefer you to press the issue and uncover why they weren't prepared? Again, this document is optional and can be reviewed in conversation if it'll be better received by the executive.

Templates for Success

Template 1-4. Client Interview
A conversation guide to learn all you can about a new client, their life as a leader, and their company and industry. This agenda is the framework for your first one to two conversations, depending on the amount of time you initially secure with your client.

Template 1-5. Client Intake Form
An intake form to learn a few basics about your client.

Template 1-6. Coaching History Form
A form that summarizes a client's history and results with prior coaches. This helps you understand their experience and engagement with other coaches to bring additional insight to your engagement. It also gives you perspective on how they think about a coach and early and helpful hints about the topic of relationships.

Templates for Success (Cont.)

Template 1-7. Expectations of Coaching Engagement Agreement
This sets the stage for accountability and initial agreements between coach and client. Note that a C-suite client is unlikely to want or need this, so adjust accordingly! Use this with clients who need a lot of structure and accountability. You can cover this in a coaching session and send it as follow-up for your client to complete and send back.

Template 1-8. Accountability Form
A form for the client who needs support outlining how they'd like to be held accountable.

Possible Client Personas

Many people seek coaching, and from my experience, a few archetypes can help you quickly get to the heart of the matter with different personas. After coaching executives for many decades, I have developed a few character profiles among this elite bunch of business leaders (Figure 1-1). Because they tend to be common personas among executives and can jump-start your thinking, I think they're helpful to share with the caveat that you must keep an open mind.

Figure 1-1. Common Leadership Personas

The archetypes are a good springboard as you head into the assessment step of your engagement. They can help you more quickly and deeply understand your client to the extent that the archetypes really fit them. But don't use them to stereotype your clients—

people are more complex than this! Be open to changing your mind and nuancing your judgment as the engagement unfolds. Let the process of getting to know your client be the truth in defining their unique persona.

You will likely walk away from your initial meetings with a good sense of your client and which of these personas feel like a possible fit:

- **Strategist/politician.** The strategist/politician is adept at reading the environment, building relationships helpful to achieving their goals, and influencing up. They are savvy conversationalists and quickly know who has the power in any situation. They may come to coaching to improve their peer relationships or more effectively inspire their organization to action.

- **High potential.** Many high potentials are on a steep trajectory and seek continuous growth. They may not have received development feedback before. Their skills are high and their desire for growth is even higher. They can be demanding and seek an intense level of engagement and sponsorship from their leadership. Many high potentials are part of special programs that include executive coaching to help them accelerate readiness for their next position.

- **Technical expert.** The technical expert is the person in the room who has the deep medical, scientific, or technical expertise required for the team or business to be successful. They may be an extremely talented software engineer who needs to develop some people skills, or an expert physician who wants to build stronger care teams. They bring essential technical skills to the team, and many seek a chance to round out those talents with other interpersonal competencies.

- **High performing.** Even leaders performing at a high level seek coaching. They may be on the succession plan for the CEO seat and need to grow in certain areas like managing a board or engaging with the investment community. They may be on the cusp of rotating to a completely new area of the company as part of their development and be seeking coaching to prepare. Every leader has areas to grow or improve and development is never-ending.

- **Operations.** Many operational leaders are the backbone of their company. After all, a company can't run without effective operations in place. These leaders may need to grow their executive presence or presentation skills. They may need to improve their strategic thinking to balance out their robust analytical and operational thinking.

- **Fix 'em, please!** This is a catchall for another common client—the "improve specific skills" client. This can be someone who has an area for development that needs to be illuminated to continue to grow in the company, or a specific situation between colleagues that needs special attention. The behavioral needs are clear, and coaching is called in, sometimes as a last-ditch effort to help turn something around.

Think about these individuals: Which are you drawn to? Which may be challenging for you?

Keep the Sponsor Involved Throughout

It's important to remember the person funding this work if it's not the client directly. Keep the sponsor, typically the executive or HR leader in the company who is funding the coaching, apprised at the outset of the coaching program, with optional check-ins midway and at the conclusion. You want your client's leader or sponsor involved and invested in their development and acting as a day-to-day champion of this work. Your client is most likely a highly valued employee who is receiving coaching to help them accelerate to the next level, deepen or broaden their abilities, or quickly step into a new level or position. Their sponsor might need them to be successful in this work as quickly as possible.

Be sure to include your client in all conversations related to their development. You want your client to be present because you're brokering the conversation for development with their leader or sponsor. If there is any misalignment, you want your client present to help advocate for their development and ensure continued agreement and alignment with the development areas.

It's important to keep an oath of confidentiality with your coaching client. Therefore, any check-ins with the sponsor should only include process comments. For example, you might explain that you are halfway through the first step, still gathering the assessments and the 360 information. Or, you could say that you just finished the IDP and would be happy to share the competencies you're focusing on but are not at liberty to give details.

The first half of the IDP, which lists competencies, behaviors, and challenges, is the only nonconfidential part of the document. It's high-level enough, especially without the experiments, to share. Keep the client's profiles and 360 input handy, but never, ever provide this detailed information to the coaching sponsor. This is for your confidential work with your client, not to be shared more broadly. It's imperative that you never dip into the content of the coaching conversations or the work you're doing with your coaching client.

That is their development work and their story to tell, if they choose. Keep the updates to short phone calls versus extensive notes or documentation.

Sometimes a leader can attempt to enlist you in giving confidential performance feedback about their employee. However, this is not your role and it's not appropriate given the confidential nature of the coaching engagement. You can speak to the four-step model of coaching, where you are in the overall journey, and any observations about your client related to their engagement with coaching: Do they show up to coaching sessions? Are they prepared? Have they done their homework? Do they seem engaged in the experiments and the self-reflection? If the leader asks for more information, politely encourage them to set up a three-way conversation with their employee. It's the client's responsibility to represent their development plan and progress against those goals.

CLIENT SPOTLIGHT
Keeping a Promise of Confidentiality for David

At a recent executive team strategic planning session that Becky was leading, the CEO pulled her aside to check in on one of his employees who had recently begun coaching with her. He gave the "wink and nod" look when asking about David and was curious about his progress. The CEO asked for time at a break or lunch to discuss it further.

When they met, Becky addressed where they were in the coaching process, reiterated the focus areas already discussed with this leader, and shared her perspective on David's engagement in the coaching process. After she paused, the CEO then prompted, "Well, how is he doing? You know, is he going to turn this thing around?" She replied that more exploration of David's development and learning from coaching should be discussed with David present. She reminded the CEO that they had a midpoint check-in coming up in a couple of weeks, and that if he wanted to meet earlier, they could set a meeting for the three of them to discuss the coaching program. He seemed to take the point and said he'd raise his questions with David in their next one-on-one meeting.

It can be challenging to hold your ground with a leader. Becky knew that the CEO was asking from a space of kindness and desire to help, but that keeping David's development journey confidential was of utmost priority. Also holding the space for the client, David, to hear directly from his leader is a powerful connection a coach can help make happen.

Competencies:
Leadership presence, effective delegation, collaboration skills

Some sponsors want to be apprised of progress, and some do not. Asking up front what their preference is and agreeing on the number of meetings they want to have during the coaching span is helpful. You don't want to bombard them or, conversely, leave them out. Template 1-9 provides a sample email for updating the sponsor.

Your first check-in should happen during the goal-setting step. As you align with your client on three to five competencies, targeted behaviors, and the first set of actions or experiments to begin living into these new competencies, debrief the sponsor on this effort. This can be a meeting, or the coaching client could email their IDP to the sponsor, copying you. If you are meeting, propose an agenda (such as one in Template 1-10) in your email invite to focus each check-in conversation and maximize time; attach your "Overview of the Coaching Process" document (Template 1-1) to the email as well. When you secure time with the sponsor who hired you, this agenda helps you maximize your time with the leader while still allowing you to build your relationship and better understand the client.

About midway through the program, while you're in the implementation step, it might be helpful to have another check-in with the coaching sponsor, depending on what you both agreed to at the onset. This could be a simple email status update to keep the sponsor informed and engaged. If something has significantly changed from the outset, it may be helpful at this point to have a conversation. Changes could include a shift in the competencies or focus areas, challenging experiences when attempting to role-model new competencies or behaviors, a lack of sponsor support in critical group settings, or other such "yellow flags" that would be helpful to address in person. Again, this meeting would be held with your client present and addressing any of the development content in the conversation.

Near the end of the contracted coaching program, it's important to offer a final meeting with the sponsor, again depending on what the sponsor desired at the onset. Template 1-11 offers an email you can modify for the outreach to the sponsor. After you secure time with your client's direct leader or the HR leader managing your client's program, use the "Program Completion Sponsor Meeting Agenda" (Template 1-12) to review the coaching outcomes and bring their involvement in this process to a satisfying conclusion. If those templates seem like overkill, you can use the IDP to anchor the discussion. Your client's progress can be reviewed and celebrated, and any follow-up actions or further development recommendations can be contracted with the leader. If you feel more work could be done, you can assess their interest in a check-in or further coaching in six to 12 months, which can be discussed and agreed to in this meeting as well.

CLIENT SPOTLIGHT
The Value of an Engaged Sponsor

Becky coached Lani, a midlevel manager who was having difficulty with her direct manager, despite having completed an in-house mediation to address the conflict. The relationship needed intentional focus to have a chance to repair.

When asked how to engage the skip-level executive who sponsored Lani into coaching, Becky and the client agreed to set up three calls with this sponsoring VP. In the initial call, Becky reviewed the coaching model and timeline, and Lani shared her reason for seeking coaching and the key competencies she and Becky would work on in the coaching engagement. At the midway checkpoint, they reviewed progress in a similar fashion, with Becky focusing on the coaching process and Lani focusing on the development process and insights.

In the final meeting, Lani briefed the VP on the coaching outcomes. In turn, the VP was able to share the positive feedback he had received from Lani's manager and peers about the changes Lani was making and the positive impact on the team. A beautiful thing then happened. The sponsoring VP shared more about himself, his journey in the organization, and his prior experience with coaching as a huge lever in his own development. This personal reveal was a tremendous moment of connection between these two individuals and helped galvanize their own relationship in a meaningful way.

Competencies:
Communication skills, building trust, interpersonal savvy

Templates for Success

Template 1-9. Sponsor Status Update Email
An email to contact your client's manager or the sponsor of the coaching engagement, suggesting a short meeting to share progress or provide a high-level written update via email.

Template 1-10. Sponsor Check-In Meeting Agenda
An agenda to follow with your client's manager or the sponsor of the coaching engagement to keep them apprised of the coaching program's progress.

Template 1-11. Program Completion Sponsor Email
A sample email to use as you near completion of the program, securing time with the client's direct leader or the HR/L&D program leader to review the outcome of your client's coaching engagement.

Template 1-12. Program Completion Sponsor Meeting Agenda
A sample agenda to use with either the client's direct leader or the HR/L&D program leader to review the outcome of your client's coaching engagement.

The Power of Relationships

You just read about several essential relationships, so this seems like an excellent time to dive deeper into the power of relationships and the fundamental importance of relationship skills as an executive coach. Think of this as the essence of executive coaching, the core capability that will make or break your coaching engagement. Your relationship skills are key to differentiating yourself in an increasingly crowded market.

The stronger and more genuine the coach-client relationship, the easier, deeper, and faster the client progress will be. This is a key premise of my powerful and intimate method of coaching, which is also backed by clinical research.

This relationship, rooted in the X-ray of the client from their psychometric profiles and 360 input (which we'll dig into in the next chapter), is tender and vulnerable and requires continuous attention and development. This is the primary way you can help the client achieve their IDP goals and dreams.

Why the Coaching Relationship Is Critical

Research shows that the strength and quality of the coach-client relationship is the best predictor of positive outcomes (DeAngelis 2019). A caring, trustworthy, and skilled executive coach builds a strong, positive relationship to support their clients in achieving their desired future version of themselves. There is empirical research about the power of relationships, and it mirrors the link I have found between a positive relationship and excellent coaching outcomes.

For example, I often win bids over other coaches or I'm brought in without a request for proposal because of someone's direct experience working with me or through word of mouth. It's true that clients sometimes remember that there are four steps in the method, but they always refer to the relationship as what made the most difference. My ability to care and commitment to going the extra mile as part of the coaching experience made a lasting impact.

The Main Emotional Aspects of the Relationship

My approach is client-centered and bespoke. Taking the relationship from the client's perspective, we see the following three main elements:

- First, the power of being *understood* is a relationally transformative experience for clients, because people around them usually see the executive through their own lens of projections, needs, or power structures. To listen fully to your client, to slow down and fully understand what they are saying, experiencing, and hoping for—and why—is to deepen the relationship in a positive and unique way.

- The power of being *remembered* is the next, deeper layer. As the coaching work progresses, there is an evolving bank of the client's stories, facts, IDP experiments, and insights. The coach is often the primary keeper of the memory bank, leveraging that to underscore, place in context, or celebrate new competencies and the client. It can be hard for the client to simultaneously build competencies and reflect on themselves. So the coach provides this remembering in an unbiased way, reflecting the client's experiences, feelings, goals, and transformations across time, which deepens the relationship. This is a rare kind of relationship in the executive's life, and perhaps only their physician or therapist would serve a similar role. So it will feel intimate, validating, and reassuring, and ultimately provide a sense of belonging.

- The power of *caring* is the third element of the relationship. Caring involves investing emotional labor, emotional intelligence, and authenticity. It is unconditional and requires the emotional capacity for both the client and coach to receive and allow each other into their hearts. Demonstrating care can take many forms, such as verbalizing feelings or carrying out the coaching method with care embedded and expressed as appropriate throughout. It's important to be cognizant of the theoretical framework of human motivation covered later in this book. Because it can be received as a reward by the client, it's important to show caring both when things are looking up and when things are looking down, being unconditional in your care in all circumstances.

As an example, I coached a client through several promotions, from VP to SVP and eventually to CEO of a biotech company. She was a scientist originally. It's lonely at the top, especially when new CEOs are promoted over their peers and have multiple parties, like the board and the public, to answer to. I suggested we prepare her inner-circle list of advisors and loved ones, and I saw my name on the advisor list along with attorneys and other key members of her inner circle. There was an asterisk by my name and her personal note: "She cares about me."

From the coach's perspective, to fully deliver on the three main aspects of the relationship, you will have to ensure that you clear your mind of baggage and biases, such as your own past executive experiences, preconceived notions about a client, or concerns about the company they work for. You will need to make room for the relationship, which requires time, mind, and heart.

Relationship Superpowers

Seeing this situation now from the coach's perspective, there are relationship competencies that the successful coach will need to build and continuously develop to have a positive relationship with the client. Let's first turn our attention to the superpowers of relationship skills in coaching. I believe so strongly in a coach's capabilities and continuous learning in these areas that I feature them above all other relationship capabilities. Deepen your strength here, and continue to work on these relationship superpowers, and you will have done a very good deed for yourself and your business as an executive coach.

Beacon of Hope

Remember the beacon of hope mentioned earlier in the book? It's back, now within the context of the emotional tone of the relationship. The idea of partnership is important to set out at the beginning, and within that partnership, the coach is a beacon of hope. Partnership is the emotional construct of the relationship, with the recognition that you are each skilled in different areas, and the partnership is what enables you to work through the four steps of the coaching engagement to yield great results for the client. Partnership includes many relational risks, such as coach feedback to the client (and vice versa), trust, and vulnerability. Being the broker of hope in the partnership involves being able and willing to put forth alternatives or more hopeful situations than the client finds themselves in. Imagine shining a light down the path to help the client see their way through a thorny situation. That is the essence of showing up as a beacon of hope in this partnership.

Customer Focus

You need the ability to deeply understand your client and tailor the relationship to their individual characteristics, such as their cultural background, coaching preferences, emotional style, gender identity and sexual orientation, learning style, and religious or spiritual beliefs. Pay attention to different coaching methods, stances, and gestures appropriate to the client and the context. Be flexible, responsive, and willing to educate yourself on areas of life you perhaps know little about. Customer focus also involves emotional labor, being truly open to understanding and working with your client in an emotionally open and informed way. Customer focus is also demonstrated by how you structure your business and time.

Monitoring and Building the Relationship

It's fairly new to talk about these human conditions in a work setting. I meet people all the time who have no idea what an executive coach is or why you'd need one. So, working on the relationship in small bits and large sweeps is what "monitoring and building the relationship" is about.

There are power dynamics at play in a work setting that make it potentially risky to be vulnerable and share what's real in terms of relationships. The company and, by extension, the executive leadership (board or C-suite) hold most of the cards for salary, benefits, investment strategy (the company's and your own 401k!), when you can take earned vacation time, bonus structure, and many, many other aspects of earnings and job satisfaction. It can feel risky to give difficult feedback, ask for help with a board presentation, challenge a terrible boss, work toward a promotion that moves you out of your department, handle a tricky employee situation, and other leadership and management tasks a leader faces each day. How can you feel like a fully empowered free agent when there is such a power imbalance?

That is an essential job of a coach: to provide a safe space to address these obstacles and more. Focusing on the health of the relationship, in small and vast ways throughout the coaching journey, will help the coach care for the relationship while also teaching the client how to do some of the relationship work themselves.

Pay attention to how much the client opens up, trusts, and reveals. Do you start at the first step in trust-building at the beginning of each coaching session, or is there durability in the trust you have built so far?

Micro- and macro-monitoring of the relationship also includes listening for cues from your client about the health of the relationship. Watch their mood, energy level, and general outlook. Where are they placing the coach in the context of their life—as an essential relationship, an employee, a confidant, a glorified assistant? They will give you hints about how they think about you and the coaching relationship if you listen for them. Pay attention to how your client orients toward you or away from you during the coaching journey. Are they excited to tell you something, eager for the reward from you as their coach? Or do they dread telling you (or even don't tell you), because something didn't work out or they didn't do the practice exercises as agreed to? Remember to accept them as they are, in that moment, and ensure that they know they will be accepted by you as their coach no matter what they do or say. You may be the only unconditional acceptance they experience. Pay attention to how they receive it.

Integrity and Trust

I am not sure if this is a competency one can build or something one is born with; perhaps both. The coach's integrity needs to be obvious for a solid relationship to build. Being able to present options or feedback to your clients in a truthful and caring way is an important competency that helps build the relationship and establish or strengthen trust. Other aspects include admitting mistakes, keeping confidentiality, and using interpersonal savvy. Following through on commitments is important as you model integrity. You want your client to also follow through on their commitments, so it's essential that you role-model this from the beginning.

Perspective

Relationships are complex and dynamic. You may even experience shifts in the relationship within one coaching session. Perspective is also multifaceted. It's about tuning into the micro-feedback you may get from your client and attending to the relationship with a particular point of view. How is today different in tone or tenor? Did something just shift that you need to attend to? What is your perspective on the state of your relationship and dialogue at this moment?

It's also your job to offer alternatives or a new point of view to the client about their situation. Give advice, stepping in to help your client see something in a new way. Use your experiences to inform the situation and support your client in their development. This is a key competency for coaches and explored throughout the book, especially in the implementation step.

You can also directly seek feedback from your client, proactively getting their perspective, then incorporating that into the coaching goals along the way. Asking for their perspective on the relationship and how things are going is a powerful way to build trust and nurture the relationship. It also gives them a moment to pause and reflect, ensuring that any minor (or major!) irritations or missteps are discussed, versus being held in by your client.

More Relationship Competencies

For those wanting even more (gold stars!), many other relationship competencies can be useful in a coaching relationship. I briefly mention them here as encouragement and inspiration to go for more in this area of relationships.

Humor

Humor is such a stress relief and a means to build rapport and connection. It's healthy to laugh at oneself, both coach and client. The world these leaders operate in is complex, moves quickly, and is full of unseen potholes. Bringing humor into the coaching relationship helps your client find some peace from the intensity of their work world, releases endorphins, and helps strengthen the relationship. There are important cultural differences and context to pay attention to, however, and if the client says something inappropriate or offensive to any group, it's important to call that out. It's up to us to educate our clients. This can be a powerful teachable moment.

Look for a nervous laugh from your client as a potential opening. Known as Gallo's laugh, this is the nervous giggle some people let out before they do something new or are about to share something they're scared to share. If you have established a rich relationship, you will have an opportunity to ask your client, "I see you getting a bit nervous. What's coming up for you?" or some other skillful question to open the dialogue. Or maybe you leave it alone and come back to that exploration another day.

Patience

Development takes time, and busy executives are not always the most patient with themselves or others. They want to see progress quickly and can get frustrated if they don't. This is where you can support them with patience and kindness, helping them see how to give themselves these gifts. Clear out your own agenda for performance—your expectations of how quickly or efficiently this leader will "get it." They are on their own development timeline, and you are there to support them through their huge development spurts as well as help them navigate their obstacles. Remember to capture the obstacles in the IDP so you can have ongoing conversations about how to overcome them.

Handling Negative Outlooks and Emotions

Clients probably wouldn't be in coaching if they didn't have some negative feelings about the obstacles they need to overcome to achieve their goals and deepen their competencies. Unfortunately, it can be difficult for coaches to address clients' frustrations or their negative outlook. Some coaches can become frustrated themselves, which clients can take to mean there's something wrong with them. It's important to pay attention to your reactions and learn the early warning signals that you are building toward frustration. If you're distracted, bored, or wanting the coaching session to end, you probably are not in the best coaching posture to support your client. Be aware that clients can often pick up on your feelings, facial expressions, and tone of voice. Make sure there is alignment in these nonverbal and paraverbal forms of communication. If you need more time to prepare for a client and set aside your personal frustrations, build that into your preparation time.

Work-Life Balance

Pay attention to your own relational capabilities. The concept of self-care is also about your life and career as an executive coach. Where do you put the client in your life? How do you prioritize that relationship? Coaches can get overwhelmed with the emotional work that clients exact. It's important that you learn the right number of clients you can effectively serve. I'd recommend starting small and building up to a larger client base, always paying attention to your own relational capacity. As an example, someone I mentored to become an executive coach with my four-step method takes a maximum of six to 12 high-priced contracts with unlimited access per year. This allows him to be available and maintain customer focus. This approach is not for everybody, but it suits his and his clients' coaching needs.

Relational Capacity

The best coaches have the emotional capacity to engage deeply and proactively, both in the session and in between. They always keep the client in their thoughts. This helps the client feel special and important, knowing you are constantly thinking about them and their development. Relational capacity is not infinite. We each have a limited amount of capacity to care for others, attend to others' needs, and personalize learning and growth. Some clients need more of this attention than others. If you're going through a lot in your own life, that can affect your relational capacity. It's important to attend to your relational capacity in an ongoing and honest way to ensure you have the ability to care for your needs and those of others in your life and work.

Emotional Resonance

Paradoxically, it's important to maintain some distance between your client's challenges and your own experience of the same challenge. Keeping the focus on the client and their experience and interpretation of the challenging situation helps both parties to be clear about the work. Don't muddy your client's experience with your own unless it will benefit them. Stay in the space of expressing compassion and empathy for the challenge, be curious about what comes up for your client when talking about this situation, and remain laser focused on your client.

Be Real

It's tempting, especially as a new coach, to put on a facade of what a "good coach" looks and sounds like. Perhaps you think of your own coach, who had such an impact on you, or someone you saw presenting at a conference, who sounded like an awesome coach. This draw to adopt a persona can help people overcome a sense of imposter syndrome and adopt a way of coaching that they believe will be successful. The fact is, this doesn't work all that well. Putting on a face inserts a separation into the relationship. You are asking your client to trust you with potentially deeply held thoughts and challenges. You need to enter that relationship in an authentic way. Being real connects us all and keeps the focus on the client instead of maintaining a front. We are all on this planet trying to do our best, and I think it's best for you to keep it real with your clients.

Emotional Capability to Have Effective Endings

When it's time to end the coaching relationship, research by Norcross and colleagues (2017) finds that some key actions tend to promote better client outcomes. This includes having a mutual discussion about how the client did during the coaching journey, giving both the client and coach time to look back and reflect on the entire journey over several weeks or months. Then take some time to look ahead. Discuss the client's future progress without coaching, and how they will continue to use new skills and engage in competency development. Help them understand that setbacks are completely normal. And talk through how they'll recognize a setback and reengage with their practices and experiments to continue to develop through this setback. Put some forethought into how you want to celebrate and honor your client and their commitment to working toward their goals. Reflect on their gains and express pride in their progress. Be honest about your feedback and your own feelings about the relationship coming to an end, for now at least.

How to Handle Mistakes

You're going to make mistakes along this journey. Set aside the idea of perfection. You're working with humans, you're human, and mistakes and misunderstandings will happen.

When you mess up, it's crucial that you say it, own it, don't stay stuck, and move on to what it meant to the client. Eventually, at your client's pacing and preference, you'll work out a path forward, decide how to resolve the mistake or misunderstanding, and truly move on, perhaps with a deeper relationship because of the authenticity you showed in handling the misstep. Outside the client engagement, if you're having a hard time moving past this issue, discuss it with your own coach or other support to learn what you can glean from this upset. There may be times when your client can't or won't discuss the issue or holds back forgiveness. This is a moment of truth about the future of your relationship. If they can't (or won't) forgive you, it may be in the client's best interest to be referred to another coach.

In more than 30 years of coaching, I've made my share of mistakes. The concept of continuous learning applies to my coaching clients and to me, and I know every client makes me a better coach. I've probably made a few other mistakes that I didn't even realize.

For example, early in my coaching career, I had a client whose MBTI profile was the opposite of mine. I have a fairly strong J, which means I like to build and finish projects on time. My client was more on the P side, and enjoyed spontaneity and an exploratory approach. Her IDP included getting her doctorate of nursing, and the deadline for application was fast approaching. She had time management as a competency on her IDP, which we revisited each time we met. One day, instead of bringing up the topic for full discussion and planning as I usually did, I let my need for finishing projects on time get the best of me and assigned her as homework the task of applying to the program by the deadline. Not only did she not apply, but she also canceled the next two meetings with me. We were able to discuss that she was avoiding me, because she didn't apply. I owned my mistake, apologized, and fully listened to the impact my mistake had on her. We were able to recover and eventually laugh as we compared our MBTI profiles. She applied for the next deadline—three months later—in her own time and way. This was a lesson I continued to remind myself of as she continued to struggle with papers and other deadlines. But I am relieved to say that by the second year of her herculean degree and our coaching relationship, we had figured out a way for her to make and stick to her own timelines. She finished that doctorate in nursing! And I was so proud (and relieved) at her graduation.

Another example: At the first meeting with a coaching client, I mistook his umbrella for a cane. I was used to the umbrellas that fold and are brightly colored, and this was a long, nonfolding umbrella with a wooden handle. The new coaching client was perplexed, and offended that I would think he was old and needed a cane to get by. He was (fortunately) vocal about this, so we could discuss it. I listened hard and deep. I asked questions, and he relaxed. At the bottom of it, his reaction to my misunderstanding had to do with feeling old and passed by at work. It turns out that he was actually overlooked because of his age, as we learned later. But when the time was right, I apologized. I owned it all. I also mentioned the umbrellas I was used to (without trying to excuse myself), and that it was a lesson to me to look more closely. I inquired about the impact on our relationship. He laughed and said I looked like I felt so bad, how could he not forgive me? We moved on, and into a much deeper relationship than if that hadn't happened in our first meeting.

As an example of being on the receiving end of a mistake, I joined a new gym, and the new membership came with a free session with a fitness coach. I filled out the required intake form, which included my fitness goals. As we were finishing the session, the coach mentioned something like, "And you will be able to lose the weight, no problem." Now, I had not listed or mentioned weight loss as a goal, and I said so to him. He quickly apologized for his assumption, and nervously spluttered that it didn't seem like I would need to lose weight anyway. He then said, "Did I totally eff this up, or is there a chance you would still want to work with me? Because I would like to work with you." I hired him for 10 sessions on the spot. He was a great coach. I remember him more for our banter than his technical skills. He talked about life, encouraged me, and even selected music he knew I'd like. Learning from others' mistakes and forgiving others has freed me up in life and helped me be a better coach.

Key Relational Milestones

The coaching model is bookended by the "getting started" and "client retention" steps. Key relationship competencies are called upon at each step of this four-step process. Underscoring the entire coaching life cycle are three of the relationship superpowers we discussed: beacon of hope, customer focus, and monitoring and building the relationship.

Then, more specific to each step are key relationship competencies, as mapped out in Table 1-1. There will be variations and perhaps additions to the relationship skills most critical for each step. These will be different for each client and per the coach's individual skills and growth. Each step builds upon the prior steps; consequently, the relationship skills build as well.

Table 1-1. Relationship Competency Milestones

Relational Milestones	Relationship Skills
Getting started	• Integrity and trust • Being real • Work-life balance
Step 1: Assessment	• Listening • Micro-monitoring the relationship • Handling negative outlooks
Step 2: Goal setting	• Perspective • Emotional resonance
Step 3: Implementation	• Patience • Handling negative outlooks and emotions • Relational capacity • Handling mistakes • Humor
Step 4: Ending	• Emotional capability to have effective endings
Retention	• Being real
The Superpower Foundations	
• The Superpower Foundations • Beacon of Hope • Customer Focus • Monitoring and Building the Relationship	

When the Client Isn't Coachable

You'll occasionally come across someone who is just not picking up what you're putting down. They're not responding to coaching, and you can sense early in the situation that they're not fully engaged, willing, or able to do the work of competency development. There could be several reasons for this.

First, a client could simply be unwilling to do the work. They may resist doing something new or find little utility in the exercises, reflections, and practices. This situation is best resolved head-on to find out if there is any motivation or meaning you can connect with to spur action and engagement. Sometimes, someone is just uncoachable, but as the beacon of hope, you need to try several interventions to engage them and inspire action before you simply write them off.

Second, a client may not be able to engage with the practices or coaching conversations in a meaningful way. They may have too many competing priorities, like the first weeks of opening a new business line while caring for an aging parent or struggling with their own health condition. There are many aspects to a leader's life, and sometimes the timing is just not right for coaching to be as effective as possible. If this is the circumstance, have an honest conversation about what's going on with your client and decide together if now is the best time for the intense work of coaching.

CLIENT SPOTLIGHT

Too Busy for Homework?

Janelle came to me for executive coaching as part of a leadership academy at her company. In an odd way, being identified as high performing and high potential weakened her motivation—she felt too good to be coached.

She had clear goals in her IDP that were within reach and clearly in her self-interest to attain. The problem was that she did just enough of her homework and assignments to skate by. All executives are super busy, but others in the program managed to find or make time for their homework. Their hearts were in it; they were motivated and engaged at a higher level. I wondered if something was going on behind the scenes that was affecting Janelle's ability to fully engage.

I had a choice: Continue to find tactics for her to make time, or tackle the problem at a deeper level and maybe even risk the relationship. As you might guess, I chose the deeper path. I decided to approach her directly. I asked for her permission to offer an observation. When she agreed, I shared what I was seeing from her and others in the program. And then I was quiet.

Janelle opened up and let me know she had been eyeing another job in another company. We discussed the opportunity and concluded that our work together here, building her competencies toward her leadership goals, would help her in her new job as well. And we cleared out any guilt about her jumping ship from her current company and released any fear she might have been holding in telling me about this other opportunity.

From that day onward, she did every bit of homework and more. She engaged with intention and enthusiasm. To this day, she has continued to grow with the same organization, because they saw even more of her potential when she was fully engaged. And the best news? They promoted her!

The lesson here is that it pays to do homework, and it pays to take relationship risks to go deeper into why a client appears to not be showing up fully.

Third, a client may find it difficult to learn how to do something. Their behaviors may be so deeply ingrained in their family system, culture, educational background, or path to success (to name a few unconscious behavioral anchors) that they can't imagine behaving in any other way. The path of growth being offered by coaching may be asking them to operate in a way very different from what they have done up to this point. This is a beautiful chance to describe to them the opportunities that lie ahead with a broader and deeper set of capabilities, and how learning new skills can only enhance their leadership potential.

Fourth, the environment may not be conducive to supporting the client, the coach, or leadership development in general. Sometimes the organizational support is lacking, which can make it difficult to engage at the fullest level with coaching. This is an opportunity to discuss with your client the realities of their situation and how to navigate those together. This could even turn into a competency to focus on, so they face their challenging climate with more skill going forward.

Lastly, your client may continue to be unaware of their limitations, or they may stubbornly hold on to the idea that whatever negative situation they perceive is someone else's fault. This is another example of what "uncoachable" might look like, but you have many interventions you can engage to try to break through to your client. Take many runs at finding a way into their thought process and determining their motivators.

If, in the end, your actual or potential client refuses to move off their position and remains steadfastly committed to the status quo, it's best to raise this with your client with a recommendation to not start, to pause, or to end the coaching engagement. This will affect your income, but it's best to act from a position of integrity, caring more for your reputation than revenue.

Summary

As you can see, a lot happens in this initial step of getting started. I wanted to include everything, but the main focus is to meet your client and sponsor; understand their goals related to coaching; establish expectations for the coaching program; broker initial agreements, including administrative details and meeting schedules; and complete the initial conversations using the templates as guides. There is a lot of relationship building, establishing trust and rapport, and setting the context for the overall coaching engagement that sets you all up for success. When these goals have been achieved, you've successfully set the context for the coaching engagement and can move on to the first step in the executive coaching model: assessment.

Chapter 2
Assess Your Client

"The most fundamental harm we can do to ourselves is to remain ignorant by not having the courage and the respect to look at ourselves honestly and gently." —Pema Chodron

"Without the proper self-evaluation, failure is inevitable." —John Wooden

"If you want to really know somebody, talk to who they live and work with." —Granny Greiner

In this chapter, I cover:

- Building or deepening the rapport you have established with your client: Keep the relationship going, always brokering hope to the client.

- Gathering 360 feedback: Select interviewees and conduct interviews, as well as soliciting self-assessments.

- Administering psychological assessments: Select the right ones for your client.

- Synthesizing and presenting the results to your client.

The assessment step sets the stage for the entire coaching program and provides insight into the competencies that your client can benefit the most from developing. Working as a broker of hope for your client, you create and hold space for what's possible for your client in learning more about their strengths, gifts, and additional opportunities for growth as a leader. During this stage, you'll start to get an idea of some appropriate competencies for your client—communication skills, team effectiveness, executive presence, collaboration, prioritizing, delegating, and many more!

The initial assessment process is meant to help you gain a full and true picture of your client: their strengths, areas for potential growth, and even behaviors they are unaware of. Many of us lack true self-perception, but these assessments allow you to quickly uncover the opportunities that coaching is uniquely positioned to identify and support. After a good assessment, you can quickly and objectively align with your client on the priorities for the coaching program and their role in the development journey. This step is like an X-ray of your client: no secrets and no surprises.

Although this chapter focuses on assessing your client at the outset of the coaching program, it's important to note that, as a coach, you're always assessing. You're always building the relationship with your client and gathering more information. Stay curious about your client and their experiences, because your client will evolve during their work with you. Assessment is not a point in time, but something you're doing the entire time you are coaching your client.

Set the Foundation by Building Rapport

Many of the early coaching conversations with your client and key members of their circle should be focused on the relationship: building rapport, developing trust, and listening to understand. Initial meetings take a conversational style that is deeply inquisitive about what is said *and* not said.

Most of our understanding comes from speech variations, tone, pace, gestures, and facial expressions, more so than the actual words spoken. So pay attention to these inputs. For example, your client may have some preliminary topics and goals for coaching. Be sure to acknowledge and paraphrase them. Express confidence that the two of you will be able to achieve them, that they are in good hands, and that you have had success with other coaching clients with similar goals. Keep a tone of optimism, which will signal you're looking forward to being on this journey of success together. You are having both a cognitive conversation and an emotional one. The cognitive conversation is about the goals; the emotional conversation is about you two connecting with warmth, comfort, and enthusiasm.

Interviews and client meetings are an excellent time to use some of the key coaching skills mentioned in the introduction, in particular listening and courage. During assessment, you'll explore a wide range of topics relevant to your client. You're trying to understand your client's current responsibilities and the competencies necessary in their day-to-day work. Your approach to coaching should focus on how clients use their current skills to grab opportunities and face their challenges.

An essential step in building rapport and keeping trust is establishing clear agreements on confidentiality. All aspects of the client relationship are confidential—outside the client engagement, you do not share or publish your client's name, title, or organization without their express permission. You do not speak to anyone about your client's goals, the details of their development plan, or how the practices and experiments are going during implementation. This is your client's development journey and theirs to share as they see fit.

At the end of a successful coaching engagement, you may seek a referral or an endorsement from your client. This is a specific request for you to use their name in promoting your business. That is done outside the coaching engagement.

The Phases of the Assessment Step

A key differentiator of my coaching method is that the process is faster and deeper than other methods, hence yielding more positive outcomes for coaching clients. It takes a long time to know a client if you're relying only on what they tell you. Gathering input from key members of your client's circle will help you immediately grasp your client's strengths and areas for growth. The assessment step requires a bit of work up front, but ultimately it saves tremendous time throughout the coaching program.

Another key differentiator in the method is that the psychological, leadership, career, and stylistic profiles offer deep insights grounded in research that provide a full picture of motivations, professional interests, interpersonal needs, patterns, and values. These profiles help uncover key elements of your client's personality and competencies and can shed light on how they come across to colleagues. Some tools target career choices and professions, which reveal jobs that best align with your client's passions, values, and personality.

Before you can offer coaching advice or create an individual development plan (IDP) with a client, you must compile information using self-assessments, 360 feedback, and psychological assessments. This gives you a fast and well-rounded view of your client, their strengths, and their opportunities for growth. You'll find answers to questions like:

- Which similar traits show up across multiple inputs?
- Are there key themes from the psychological assessments that are worth further exploration?
- Are there discrepancies in the feedback or reports that may highlight some behavioral inconsistencies?
- Does your client have a realistic self-perception or are there significant gaps in their awareness?

The assessment step has four phases involving varying stakeholders and desired outcomes (Figure 2-1).

Figure 2-1. Phases for Assessing Your Client

Gather 360-Degree Feedback	Administer Psychological Profiles	Synthesize the Results	Share Findings
• Share a self-assessment worksheet • Seek other inputs, like performance reviews • Interview 5 to 8 stakeholders • Focus on strengths, areas for growth, and blindspots • Anonymize the results	• Select the tools appropriate for your client • Look for themes or inconsistencies in habits, patterns, and personality traits	• Summarize findings from the 360 and psych profiles • Begin with overall themes, and especially seek out what is positive • Begin to identify recommended competencies	• Present the report to the client in at least two meetings • Assign small actions to take between meetings • Set context for coaching engagement • Reinforce safety and trust

Gather 360 Feedback

Gathering 360 feedback is the first phase in the assessment step. You'll compile your findings into a final assessment summary. The phrase *360-degree feedback* (or 360 for short) simply means collecting input from multiple perspectives: the client (self-assessment), their peers, direct reports, partners, and an immediate manager. Depending on the client's role, it may be important to also include key internal or external stakeholders, as well as another level of management for input and engagement. These decisions are strategic and specific to the client and their role in the organization. For example, if you determine that your client would benefit from visibility with more-senior executive leadership or a board, coaching is an excellent opportunity to engage those leaders for input on your client and increase their interest in and awareness of your client's strengths and growth trajectory.

CLIENT SPOTLIGHT

The Fruits of Jose's 360

I will always remember a client, Jose, who got feedback that his presentations at meetings were dry and lengthy. We worked on making his presentations shorter and more story-like, visual, and upbeat. His colleagues immediately noticed and celebrated this, which created a great feedback loop. This would not have happened without the investment from others built into the 360 process.

Competencies:
Presentation skills, executive presence, communicates effectively

---

There are many tools for administering 360 reviews. Some measure various competencies, while others are quite simple. Some competencies are tied to levels of leadership, such as first-time managers or experienced senior executives, and some are tied to industries or functions. I recommend keeping it simple by using the process outlined in this chapter. After all, you're looking to deeply influence only a few competencies during the time you have with your client. Doing just that is a huge success.

Administer the Self-Assessment

This is the first step in collecting 360 inputs. You can assign a self-assessment worksheet (Template 2-1) to your client as homework after the first meeting; if appropriate, share the leadership competencies self-assessment (Template 2-2). Additionally, you could ask your client to provide other inputs, such as current performance reviews, their professional development plan, any previously completed leadership assessments, and client or team recognition. And, you have the information from the in-depth, one-on-one exploration of your client you did during the first meeting to understand the reason coaching was sought, and have begun to explore what growth opportunities are available to your client.

ON THAT NOTE
Continuous Assessment

Remember that although you're now in the formal assessment step, you should always be in "intake mode," gathering more insight and information to understand your client as a unique human being. Each conversation is a chance to get to know your client more fully and deeply.

The results of self-assessments don't often come as a surprise to coaching clients. For example, they know—or suspect—that they're extroverts, technical wizards, or averse to conflict. The addition of the 360 brings another dimension to this knowledge and can uncover the impact these behavioral preferences have on others. At times, this more comprehensive and directed feedback can be news to a client.

Templates for Success

Template 2-1. Self-Assessment Worksheet
This self-assessment is an alternative way to jump-start the process to get to know your client. It invites your client to think about their goals for coaching and to evaluate their performance as a leader. Note that there is some overlap with this worksheet and the client interview.

Template 2-2. Leadership Competencies Self-Assessment
A detailed review of 12 key leadership competencies, highlighting several core skills within each competency. If your client seeks more detailed development aligned with leadership competencies, you can use this in both the client self-assessment and the 360 interviews to gain a very detailed view of your client's strengths and areas for development.

Conduct Interviews With Key Co-Workers

Next you'll solicit additional inputs from your client's circle of co-workers and colleagues in a series of one-on-one interviews. You will later anonymize and share the feedback you collect.

This is an excellent time to deepen the relationship with your client, building on the trust and rapport you have already developed. Make sure to check in on how they're feeling about this feedback process. What are they imagining? Do they have any concerns? Are they looking forward to hearing the 360 inputs?

You may also choose to show your client the three questions that you'll ask interviewees and talk through how the answers will be recorded. Reassure them that the intention of this process is to gather actionable and detailed feedback that supports their growth as a leader. You can share how this process has been instrumental with prior clients or even share your own experience receiving 360 input from your coach.

Let them know that the feedback is extremely affirming and underscores their gifts, while also pointing to improvement areas that will help them be even more effective as a leader. Although some of the feedback may sting a bit, it's given with the intent to be helpful. You will then work together to ground the feedback in the language of competencies, which becomes instantly actionable in a proven model of helping leaders achieve their goals.

I recommend gathering these 360 inputs from five to eight colleagues who have recent, routine, and relevant interactions with your client. The two requirements for qualifying as a 360 interviewee are:

1. **The colleague knows the coaching client well.** The vendor from last year's project is not very helpful for your purposes. The senior manager who only worked with your client twice during a multiquarter project would also not be helpful. The depth of insight would be lacking in these examples. Instead, look for those who are intensely connected to and regularly interact with your client.

2. **The colleague is able to provide articulate, direct, constructive, and honest input.** It's important that the interviewee does not have a "fan club" mindset—giving feedback like that of a big believer. Instead, seek people who can offer candid, detailed, relevant, and balanced feedback. Conversely, a colleague who is completely disenchanted won't be of much help either.

At a minimum, consider requesting input from:

- Your client's direct manager
- One to two peers on their immediate team
- One to two direct reports
- One to two key partners outside their immediate team

Your client is responsible for requesting these interviews for you, so help them select the right people. Use Template 2-3, "Initial 360 Interview Outreach Emails," to craft an email to send to the client, asking them to begin the outreach. You will then reach out to the interviewees who have agreed to be interviewed using the email in Template 2-4. Once you agree on a time, send a calendar invitation using Template 2-5, "360 Interview Meeting Invitation, Agenda, and Attachments for Interviewees."

These stakeholder interviews should focus on three main areas:

- **Your client's strengths**—what are their gifts, and what do they do consistently well?

- **Their areas for improvement**—what are their challenges, what holds them back, and what behaviors negatively affect the business, organization, or team?
- **Three changes your client could make immediately** that would have a positive impact on the company, organization, their team, or themselves.

You'll pose this same set of questions to your client in their self-assessment, giving you a structure to understand your client and their gifts and opportunities for growth from many meaningful perspectives. Use Template 2-6 as a form for conducting the 360 interview and collecting your notes. Template 2-7, "360 Interview Notes Completed," provides a sample of what completed notes might look like.

Be sure the stakeholders know the purpose and intended use of their feedback. Assure them that their feedback will be anonymized and summarized for your client for the purpose of the their growth as a leader. You can even show them briefly how you take your notes. Be sure to honor their anonymity by removing specific examples or even phrases that might identify their comments. Also, mix up the feedback to prevent someone from reading across the bullets and identifying who gave the input.

Take a moment to explain the four-step coaching process (Template 1-1). You want to build understanding and trust to make sure that you get great information about and for your client. This is also a good way to let these colleagues know a bit about you and your method, in case they need a coach in the future. Think ABS: Always be selling!

CLIENT SPOTLIGHT
Engaging Leaders in Shankuri's Growth

I had a client who experienced an unexpected dip in her presentation quality at the monthly senior leadership meeting, and her reputation was taking a hit. Shankuri sought out coaching, and I intentionally engaged her senior leadership to remind them of her capability and leadership capacity. That strategic decision paid off, and because of Shankuri's engagement with coaching, her learning posture, and the immediate improvement of her presentations, she was quickly back on track with upper management. She was invited to join the high-potential leadership accelerator and was soon well on her way to her next promotion. This is a great example of why you should consider engaging senior leadership to help sponsor your client in their progression as a result of coaching.

Competencies:
Executive presence, confidence, communication skills

Sometimes it's helpful to have an idea of the personality profiles of the people you're interviewing. You can ask the interviewee their Myers-Briggs type or do a little sleuthing during the interview—using Template 2-8, "360 Interview Myers-Briggs Short Assessment"—to see if that uncovers anything useful. Sometimes a conflict between colleagues can be attributed to their different approaches to the work and relationships. This simple insight of "we do things differently" or "we think differently" can help colleagues understand each other better.

Sometimes you may get contradictory feedback from key constituents. A direct team member may experience your client one way, and a partner on another team may have the exact opposite feedback. Your knowledge of the business, of how work gets done, and of the relationships and connections critical to the team's output will help diagnose why you may be getting conflicting feedback. There are natural dynamics and tensions in any business—for example, between product development and sales or between customer service and billing. Use your executive experience and insights about the business to distinguish where these opposing bits of feedback may be coming from.

CLIENT SPOTLIGHT
Maggie's Contradictory Feedback

Maggie is one of my clients who works in healthcare. She received conflicting feedback on her communication style. From leaders she occasionally interacted with, the feedback was positive. These key stakeholders appreciated, even admired, her clear, concise, and factual communication style. Conversely, from those she regularly worked with as peers, the feedback on her communication style was lukewarm. That group was seeking a more warm, engaging, and collaborative style. As a broker of hope—her coach—I helped her reconcile this apparently conflicting feedback by thinking about how work gets done, the frequency of interaction, and team dynamics. This was a great example of situational communication styles and recognizing that the leadership preference was for short and focused communications. Her team and colleagues, however, wanted a more connecting and compassionate communication style. This distinction helped to open the dialogue with Maggie about adaptive styles and when to be warmer and more congenial in her interactions.

Competencies:
Communication, situational leadership, relating to others

Although this step takes significant time and effort for you, the client, and their colleagues, the importance of the personalized stakeholder perspectives cannot be overstated. The engagement of others in this coaching process achieves numerous objectives:

- Creating a more complete picture of your client
- Enlisting others in the development of your client—they are invested now and part of your client's improvement efforts, as illustrated by Jose's story
- Engaging leadership in a deeper understanding and evaluation of your client's talents and ability to grow
- Building stronger partnerships, internally and externally, through the shared journey of growth

Templates for Success

Template 2-3. Initial 360 Interview Outreach Emails
An email template for you to send to your client to jump-start the interview process. It also contains a pass-through template for your client to send to their selected 360 interviewees.

Template 2-4. Email Invitation to 360 Interviewees
An email template for you to send to your client's 360 interviewees to begin scheduling the 360 feedback interviews.

Template 2-5. 360 Interview Meeting Invitation, Agenda, and Attachments for Interviewees
A template for booking the meeting time with your client's 360 interviewees. It includes the agenda and recommended attachments for the interviewee to prepare.

Template 2-6. 360 Interview Notes Form
A form to collect feedback from your 360 interviewees. You can include the responses from your client's self-assessment in this template as well.

Template 2-7. 360 Interview Notes Completed
A sample 360 notes template completed for Simone, whom I use as a case study throughout the book. This gives you a good idea of what a completed 360 should look like.

Template 2-8. 360 Interview Myers-Briggs Short Assessment
A summary of the Myers-Briggs Type Indicator. Knowing MBTI types can help illuminate where there may be conflicts between your client and some of their colleagues.

Online 360 Tools

You may be asking yourself, *Isn't there a tool for this?* The short answer is yes. Many 360 tools are available online that could eliminate the need for one-on-one interviews. Some tools are stand-alone applications, and others are embedded in performance review systems. Some are tied to competency models, and others are more aligned with values or even supposedly tied to business outcomes. I have tried many of them, and each has its benefits. However, even though the stakeholder interview process can be time-intensive, the data gathered for and about the client through this method is deeper and more detailed than that from any online tool. Interviews also afford you the chance to ask follow-up questions, clarify any necessary points, and get buy-in. This is the power of relationship and dialogue that is not possible in an online form.

The benefits of online tools are most evident in a programmatic approach, in which large numbers of people are being reviewed or participating in 360s. Collecting 360 data online is not only efficient, but also a powerful way to compare data year over year and across teams. In that case, while the data might not be as qualitatively rich, it's very quantitative and useful. Other benefits to this approach are that the reports can be well designed and matched to core competencies or values across the organization.

For the coach on a budget, work out the cost of your time versus the cost of the online tool. Experiment and see what works best for you and your clients.

Administer Profiles

An essential part of the assessment step is administering psychological, leadership, career, and stylistic profiles. These profiles accelerate, clarify, and deepen your understanding of your client and invite them to examine new dimensions of themselves. It can bring to life leadership competencies to help achieve their goals. Profiles help you understand the client, create the IDP, leverage strengths, identify levers to stimulate motivation, and use a common language.

It's important to note that no single assessment is the answer. Psychological assessments are imperfect by their very nature because their validity and reliability are imperfect. No tool, no matter how tested, is 100 percent accurate 100 percent of the time. Tools are simply an exploration into your client's fields of passion, behaviors, communication styles, drivers and needs, patterns, and preferences, and often illuminate opportunities for growth that other data don't reveal. Use these tools as diagnostic aids and correlate the data from the profiles in your overall evaluation. This is where seeking themes or trends across these tools can be helpful. Be sure to see how the profiles line up with what you learned during the 360, or if they reveal another perspective to what you have learned so far.

Explaining the purpose and utility of the psychological assessments, as well as your reasons for using them, can help you continue to deepen your relationship with your client. You have a command of these profiles and know which ones are used for which topics. Nobody wants to feel like they're about to get their head shrunk by a random psychological profile, so explaining a bit about the background and application of each profile really helps reduce the mystery for your client. For example, FIRO-B is used extensively in the military to ensure compatibility for submarine sailors. DiSC is regularly used in hiring for specialty positions—to ensure key behavioral traits are prominent for new hires to a high-performing sales team, as one example. And assure your clients that the results will go straight to them and nobody else.

You can also share your own results as an example to give them a feel for the output and how it may be interpreted. No need to go into huge detail, but just seeing it can be comforting. In my experience, it's really only one client out of 20 who has that much concern.

These are the top five assessments I use in my coaching practice:

- **DiSC assessment** measures a client's personality and behavioral style related to responding to challenges, influencing others, pace of work, and relationship to rules and procedures. It is also widely used in companies for individual and team development.

- **FIRO-B assessment** identifies how a client tends to behave toward others and how they would like others to behave toward them. It's currently one of the only instruments that can uncover a person's expressed behavior versus wanted behavior, which can be very helpful in coaching. It reveals how a client handles interpersonal relationships, social needs, and social perceptions.

- **Myers-Briggs Type Indicator (MBTI)** shows preferences for how your client perceives the world, relates to others, and makes decisions. It's widely used in companies for individual and team development.

- **Strong Interest Inventory** helps a client understand their work interests and industries best suited for their preferences. This tool doesn't test abilities. Rather it inventories interests and showcases occupations, types of work, and industries that are aligned to those interests.

- **Thomas-Kilmann Conflict Mode Instrument (TKI)** helps a client understand how different approaches to handling conflict influence interpersonal and group dynamics. It illuminates the different conflict styles and invites a client to choose a style better suited to a particular situation.

There are many other valuable assessments on the market, such as the StrengthsFinder, Denison, Hogan, Birkman, Enneagram, Five Dynamics, and 16 PF. Choose what you have found useful in your own development as an executive and bring in two to three more to round out the insights for your client.

Some assessments require certification to use the tool, administration costs, and reporting costs. In all, establishing and maintaining certification can be rather expensive. I advise you to research, experiment, and see what feels comfortable for you. As I said, no single assessment is completely reliable and valid from a clinical perspective, so variety is helpful in painting a complete picture.

In addition, some of these assessments can be found online for low or no cost. Ask friends and family to try them out to see if they work for your purposes. Alternatively, you can become intimately familiar with one or two of the tools and use insights from your client engagement to estimate their preferences. For example, with Myers-Briggs, you can ask questions about how the client refuels after a long day (introvert-extrovert preferences), how they plan a vacation (judging-perceiving preferences), and so on. While this is less reliable than having your client formally complete the assessment, it's a low-cost way to gain some additional insights. Lastly, if you share a coaching practice, you can divvy up the certifications and run profiles for each other.

There are also companies that administer profiles and will even debrief your client on the results of their completed profiles. They'll send you a copy of your client's results so you can be in the loop and include the information with the 360 input.

I highly recommend using three to five instruments to get a well-rounded picture of your client. Each instrument evaluates something different, and they all have varying levels of validity and reliability. Use Template 2-9 to craft the email inviting your client to complete the assessments you assign them.

Once you receive the results, take the conclusions lightly, not as hard facts about your client. Avoid language like "you are" or "you will do this." It's better to use the information as a conversation opener, like "Given this result on introversion on your MBTI report, I'm guessing you like to refuel by yourself with quiet time instead of a big group activity. Does that sound true for you?"

Template for Success

Template 2-9. Email Invitation to Complete Profiles
An email to send to your client to begin the process of collecting their profiles.

Synthesize the Results

Your next step is to synthesize the results of the 360 and profiles, identifying patterns and themes to apply to the goal-setting step. As an example of how to synthesize the results, let's review a case study focusing on one key client: Simone, a valued executive, was sponsored into coaching to improve her effectiveness so she could continue to progress in her career as a high-performing technical leader in the healthcare sector. Her detailed case study illustrates the four-step coaching process and how coaching can be part of someone's ongoing leadership development, not necessarily an intervention or acceleration.

For now, we'll discuss the results of her 360, her self-evaluation, and four psych profiles. Simone's IDP is referenced throughout this book, so we'll call out the key themes and trends from her profiles and 360 that helped set the priorities for her IDP.

The 360 input from Simone's peers, team members, and senior leader indicated a few trends, both in strengths and areas for development (Table 2-1).

Table 2-1. Simone's Strengths and Opportunities

Simone's Strengths		Simone's Opportunities	
• Work ethic	• Highly competent	• Dismissive	• Defensive
• Goes above and beyond	• Dedicated	• Harsh tone	• Controlling
		• Perfectionist	

Her self-evaluation was important to determine her self-awareness and any potential distortion she had of her strengths and areas for development. In this case, Simone was aware of her opportunities and was not surprised by any of the feedback. For the full summary of Simone's 360 input, review Template 2-7.

Simone's MBTI report indicated that she was an ISFJ: introverted, sensing, feeling, and judging. Additionally, a few interesting themes emerged. Simone is not one to initiate, because she's high on the introversion scale, but she has a very strong need for closure, because she measures high on the judging scale in several categories, including systematic, early starting, scheduled, and methodical. Simon has a driving need to structure her day and will double- and triple-check work—her own and that of others. She'll also look for evidence that you can do the work, confirming your competence to do your job.

Simone's TKI report showed a very high competing style, which means any conflict will result in a strong drive toward her way (or the highway). Combine this with her high need for closure and driving need to structure her day, and you start to get a sense of what it might be like to work with Simone.

More behavioral tendencies were revealed on Simone's FIRO-B profile. Although the MBTI report identified her as an introvert, the FIRO-B profile showed a high need for one-on-one interaction and relationship. Simone has a high expressed affection, but a low score in wanted affections, meaning that she gives graciously without expecting much in return and has a higher-than-average capacity to include others.

This is a great example of the assertion that several reports are important. If I had not completed the FIRO-B with Simone, I would have no idea she had these tendencies toward warmth and generosity in small groups or one-on-one interactions. And this capacity for warm one-on-one interactions is a great lever for the coaching relationship and for developing direct reports. This was really her saving grace, because the rest of her profile revealed a combination of challenging traits and behaviors that were also evident in some of her 360 results.

The more you work with whatever profiles you choose, the more you will understand what they mean and how to stitch together themes and opportunities to share with your clients.

The assessments evaluate how the client mentally and emotionally constructs and takes in the world. Each tool offers "questions to ask yourself" and personalized summaries as part of the individual report. Use these to start developing themes that you'll validate using themes from the 360 input.

In this summary stage, it's helpful to consider why your client originally sought coaching. For example, if they are seeking a career change, you might lean on the Strong Interest Inventory to serve their presenting need of making a career shift. Summarizing enables you to cross-reference across all the tools to identify top themes that may be the richest areas for development with your client.

Present the Results

At this point, you've completed numerous interviews, reviewed your client's self-assessment, reflected on your notes from the initial client conversations, and summarized the results of the assigned psychological profiles with key themes and focus areas. It's now time to engage your client and share your insights and findings.

Focus on key themes revealed in the overall assessment and set the context for coaching as a safe place to learn new things and engage with development. You should review the results with your client over two one-hour sessions, or several if needed. Give your client enough time between these sessions to review the reports, reflect on their insights and learning, and bring that increased self-awareness and openness into the rest of your conversations.

It's key to offer a support structure for your client to feel safe and trusting so that they may engage more fully with the coaching program. It's rare to get this much feedback at once, provided in an extensive and detailed report, so take your time. Sometimes you might take multiple sessions, stopping to discuss in detail what comes up for the client. The depth and breadth of the assessment can be celebratory and unsettling for some clients, all at once. Although you have a lot of information to share, your focus must remain on the client, meeting them where they are and continuing to create a safe and trusted space for growth.

In your first conversation, begin with an overarching summary of the 360 inputs, the psychological assessments, and your insights. Highlight what is great about the profiles, the strengths that the stakeholder community shared, and the capabilities revealed in the psychological assessments. This helps clarify your client's capabilities and the many strengths they have. It can also help keep their self-esteem intact and their confidence high leading into the sometimes more difficult feedback around areas of growth.

You can then turn to the development topics or themes. This is where insight from the 360 input and profiles begins to turn into action, which is how your client will change and grow. This conversation is building toward the IDP that you will partner with the client to create. Some of the feedback may sting, and that is a moment they may never forget. Your role is to give them a path forward and a proven model to help them address any pain points. Remember, you are the broker of hope for this executive, and that starts with helping them address their areas for development.

Frame the information into the language of competencies as soon as possible. For example, it's much easier for a client to talk about "executive presence" or "managing meetings" as competencies rather than linger on comments about their shyness or inability to focus. These conversations about the 360 input and the profile results are crucial, relationship-building experiences. Demonstrate care and respect for your client as they absorb this information and begin to think about how to work toward their goals.

Recall the information in chapter 1 about relationship skills as the essence of your coaching work. In the assessment step of the coaching model, the foundational relationship skills of beacon of hope, customer focus, and monitoring and building the relationship are in play, with a key focus on listening as an elevated competency. You'll also call upon your skills for handling negative outlook, because your client may be learning things about themselves from the 360 input and the profiles that could be difficult.

It can be challenging for a coach to be with a client if the client has a hard time accepting themselves as they are, or if the coach senses the client's frustration with themselves. Your client can learn from you if you accept them unconditionally; it shows them the way forward to accepting themselves, their strong suits, and their areas of opportunity. Change comes more fully and quickly when your client can accept themselves in their current state. Resist the urge to jump in to solve the struggle. While you may care about them and want to help them get out of an uncomfortable situation, don't rob them of their development opportunity. Let them sit with the feedback, and learn to accept themselves and consider this powerful information as a way forward to achieve more of what they want in their leadership roles.

If your client has a difficult time with new feedback, help them see what could be possible with an expanded view of themselves. Show confidence in the four-step coaching process, which will guide them through this. New feedback, even positive feedback, can be hard to accept and integrate into an evolved sense of self. Your job as a coach is to help with this exploration and weave together what is helpful for the client in their development.

It can be tough to sit with feedback without having access to solutions. During and at the end of the first assessment conversation, use *FYI* (a leadership competency book) or another resource to steer the client's thinking toward solutions and building competencies. Suggest some small actions to take before your next conversation, such as reviewing the competency list. This keeps the client engaged in processing and integrating the feedback. Other examples of small actions include reading the summary report in full and reflecting on the feedback, seeking additional insight from a trusted colleague or friend, reviewing a few remedies in *FYI*, or journaling about their response to the feedback. This gives your client ways to process and move through the initial stages, which could include anger or denial. You will gain a sense of which meaningful small actions to recommend as you conduct the first conversation.

ON THAT NOTE
Securing Your *FYI*

FYI: For Your Improvement: A Guide for Development and Coaching, by Michael M. Lombardo and Robert W. Eichinger, was originally published in 1996 by Lominger. Newer editions are now published by Korn Ferry, which is a reputable talent management consulting firm founded in 1969. It acquired a competency model known as Lominger that was developed by numerous nonprofits, academic researchers, consultancies, and corporations, and grounded in applied research at the Center for Creative Leadership.

I recommend you buy the most current edition to ensure all the recent research is included in your copy. The book is available new and used. There is also tremendous content on Korn Ferry's website. You'll find more about how to use this book in the next chapter.

There are three typical responses to the first assessment conversations:

- **Your client is open to the feedback,** takes the inputs as constructive, and is enthusiastic about getting started with a program that will help them address their areas of concern. This is the most frequent response—about 85 percent of the time.

- **Your client has some initial questioning of and reservations about some of the feedback,** but takes time during the breaks between the conversations to reflect. Sometimes they try to piece together who said what, or say, "This was situational." That's fine. Perhaps they'll get some additional insight from a trusted source, or journal about their reactions. They might come back to the second conversation cautiously open to the coaching program. There are other competencies to focus and work on.

- **Your client doesn't take the assessment well** and engages in evidence gathering to prove that the input was wrong, unfair, or biased. They push back on the feedback and maybe even on the whole concept of coaching as a valid development methodology. They're not willing to hear what you have to offer, and that behavior is itself ripe with opportunity for growth. This has happened maybe twice in my 30 years of coaching, mostly because the coaching was somebody else's idea and seen as remedial.

Humans are always resistant to change, whether it's up front or buried, conscious or unconscious. Remember that it's your client's nature, and yours, to resist change. Mostly, the resistance is temporary. This can even happen for great feedback. Learning something new about ourselves can challenge our identity and confidence, and your job as a coach is to help your client see the gift of feedback.

Throughout the remaining review sessions, offer your client a high-level summary of the top three to five areas for development you recommend as a focus for coaching. It's essential to offer just a few growth areas, because it increases the likelihood your client will engage in the work, and the chance for successful change in the limited coaching engagement. While it may be helpful for your client to deepen or develop other competencies too, be disciplined and identify only the top ones at the beginning. Think about the highest-yield behavioral changes that are most likely to assist your client in achieving their goals and meeting the overall objectives of the coaching program set forth by their leadership.

Finally, remember to revisit the assessment summary often throughout the coaching journey to celebrate the areas that are working out great for your client and as a motivator to continue to work on the key areas that need to evolve.

Coach as Broker of Hope

The work of coaching is a journey together and a commitment from both parties. You're a broker for hope and a champion for their progress. This is a foundational relationship competency covered in chapter 1 that really comes to life in this assessment step.

As a coach, you have expertise, experience, tools, and processes to maximize strengths, enable development, achieve goals, overcome obstacles, and reduce the behaviors that are holding your client back. You're a support system, a sounding board, and an expert guide in their process. You're their trusted advisor and a witness to their growth, unfolding, and becoming.

It's helpful to remind clients, especially those few who have serious trepidation, that coaching is a tremendous gift. If a company invests in a client for their development, that is an important signal of the leaders' perspective on your client's current and future capability. Help them see that sponsorship as an affirmation and invitation.

In your conversations about the assessments, it's important to help your client feel safe and know that you're creating a confidential space for their development. You welcome whatever is coming up for them. You are always deepening the relationship, and the client knows you're there to help them work through feedback with targeted practices. Feel free to weave in examples of similar clients who made similar changes successfully. Perhaps it's Jose and presentation skills or Maggie and situational communications. Perhaps it's problem solving or measuring and managing work. There are many leadership competencies to deepen or develop. Remind your client that they have tremendous talents already that are being expanded through coaching. It's a journey, and you are on that journey together.

Coaching is an opportunity for growth that will help your client in work and life, inviting them to live more fully into their vision for their life, and that takes work. It may mean undoing patterns that have built up over many years. It may take renegotiating relationships that are based on old habits. It's stepping into a new way of being that has ripple effects in every aspect of life. Because of this, the coaching experience can be transformative.

Summary

The assessment step is a rich body of work that will bring together insightful 360 input, the client's self-assessment, and the profiles that provide an X-ray of your client and their strengths and development opportunities. You may also receive additional input from your client, such as annual reviews, customer feedback, or other profiles they may have completed recently.

You'll synthesize and discuss all of this at length with your client. You'll explore themes from this body of work and discuss what matters most to them from a competency perspective. This work is highly relationship-based and sets a strong foundation of trust, honesty, and support for the entire coaching engagement.

In the next chapter, we'll work through how your assessment feedback report becomes the foundation for the overall coaching program design, identifying specific competencies for development and setting goals. This is all part of the IDP.

Chapter 3
Set Goals for Coaching

"Everything is practice." —Pele

"The big secret in life is there is no secret. Whatever your goal, you can get there if you're willing to work." —Oprah

"I am guided each day by these three questions: 'What are you fixing?' 'What are you making?' and 'Who are you helping?'" —Juliana Rotich

In this chapter, I cover:
- Letting your client set the groundwork: Following the assessment step, learn what the client is most eager to work on through coaching.
- Exploring and selecting competencies: Use the assessment results, along with some trusted resources, to select the three to five competencies that meet your client's goals.
- Creating the IDP: Guide your client in high-level thinking about their competency development, including corresponding behaviors and obstacles. Cement the goals of coaching in the IDP.
- The power of relationship: Explore and experience how the relationship increases the accuracy and drive for goals.

After doing extensive work getting to know your client through the profiles, the 360 input, their environment, and some of the key people they interact with in their work, you've arrived at a significant stage in coaching: goal setting. This is where all the opportunities uncovered in the assessment are prioritized, and the capabilities you see as most meaningful for your client get intentional focus and effort. This is the foundational work of coaching.

In this chapter, step 2 of the four-step process, I further explore our case study, Simone, and dig into the individual development plan (IDP) process and competency selection. My favorite competency-development resource is *FYI*, and I'll also share some leadership models and other key tools for your competency-selection toolkit.

The exploration made possible by the assessment process gave you a deep understanding of your client and now allows you to align with them on top priorities for their growth. In the goal-setting step, you and your client will agree upon the top three to five competencies to focus on for the duration of the coaching program, establishing accountability for the work and creating practices that begin a new way of thinking about their work as an executive.

Recall that there are many paths that may have brought your client to coaching. They might find and engage with you on their own, or their company may be investing in their development. They could be part of a leadership acceleration program that includes personal coaching, or they could be on a "corrective action plan" to get themselves right in some way important to their company. You can imagine that someone who is a high-potential executive on the succession plan for CEO will have goals and an overall coaching program design that is very different than someone who has been sent to coaching for intensive development and performance improvement.

Therefore, the work of goal setting is deeply individualized—it's tricky, if not impossible, to describe the process in a simple one-size-fits-all approach. Each human being you interact with is unique—their combinations of profiles and 360 data, the journey they have taken to arrive at your door, the work they do, the level at which they operate, and their educational experience, global exposure, childhood experiences, social support system, family of origin, culture, and so much more—so goal setting will have to be designed intentionally for each individual in order to be effective.

As we discussed in chapter 1, the relationship between coach and client is the core of coaching. It is how and why coaching is done, or the train that gets you down the tracks, so to speak. During this phase, the skills of perspective, emotional resonance, beacon of hope, customer focus, and monitoring and building the relationship should be used for effectively setting goals with your client.

At this stage in the process, you are working with your client to develop goals related to competencies they want to strengthen. Being a coach, you are very familiar with the language of competencies, which will be comforting and inspiring to your client. Don't be shy to mention a few, especially those that pertain to their goals or might help address some of the 360 feedback. Self-acceptance is hard for most coaching clients, but you can make it easier by normalizing, offering perspective, and always conveying your skilled dedication and hope.

Consider Your Client's Perspective

Next, the coaching conversation focuses on the client's perspective on the profiles and 360 inputs. Which competencies are their highest priority? It's important to hear what your client thinks is important, what is affecting their work, what they may be struggling with, and what kind of feedback they've been given at other points, like performance reviews.

Your role is to help your client stretch, but not overstretch. The client may want to do it all, but you can help them focus on the most critical three to five competencies that set them up to show improvement during the coaching timeframe. Conversely, your client may envision small steps, and your role is to challenge them to strive for more and work harder to achieve more of what they desire. You can task them with a loftier goal that may stretch them a bit and enable the possibility of more growth.

After completing the assessment step, you will have a sense of what is right for your client; now, you'll help them pull back or push to stretch, as appropriate. This is all grounded in and reliant upon a healthy, trusting, and respectful relationship. It's a good example of the relationship competency of perspective.

Then you'll engage the tools needed. Review the company model, if one exists, for leadership competencies and expectations. Explore other industry models that may be helpful and turn to a trusted resource (such as Korn Ferry's *FYI: For Your Improvement*) to build out the desired behaviors and initial practices or experiments that will be assigned to help your client improve.

Assign your client the homework to review these models and competencies as defined in *FYI*, and come back with a draft individual development plan (IDP) completed. The IDP is the client's development plan, so it's important for them to feel ownership from the beginning.

CLIENT SPOTLIGHT

The Power of Natalie's Robust IDP and Sponsor Engagement

Becky worked with a senior leader in the forest service who was on a temporary assignment at a more senior level in the agency. This is a common practice to develop high-performing employees and prepare them for their next promotion or job opportunity.

Natalie engaged in coaching because she was leaving her comfortable job to take this new role, which had a scope and set of responsibilities that were unlike what she had experienced as an already accomplished, high-performing leader.

Natalie had specific goals coming into the assignment and the coaching program. She proactively involved her new leader as her sponsor, reviewing her coaching goals with him and keeping him informed of her progress. She was incredibly engaged and transparent with her new leader, ensuring that he supported her growth, aligned to her goals for coaching, and gave her feedback throughout the six-month opportunity.

Specifically, Natalie asserted that she wanted to work on decision making, confidence, and driving results at this new level. It's not common for your clients to arrive with such a strong sense of their goals for the coaching program and a strong sponsor already in place, cheering them on. Natalie achieved all her goals for her assignment and her coaching program. She is being heavily recruited for more senior positions across the agency, giving her multiple options to explore as she continues to grow with the forest service.

Competencies
Executive presence, decision making, goal orientation

It's true that there may be some common themes for executives who seek coaching. However, it's critical to meet your client where they are. Always be in relationship and assessment mode. You won't be able to craft an IDP that will help them achieve the goals that brought them to coaching if you do not continue to cultivate an inquisitive, authentic relationship with your client.

The Individual Development Plan

This is the core of the goal-setting step. Your client will create their own IDP, with your guidance, which will become the cornerstone of implementation (Template 3-1). The first half of the IDP has three main sections: competencies, behaviors, and challenges. You'll create this first half with the client during the goal-setting step. As you move into implementation and ongoing coaching conversations, your client will continue to expand upon this high-level summary.

Let's go back to Simone. After completing the assessment profiles and reviewing those in depth with Simone, I realized that some of the behaviors her team was responding negatively to were rooted in her personality and lack of leadership competencies. Recall our summary from the last chapter:

- The FIRO-B outlined her need for inclusion, control, and affection. Simone's *expressed affection* was at the top of the scale—9 out of 9—which means she is very warm and emotionally invested in individuals and her interaction can be quite intense as a result.

- The Myers-Briggs assessment revealed how she shows up under stress, and we could see that her stress expressions were irritation, tension, anxiety, and feeling overwhelmed. In addition, Simone is a high J in Myers-Briggs, illustrating a very strong drive to closure, a behavior pattern that can look and sound a lot like "get on with it already."

- The Thomas-Kilmann Conflict Mode Instrument reviewed her conflict styles and showed that her default style was competing. This opened a dialogue about the value of flexing her conflict styles to be more adaptive to her team and environment.

The summary of the profiles led us to think about three potential areas for development: conflict management, containment of oneself in a professional environment, and listening skills.

Next, the 360 inputs revealed some critical areas to prioritize for her development—namely, the disconnect on feedback from her laboratory team and physicians about her communication style. Simone prefers short, clipped, and direct communication. This works very well with healthcare professionals, who are moving rapidly through an unwieldy patient roster and need "just the facts, ma'am" from Simone. Conversely, the team she leads day to day in a highly stressful environment wants more warmth, connection, and compassion from their leader. Softening her communication style, and even having some conversations simply to build relationships, would go a long way in building team morale and loyalty.

The assessment step culminated in Simone's IDP, which is annotated for reference in Figure 3-1 and shown without annotation in Template 3-2.

Figure 3-1. Annotated IDP For Client Simone

Coaching Individual Development Plan
Simone Smith

Competencies I want to build

- Composure
- Receiving feedback
- listening

> You and your client will pick three to five competencies.

Specific behaviors I want to adopt or strengthen

1. Composure
   a. Patience
   b. Impulse control
   c. Consciously make a choice about how I want to respond
2. Receiving feedback
   a. Manage defensiveness, pause
   b. Ask clarifying questions in a nonjudgmental answer
   c. Start to choose different responses going forward
3. listening
   a. Let people finish, don't interrupt
   b. Understand the feedback
   c. Restate the problem In my own words to everyone's satisfaction

> Ask your client to write these in their own voice, prompting them with findings from the assessment step.

Potential challenges

1. MYSELF
2. Time—rushing to the next thing rather than stepping back and taking stock
3. Working against the implicit teachings of hierarchy that medicine instills
4. Forgetting to use my new tools

> The discovery process probably gave your client a good idea about the root causes of their challenges and the obstacles they'll face in overcoming them

Templates for Success

Template 3-1. IDP Form
This blank template is a framework for your client's development plan. It's the foundation of the four-step coaching model. After deciding on competencies to focus on, work with your client to fill out this development plan.

Template 3-2. Simone's IDP
Simone's completed IDP.

Competencies

A competency is the ability to successfully perform a critical work function or task in a defined work setting. You can think of this as proficiency or capacity to apply knowledge, skills, and abilities to perform your work. Many competencies are multifaceted and can require multiple behaviors or actions to accomplish.

When working with a resource such as *FYI*, competencies are rated as less skilled, skilled, or talented (as we'll discuss later in this chapter). It's important to anchor your client's IDP to what a skilled person demonstrates in a particular competency. This helps your client grow to the first level of competency and see that more growth is available to demonstrate a competency at a more talented level.

You can also leverage outside resources to understand the possible causes of low skill in a particular competency. This gives you further insight to explore with your client the root causes or historical patterns of this lower performance and some actions to take to model a new way of being. Examples of competencies are found later in the chapter and throughout the first half of the book.

Behaviors

Behaviors are typically observable and demonstrate broader competencies. Behaviors help answer the question, "What actions must happen for me to demonstrate a given competency or ability?" Actions are the steps taken to accomplish the behavior, which we'll explore more in the implementation step.

In Simone's IDP, we listed multiple behaviors under the composure competency. This gives a sense of what challenges Simone in keeping her composure, by highlighting which behaviors need development. The behaviors become the anchor for development coaching and for the experiments or practices that will come into play with the coaching implementation step.

Potential Challenges

Your client will certainly face challenges when trying to change their behaviors and adopt new ones. Work with your client up front to identify known challenges so you can help minimize them from the outset. Sometimes the client can consciously or unconsciously trip themselves up. You can see in Simone's IDP that the first challenge she identified was herself. This shows a level of self-awareness and the grip of patterns that can make sustained behavior change quite difficult.

Self-awareness and self-reflection are key practices for the client to engage and hone during coaching, bringing the client's attention to what they may be doing to assist or hinder their own development. Some challenges will be external while others might be more innate and can be detected in their profiles or 360. There may be additional, unforeseen challenges in the implementation, which we'll cover more in the next chapter.

It's worth noting that if these shifts were easy, your client would likely have already made them. They are high-performing executives with a long track record of success; they are skilled at overcoming obstacles. As a coach, we commit to being on the journey with them, whatever it takes. You bring all your skills, education, experience, and training to support them in this process. You help them overcome obstacles in support of achieving their goals.

You can also help them with experiments or practices to mitigate challenges on a more sustainable basis. In this example, Simone identified time as a challenge, so part of our coaching conversations included how she was prioritizing, working on her time management skills, and ensuring there is enough space in her daily schedule to practice these new behaviors.

Select Three to Five Competencies

Although your client may have many competencies to improve, you both need to align on their top three to five. It's tempting to want to solve all the gaps and improvement areas uncovered in the assessment step, but that is a fool's errand. At this point, you may be thinking that there are so many competencies based on your client's assessment that focusing on three to five feels overly restrictive. Let's explore why this focus is a smart way to approach adult development.

First, you're with your client for a limited time, so it can be challenging to effect real and sustainable behavior change. Limiting the development areas will help you and your client stay focused on what truly matters, right now and in the long run. It gives your client a chance to show progress, which is an important part of keeping them engaged.

Second, it's difficult to change behavior, and insight alone doesn't work. Resolutions themselves don't work in a sustained way; otherwise, the January gym surge would last all year. Knowing something and doing something are two very different things. We've had a lifetime of operating in our patterns, and for most people, those habits have helped them achieve tremendous professional success. But, as the saying goes, "What got you here won't get you there." Coaching is often about helping your client undo habits that no longer serve them and build new habits or behaviors that are better suited for their new role, level, or industry.

CLIENT SPOTLIGHT
Expanding and Shifting Expectations as You Move Up

Becky coached a scientific leader who rose through the ranks of her consulting firm at a breathtaking pace. Amber is smart, driven, hardworking, results oriented, and acutely tuned to success in all aspects of her life. She's the person others turn to when they need to accomplish a tremendous amount of work. Amber graduated with an advanced degree from one of the most prestigious schools in the country. She pivoted from her consulting practice to a biotech startup and has held numerous leadership roles in the company. She's now a VP, and she's learning that the skills at this new level are different. She can't operate from the same play-book and expect the same outcomes.

Skills that were highly prized in her former company are now potential liabilities in her new level and company. Specifically, the mantra of "under-commit and over-deliver" served her well in her consulting practice and helped build her brand of high-achieving senior consultant. Now, in a startup that's delivering a game-changing diagnostic to the market, the ability to articulate a compelling vision, make strategic decisions, and inspire the team with what's possible are highly valuable skills. Her tendency to under-commit looks more like an aversion to risk, an inability to partner, and a gap in possibility thinking. She will have to shed what has helped get her to this point and build new skills better suited for her new company and leadership level.

Competencies
Executive presence, partnering, communications

Finally, adults learn through trying, doing, and self-reflection. This is a key reason your client should only focus on three to five development areas. Foundational adult learning theory indicates that adults retain new information when they apply it. In fact, 70 percent of learning is said to come from doing (Training Industry, n.d.), so giving your client time to try new things, attempt new practices, and experiment with a new way of being is essential for them to integrate their new knowledge and deepen their competencies. Without doing, there really is no learning (that sounds like Yoda, but you get it, right?). Also important is the opportunity to reflect on the action and intended outcomes. Engaging in self-reflection and self-awareness activities helps your client see what is working in these modifications and identify further changes that may be required to achieve the desired outcomes.

Situational vs. Intrinsic Goals: Treat the Root Cause

Many clients come to coaching with situational goals: "Help me improve my communications," or "I need to be a better presenter in high-stakes situations," or "My peers don't think I play well with others." Contrast these with the intrinsic goals revealed in the assessment process, which are the opportunities that have a deep and durable impact on your client. What really matters most to them?

For example, the Strong Interest Inventory shows personal values alongside the industries and roles best aligned to those values. This is incredibly helpful information when working with someone who is frustrated in their work situation or feels stuck. Sometimes they just aren't in the right industry or job for their personal values and intrinsic strengths. This can be a breakthrough moment.

CLIENT SPOTLIGHT
Finding Scott's Right Job Fit

I worked with a client who was finding it difficult to fit into his company, despite (or perhaps because of) the fact that his father was the CEO. He was hired into a senior leadership role, and his peers rejected him in the subtle ways that can happen in the workplace. No one included him, no one hung out with him, and he was out of the loop in small and big ways.

Scott engaged coaching to help navigate these challenges. I helped him understand where his peers were coming from, operating from a place of concern about what Scott might say to "daddy" and frustration at the apparent nepotism. All these concerns were revealed in the 360 input process. I helped Scott find ways to connect with the team and his peers in an authentic way. Ultimately, the Strong Interest Inventory and other profiles revealed that he wasn't really suited for the client-facing role he was initially hired to lead. When he pursued an opportunity in another part of the company, using his deep technical and innovation skills and passion—a better fit for his strengths—he flourished.

Competencies
Courage, relationships, self-awareness

These more intrinsic goals help you guide your client to zoom out from the perhaps urgent situational topics and develop an area with immediate positive impact as well as lasting future impact. Whenever you're pressed to help your client with something situational, make sure you're zooming out to look for the broader competencies or root causes.

For example, your client may say they need help with presentation skills to be more effective in their role. Any of the competency models discussed later in the chapter will have practices and exercises to improve this skill. In addition, there are many leadership books, TED Talks, and YouTube videos on leadership presence and presentation skills, which are all helpful and will certainly serve your client in growing competency.

But your job is to explore the unfolding of your client—the issue behind the topic. If your client wants to improve their presentation skills, explore what is *behind* that topic. What is meaningful to your client? What have they tried before? What happens with them in this setting; that is, what is their self-talk, what are their emotions, what's happening in their body? What about presenting is hard for your client?

CLIENT SPOTLIGHT
Bringing in Reinforcements for Marisol

With your client's permission, it's perfectly acceptable to bring in an expert in an area that may not be your strength or competency. I had a client, Marisol, who was seeking coaching to be better prepared for and engaged with the investment community. I have a colleague in my network who is quite skilled at this specific type of work and has coached others to be more successful in this capability. With Marisol's permission, I engaged this expert to build her capability and confidence in this essential leadership skill. Simultaneously, I continued to work with Marisol in other areas important for her growth as a leader.

Competencies
Executive presence, presentation skills, strategic planning

This is when your competencies as a coach—listening, observing, asking skillful questions—are most critical. It's also when leveraging the power of relationships can yield breakthrough moments with your client. When you display how deeply you're invested in your client's growth and how authentically excited you are to help them succeed, your client can find motivation to accept what could be for them a very unsettling root cause. Issues of confidence, insecurity, anxiety, feelings of inadequacy, imposter syndrome, and former failures, and even things like childhood speech disorders, can be revealed in this type of exploration. The answers can also be found in the profiles—for example, your client might be more of an introvert or prefer one-on-one interpersonal interactions rather than being in a large group. The 360 input may also reveal some of these "behind the topic" development areas.

These root causes offer rich development areas that your client can work on to improve aspects of their work or life well beyond the initial focus of public speaking. They add a dimension of understanding and an appreciation of the tremendous effort required to develop a new skill or competency.

Reframe these root causes as competencies that support skill-building with a totally different focus. If you help your client open up to these insights as part of a coaching conversation, they will have a chance to develop a broader set of competencies in their quest to improve the specific skill of public speaking. You will further their development and their ability to be self-aware, self-correcting, and self-sustaining long after the coaching engagement has concluded.

Blind Spots

Sometimes the 360 will uncover development areas your client wasn't fully aware of. In their seminal research on this topic, Joseph Luft (1961) and Harrington Ingham called this a "blind spot." Their model, the Johari Window, gives an approach to understanding what is known to the self and known to others (Figure 3-2). It's your job to make sure that those blind spots are clearly reflected in the client's goals.

Figure 3-2. The Johari Window

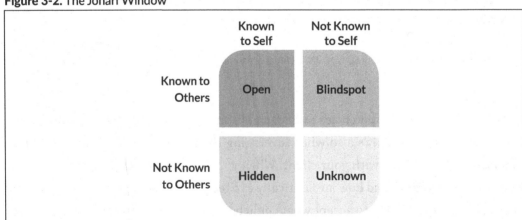

The Johari Window is one way to sort through each input from the assessment process and uncover any pieces of feedback that others have noticed but your client is unaware of. These blind spots can be powerful places for development. However, they can also be challenging for your client to come to grips with; this is feedback about the impact of their behaviors, how others see them (but they don't see that in themselves), and how a lack of capability is affecting their performance. It can be uncomfortable, but putting words to competencies can help, and you as the coach and broker of hope, can help normalize things.

CLIENT SPOTLIGHT
Tom's Blind Spots

The CEO brought me in to coach Tom, a successful sales director for a hospitality and tourism company. He has a history of achievement unparalleled by his colleagues and is highly valued by his company. However, this single-minded focus also comes with some aggressive behaviors that hurt people and himself.

Tom's senior leadership engaged coaching to help him soften the edges while enabling his high performance to continue. It was uncovered early in the interview process that I'd likely be working with some blind spots in Tom's coaching program.

In short, the assessment step revealed that Tom's colleagues thought he was mean, callous, and bad-tempered. He lacked compassion and was hard on his people, instilling cutthroat competition for sales results as his main lever for leading. His leaders valued his tremendous accomplishments in sales, but his limitations in people management and interpersonal skills were stymieing his progression.

The 360 revealed these blind spots, which were difficult for Tom to absorb. He said he had no idea. The coaching process revealed that the take-no-prisoners management style had been modeled for him from an early age and early in his career; Tom thought that's what strong managers did. And at first, it worked. But these strategies were not sustainable, and the predictable outcomes of high turnover, low morale, and declining results motivated Tom to attend to his interpersonal skills more intentionally to become the leader he wanted to be.

Tom had a choice to make: Leave, or stay and learn new leadership competencies, including compassion, developing direct reports, and ethics and values. Tom decided to stay, and we shared his IDP with the CEO, who supported Tom's development every step of the way. Tom attacked his IDP with as much vigor as he did everything else, and we were able to build his competencies and find some buried skills, including inclusion, affection, and exploration.

Competencies
Compassion, developing direct reports, ethics and values

Leadership Competency Models

As you can imagine, there are literally hundreds of leadership competency models—from those specific to a company to those in support of an entire industry. This book's recommendation is twofold:

- Leverage the client's company model (where possible).
- Become deeply familiar with a more general framework that you believe serves your client base most effectively.

Remember to pull from your own experience as an executive to inform what you believe is a top priority for leaders. This focus will help you develop your capability to work with a consistent framework to devise IDPs. Let's review several competency models you can explore with your client.

Company Models

As you engage with your client's sponsor or the client themselves, you should understand the leadership expectations of their organization. Most established companies have a set of values, leadership expectations, and competencies organized by leadership level (manager, director, vice president, C-suite, and so on). Organizations use a competency-based approach to leadership to enable clear expectations and consistent performance feedback. This is a helpful beginning point for competency building because your client will likely have received feedback about their performance against these expectations. This would be revealed in the 360, annual reviews, and your leadership interview. Refer to the data found in the profiles and 360 input because it will point to goals that need to be defined and met during the coaching engagement.

Let's use a general model to illustrate how you might engage with a client to understand their company values and leadership expectations. In Figure 3-3, a company summarizes its five values with a statement to describe "what this looks like around here." These give you a good sense of what matters at the company and what kinds of behaviors every employee is expected to model. These would be included in performance reviews in some meaningful way. We've then detailed practices in each that further illustrate what this value looks like in action. This kind of framework, along with the profiles and 360, can help your client focus on the behaviors and competencies that matter most in their world.

Figure 3-3. Sample Company Values and Leadership Expectations

	Leadership	Quality	Innovation	Teamwork	Integrity
Values	We empower each team member to continually improve their business.	We deliver excellence in everything we do.	We foster curiosity, learning, and invention by intellectually challenging one another and taking informed risks.	We win by accomplishing our goals and solving problems together, while having fun along we way.	We ensure an environment that fosters trust, respect, and transparency.
Practices	• We have a sense of urgency • We provide clear guidance • We ensure decisions are made at the right level • We ensure a safe work environment • We objectively measure our performance • We actively coach and mentor • We proactively and effectively communicate	• We are all responsible for quality • We seek to continuously improve everything • We hold ourselves accountable	• We are open to new ideas and other opinions • We seek to understand before looking to be understood • We expect respectful challenge to support decisions • We ensure a safe environment to fail • When we fail, we do so quickly and learn all we can	• We have a "can do" attitude • We demand reliability • We help our teammates • We are problem solvers • We give credit where it is due • We enjoy our time together	• We do the right thing • We treat one another with respect • We are honest and fair • We speak up • We are accountable for our actions • We are role models

Understanding leadership models can be more challenging from the outside, so your network of interviews will be helpful in revealing these expectations and how your client might be evaluated against them. This is a starting point to build out a coaching plan based on prioritized competencies. It's the coach's role to honor the competencies established in the client's work ecosystem and build upon that model to focus their client's development journey.

Table 3-1 offers a solid competency framework for working with your client. This is based on my experiences coaching hundreds of leaders, but you can bet that some version or combination of these is expected at every company. This doesn't replace the organization's model, but it will help refine the actual skills and behaviors present within that model.

Table 3-1. Common Corporate Competency Expectations

Managing Self	Productivity	Managing Teams	Career
• Executive presence • Approachability • Conflict management • Comfort around higher leadership • Interpersonal savvy • Patience	• Time management • Written communications • Planning	• Presentation skills • Hiring and staffing • Building effective teams • Directing others • Motivating others • Meeting management • Managing diversity and inclusion	• Career ambition • Boss relationships • Interviewing • Self-development • Political savvy • Dealing with ambiguity • Negotiating • Standing alone

Let's look closer at each category:

- **Managing self** includes capabilities of self-awareness, emotional intelligence, and self-regulation.
- **Productivity** is how an executive manages a workload, plans, and communicates effectively.
- **Managing teams** includes skills around hiring, developing, and retaining your talent, as well as how to manage the dynamic nature of team interactions and team projects.
- **Career** includes skills around the health and vitality of their career, both in their current job as well as caring for career goals and aspirations.

These executive competencies are defined more fully in Template 3-3.

Template for Success

> Template 3-3. Executive Competencies
> A summary of the most common executive competencies used in IDPs based on my work with clients for 30-plus years. This is most helpful for clients whose companies do not have an executive competency framework (such as startups or small companies).

Korn Ferry's *FYI: For Your Improvement*

The book *FYI: For Your Improvement* can be pivotal in your coaching engagements. It's the only industry study conducted across profit and nonprofit organizations that reviews competencies. It's a one-of-a-kind resource and the foundation for the coaching approach illustrated here in *The Executive Coaching Playbook*. If your client's company doesn't have a model, this is a reasonable place to uncover the leadership expectations that are explicit and implied in their world.

FYI can lend tremendous structure and strength to the development of your client's IDP and subsequent coaching conversations. Korn Ferry has organized its Lominger model into four groups of high-level leadership expectations, which they call factors: thought leadership, results leadership, people leadership, and self-leadership. Each group has a set of clusters containing statistically supported collections of competencies. The book outlines detailed behaviors and skills that form a path to successful demonstration of each of the 38 competencies. There are also "career derailers" and "stallers" outlined at the end, which can be valuable in a coaching situation.

Each chapter of *FYI* focuses on one competency. The recommendations and development tips within are all grounded in research and provide robust actions for your client to experiment with. The book's introduction explains how each chapter is laid out. I recommend that you read this closely to see how everything is mapped out and begin to visualize how you would use this information in conversation with your client. Let's hit on two essential sections of each competency chapter: skill level and root causes.

Skill Level

Behavioral descriptions of what a given competency looks like are provided in three main buckets: less skilled, skilled, and talented. This can help you illustrate with precision what lack of skill in this area looks like in action and gives you a chance to calibrate with your client whether these behaviors resonate. I recommend you read through this section with your client and have them share what rings true for them. You can also call forward input from the 360 to help them "see" themselves more fully in the descriptions. The *talented* descriptions also give you fodder for what role models your client may have in their environment so they have something clear to work toward. You may ask them, "Does anyone in your organization fit the description of someone talented in this competency? How might you be able to emulate them in your work?" Note that each chapter also provides an assessment of what an "overused" competency looks like, which can provide some insights if your client gets feedback that they have a strength they are over-reliant on.

Let's return to Simone's IDP and focus on listening skills. A skilled communicator listens attentively and takes input from others. The *FYI* chapter "Communicates Effectively" gives you a lot of material to navigate these growth areas aligned to the development areas in Simone's IDP.

Root Causes

The next section in each chapter covers the possible root causes of a lower skill in the competency. Root causes are drivers of the behaviors that coaching should develop or change. Many of these origination points are rooted in earlier experiences and can be unconscious for your client. It's important to tease these out in conversation with your client. Insight alone doesn't engender change, but it's a necessary first step.

The "Root Causes" section of each competency in *FYI* gives you great source material for behaviors you can include in the IDP. Reviewing this list with your client can drive the identification of the three to five areas that will be transformational for them to address or improve. For example, poor time management may be attributed to an earlier manager or work culture in which your client learned that being late is acceptable and the norm— whereas, in a new culture, this might not be the case. Obtaining this insight can help them shed any shame or fear about where they learned this behavior and can help them understand the *why* behind this gap in competency.

Returning to Simone's IDP, the topic of ineffective listening may be caused by interpersonal issues such as shyness, avoiding difficult conversations, lack of preparation, or poor examples of this competency in her upbringing or early career. Any or all of these can be places for exploration about the issue underlying the topic, and if addressed, can have tremendous knock-on effects in other competencies.

I recommend you review these root causes carefully with your client, asking them to read this section and share which ring true for them. As always, lean on the power of your relationship so your client feels supported and not rejected by this gentle but assertive exploration. Invite them to share the story of this circumstance. Pay attention to what they do and don't say in this conversation, because your client may not be fully aware of where these root causes originated in their work and life history. You can also call forward key themes from the profiles and 360 interviews to help illustrate root causes. If none of the root causes ring true for your client, and you believe them, explore what else may be at the origin of their lower skill in this area. Depending on the outcome of your conversation, you may choose to capture the root cause as an obstacle, something for you both to attend to throughout the coaching journey.

Global Leadership Forecast

Development Dimensions Inc. (DDI) has a leadership model that you may find helpful for identifying highly desired capabilities in leaders. You can use your interview notes, profiles, and 360 input to determine where your client could use some support to improve.

DDI was founded in 1970 with a focus on science-based solutions for leadership-behavior modeling. It works with 75 percent of the Fortune 50 companies to assist with leadership development, talent selection, and talent management.

For decades, DDI has published a summary of its research in the *Global Leadership Forecast*, an expansive leadership research project that offers keen insights into the leader's experience. The section on critical skills for leaders is key for executive coaching. As shown in Figure 3-4, the research is summarized in current skills shortages and future skills required for successful leadership (DDI 2023).

Figure 3-4. Global Leadership Forecast of a Leader's Most Needed Skills

	Low — Current Skills Shortage — High	
High (Urgency to Develop Within 3 Years)	Need Continued Development • Coaching and developing others • Building partnerships • Delegation • Empathy (emotional intelligence)	Urgent Future Gaps • Building talent • Managing change • Digital acumen • Strategic thinking • Influencing
Low	Well Prepared for the Future • Driving for results • Communication	Most Overlooked Gaps • Leading virtually • Driving inclusion • Business acumen • Leading across generations

Review the urgent future gaps with your client to determine if any of these capabilities are opportunities for their development. This is especially helpful if their company leadership model doesn't exist or is immature.

Industry-Specific Models

You should also consider whether your client's industry has a capability model. Because you're likely associated with the talent management community, I will highlight two models in this arena. These will be valuable in your ongoing development as a coach and helpful for any of your clients who are also part of HR, learning and development, or leadership development in their organizations. I would even argue they're generally useful competencies that every businessperson should master.

ATD's Talent Development Capability Model

The Association for Talent Development (ATD) is the world's largest industry organization dedicated to those in talent development. It serves a global community of people just like you, focused on developing great talent for teams and organizations around the world. ATD's Talent Development Capability Model guides practitioners to develop themselves and others with focus in three domains: professional, organizational, and personal.

Each of these domains offers capabilities and outlines knowledge and skill statements to bring the capability to life. An assessment helps you understand your strengths and areas for continued growth. The model also offers an expansive list of learning resources to further explore each skill area.

SHRM's Capability Model

The Society for Human Resource Management (SHRM) is an HR industry association founded to elevate the HR profession. Its model offers nine competencies necessary to be an effective HR practitioner, based on SHRM's global research of HR professionals.

SHRM offers an assessment to complete and a learning plan to support you in your continued development as an HR professional. SHRM also offers behavioral competency articles, books to help you develop key competencies, and seminars aligned to competency areas. These can be a great source of inspiration for practices and exercises for yourself or your client working in the HR domain.

Summary

The goal-setting step is when all the preparation moves into action. The IDP establishes focus areas and the framework for building new competencies. Using the profiles and 360 input as your compass is a proven method to improve in three to five areas that are deeply important to your client. The IDP becomes a living document and the foundation of many follow-up coaching conversations during the implementation step. Stay focused on the competencies that your client is working to improve, and don't get distracted by the crisis du jour. You're going for deeper change, and you can help your client stay focused on what matters most in their own development journey.

In the next chapter, I explore the coaching program's implementation, including subsequent coaching conversations, what happens when your client gets stuck or has a breakdown in their practices, what may come up for you as a coach in this process, and how to navigate the waters ahead together.

Chapter 4
Implement the Coaching Program

"Ideas are easy. Implementation is hard." —Guy Kawasaki

"You never know if you can actually do something against all odds until you actually do it." —Abby Wambach

"Have a vision and passion. Be courageous, focused, and disciplined. Lastly, persist. . . . It's definitely not easy." —Monica Musonda

---

In this chapter, I cover:

- Leaning on coaching theories: Learn about theories of adult development as your methods for working with your client on their development journey.

- Staying centered on the IDP: Use it as your compass throughout implementation, including actions for your client to practice and key behaviors aligned with the leadership competencies your client is focused on.

- Continuing to build the IDP: Help your client with their self-observations of how their practices are going and what they are noticing about themselves and others in this process; lead them toward supportive tools, such as books, research, practices, videos, and people.

- Running each coaching session: Prepare for, conduct, and wrap up each session.

- Implementing key interventions: These are your client's fuel; learn some invaluable practices and exercises that can help the client develop skill in their competencies.

- Using the power of relationships: Build, refine, leverage, and reflect on the relationship. You call upon a breadth of relationship skills during implementation.

- Navigating unique coaching situations: Help the client through a job transition or decision making, and learn how to navigate team or corporate coaching engagements.

The implementation step is the bulk of the coaching program—about 75 percent of the total engagement. All the hard work invested in assessment and in designing a meaningful individual development plan (IDP) has led you to this critical phase, where the real work of application and experimentation begins.

Implementation is where you set a cadence for coaching sessions, begin to assign homework such as exercises and experiments, and see how your client makes progress in developing competencies (or doesn't) with these expectations. The learning and results set the context for further exploration, intervention, and conversations that continue through the whole implementation phase. Looking at the entire coaching journey, this is a rich and varied phase.

For example, your client may be preparing to promote a direct report, so part of their coaching journey is to develop persuasion and presentation competencies in support of this near-term goal. Simultaneously, they may be working on their boss-relationship competency and HR-partnering skills to engage sponsors and galvanize support for the direct report's promotion. These competencies are short-term focused with one goal in mind—promoting the direct report—but will yield benefits down the road for their own skills as a leader.

Because every coaching situation is unique, every implementation can be quite varied. I cannot possibly cover every need, practice, distinction, or breakdown you may experience in implementation. However, I have prioritized those I think are most helpful to you and include a treasure chest of templates to support you in implementing meaningful coaching programs.

As a coach, you bring forth a focus on the continuous learning and improvement mindset. Mistakes happen; remind your executive that the key is how they as a leader, team, and organization respond to experiments. Are these experiments a chance to learn and improve, or a source of punishment? Can you help your client show resilience amid challenges and make necessary improvements to people, processes, or technology to continue to evolve? Great leaders are always building competencies and skills within themselves and among the team. The best leaders are self-aware and always looking to challenge themselves and their teams to improve.

CLIENT SPOTLIGHT
Sandra's Bad Boss

It's common for leadership to change with some frequency, which creates an opportunity for people to learn to work with new types of leadership styles. However, new styles don't always jibe. That was the case with one of my clients, Sandra.

Sandra was a chief marketing officer at a well-known technology company. She reported to a CEO who had grown up at the company in sales. The CEO thought he knew marketing because he'd led sales and came across as knowing it all. He'd routinely wade into Sandra's work, question her ideas, and want to revisit her decisions. This was particularly challenging because he never did this with any other member of the executive team. He also had a looser communication style—telling inappropriate jokes, acting in a slightly leering way, and interacting with her male counterparts in a very different manner. It seemed some gender bias was at play.

Sandra worked with me to set healthy boundaries with her new boss, learn to control the meeting environment, and gain tactics to create safety for herself in an increasingly unsafe work environment. This included things like holding meetings in all-glass conference rooms to ensure that behavior was appropriate. This work also included more strategic skills, like setting good boundaries and professionally pushing back when he waded into the marketing work. When he challenged her work later in the process, Sandra learned to ask if he wanted to see the market research again or bring the vendor back to present the strategy in a different way. This allowed her to keep the work moving forward and respectfully encourage her leader to stay in his lane!

Competencies
Comfort around higher management, courage, setting healthy boundaries

Coaching Theories

The coaching you do in the implementation phase is grounded in cognitive and behavioral learning theories and research. As with many things, one approach doesn't fit all clients—a blended approach is often most appropriate. For the most effective coaching practice, integrate classical conditioning, reinforcement, transformative learning, and experiential learning theories to make lasting, deep changes in your client.

These theories offer constructs for effective coaching. The crucial point is to not wade into a coaching engagement without knowing what you're doing. Turn off autopilot and engage all your wisdom to meet your client where they are, uniquely, in each coaching session. Think about their goals. Review the assessments, profiles, and 360 input. Be thoughtful and intentional about where you left off and have a plan for continuing to deepen their learning in subsequent coaching conversations.

Recognize that development is neither tidy nor linear. Just because your client was experiencing sure-footedness or grounded confidence last time doesn't mean they will be the next time you see them. Meet them new and fresh every time, and simultaneously hold the thread of development through every session. Your client needs to count on your ability to maintain the container of development and stay focused on their growth in the critical competencies you've identified.

Power of the Relationship

Research shows that the only reliable predictor of a good clinical outcome in psychotherapy is the relationship with the therapist. Coaching is not psychotherapy, but it is related. Until someone does similarly robust research on the outcomes of coaching, we can borrow from the related field of therapy to underscore the importance of relationship skills.

This passionate focus on relationships is a key part of my coaching method and something that sets my approach apart from others. It's part of the theoretical underpinning of my executive coaching method. The stronger and more genuine the coach-client relationship, the easier, deeper, and faster the client progress will be.

Classical Conditioning

Classical conditioning is a type of unconscious or automatic learning. It involves forming an association between two stimuli, resulting in a learned response. The godfather of classical conditioning, Ivan Pavlov, discovered this learning process through experimentation with bells, dogs, and food.

Classical-conditioning techniques can be very useful in helping your client cope with stress, for example. Pairing something that provokes stress (such as giving a presentation; the first stimuli) with relaxation techniques (such as meditation or breathing exercises; the second stimuli) can create a positive association of relaxation and calm with a previously challenging situation of public speaking.

Operant Conditioning

Operant conditioning is about associating a voluntary behavior with a consequence. The learner is rewarded with incentives for demonstrating the desired behavior, thus building a strong positive association with this new behavior.

Operant conditioning increases the element of choice and helps your client know they're not stuck in a conscious or unconscious pattern. You can embed rewards for new behaviors and for successfully demonstrating new practices related to the coaching program. For example, a client may be working on establishing a more organized and efficient meeting structure for their team. Once they successfully implement this new set of behaviors, encourage a small reward, such as a walk outside or their favorite beverage.

CLIENT SPOTLIGHT

Jean-Francois Learning to Operate at a New Level

I worked with a leader, Jean-Francois, who was transitioning from director to vice president. Despite moving to a new level in the company, he found himself tempted to dive deeply into the details of his skip levels' work and even take some tasks on himself instead of building his delegation skills and managing through systems competencies—an example of his hardwired response to change was to work in overdrive.

This was not going to be sustainable at his new level and was causing issues on the team as well. As I worked with him to build his delegation skills, Jean-Francois experienced an immediate reward by delegating: free time! Other rewards from these new competencies were more delayed but just as powerful. For example, he was able to be more strategic, operating at the VP level more fully. He watched his team accomplish amazing things, better than even he could have done. When he stepped into his VP shoes more fully, he empowered his team to step into their shoes more fully as well.

Rewards were important motivators for Jean-Francois to continue with new competency development. He could see the improvements and changes almost immediately, which kept him in the game of practicing, taking more actions, and observing the results.

Competencies
Managing through systems, delegation, building a strong team

Reinforcement Theory

In short, reinforcement theory stipulates that behaviors are shaped by their consequences and can therefore be changed through rewards and punishments. This theory was originally published by B.F. Skinner and is a version of operant and classical conditioning.

In coaching, you primarily focus on positive and negative reinforcement. Positive reinforcement is when a desired behavior is followed by positive consequences. It can be powerful to have your client identify people in their network who can give real-time positive feedback when they see your client practicing new behaviors. Simone's IDP notes that she is seeking feedback from her colleagues on how she's doing with her composure (Template 3-2). That support structure is positive reinforcement at work in Simone's development.

Negative reinforcement is when a desired behavior is followed by removal of negative consequences. For example, a manager may stop giving constructive or developmental feedback on a behavior from your employee (the negative consequence). This is a desired result from the productive work of coaching. In your coaching conversations, explore what negative things were happening before that are no longer part of your client's day-to-day work experience.

Cognitive Behavioral Theory

Cognitive behavioral theory (CBT) is integral to coaching from a whole-person perspective. CBT suggests that our thoughts, emotions, body sensations, and behaviors are all connected, and that what we think and do affect the way we feel. Thousands of research studies have demonstrated that CBT is an effective treatment for many conditions, including anxiety, depression, pain, and insomnia.

In a coaching context, CBT helps clients see that beliefs affect thoughts and actions. We all carry innumerable unconscious beliefs that guide our actions day in and day out. Sometimes, these beliefs can be limiting.

For example, one client believed that he needed to be an expert on a topic before he could effectively present in front of others. In helping him tease out this belief, we could help him see that it was affecting his ability to speak in public. I offered the distinction that mastery of a topic is not required to be an effective speaker, but knowing enough to be credible and helpful was a more reasonable and accessible goal.

CLIENT SPOTLIGHT
Tackling Limiting Beliefs

I coached Leilani, who wanted to branch out within her company and expand how she saw herself. Profiles showed that she was deeply analytical, had an independent mind, and was demure, which was largely culturally developed.

She valued our coach-client relationship because she said she could talk to me about anything and she could be herself with me. Again, the power of a strong relationship! I continued to build up that relationship, focusing on the intimacy she valued, and then leaned on it to stretch her vision of her self-image.

By highlighting the parts of her profile that showed her analytical capabilities and independent mind, while simultaneously tackling some ingrained cultural limitations, we were able to get to a place where she didn't need permission from anybody else to think about herself in a new light. She developed an ability to think outside the box. I helped her envision herself as an independent, analytical expert (how I saw her), which was a bit of a stretch for her at first. With the experiments in the IDP and seeing herself through my eyes, we were able to work on her independent decision quality, her business acumen, and her managerial courage. Effective CBT helped Leilani change how she thought about herself and her vision for her future.

Leilani ended up branching out on her own and setting up shop as a business transformation consultant. A couple of years later, she returned to me to become an executive coach as well, rounding out her offerings. She continues to soar because her career is now congruent with her innate sense of self and natural competencies.

> Competencies
> Decision quality, business acumen, managerial courage

Stages of Psychosocial Development

For coaching engagements that are longer in duration, a coach can use psychologist Erik Erikson's research on the stages of psychosocial development. Erikson believed that personality developed in a series of stages and in the context of a larger community (Table 4-1; Cherry 2022). In each stage of development, he said a person will face a conflict that serves as a turning point in their development.

Table 4-1. Erikson's Psychosocial Stages

Age	Conflict	Important Events	Outcome
Infancy (birth to 10 months)	Trust vs. mistrust	Feeding	Hope
Early childhood (2–3 years)	Anatomy vs. shame and doubt	Toilet training	Will
Preschool (3–5 years)	Initiative vs. guilt	Exploration	Purpose
School age (6–11 years)	Industry vs. inferiority	School	Confidence
Adolescence (12–18 years)	Identity vs. role confusion	Social relationships	Fidelity
Young adulthood (19–40 years)	Intimacy vs. isolation	Relationships	Love
Middle adulthood (40–65 years)	Generativity vs. stagnation	Work and parenthood	Care
Maturity (65 to death)	Ego integrity vs. despair	Reflection on life	Wisdom

As coaches, we are deeply involved and connected to our client's development, so understanding the stages of development that Erikson codified in his research is a helpful compass for your shared journey. Based on this model, most clients you encounter will be in the stages focused on relationships and work and parenthood. The outcomes for each of these stages are love and care. This gives you some clues about what your client may be grappling with and places to jump in with skilled questions around these topics and outcomes.

CLIENT SPOTLIGHT
Preserving Keisha's Legacy

Becky coached an executive at a large insurance provider in California. Keisha had a more than 40-year career at this company and was pondering retirement. It was becoming increasingly important to her to preserve her legacy—to have her time and experience mean something for those she would leave behind upon retirement. She had "seen it all," as they say, and she didn't want her experience to go to waste.

This is a classic example of the maturity phase in Erikson's model. As Becky worked with Keisha to tease out this urgent need she had but couldn't clearly express, Keisha became more engaged with capturing her wisdom in a meaningful way. She reflected on her four-decade career and began capturing key experiences from the past that were relevant to big change efforts on the horizon. She briefed her team and colleagues in short conversations and shared documents as a way to transfer this knowledge before she retired.

Keisha experienced greater satisfaction in her final months with the company because she found a way to capture and share her relevant experience. This also allowed her to show up with more positivity and enthusiasm about the work ahead, confident that her experience would not be wasted.

Competencies
Knowledge sharing, collaboration, communication

Transformative Learning Theory

Transformative learning theory focuses on adult education and young adult learning. The core idea purported by Jack Mezirow, the primary creator of transformative learning, is that learners can adjust their thinking based on new information. This is a cognitive ability available to adults that is not as readily available to youth.

By studying adult women returning to school, Mezirow observed that critical reflection and review could lead to a transformation of students' understanding. He observed that adults, as compared with youth in a learning setting, are more capable of seeing distortions in their own beliefs, attitudes, feelings, and values. Adults are insight-oriented and can identify obstacles and challenges with more skill and immediacy than younger counterparts. These skills of reflection, self-awareness, and self-correction are core to effective coaching, revealing perspectives that create aha moments.

An example of this is our case study, Simone. As you might recall, Simone prefers short and direct communication, and this style worked well for years. However, when she started leading a new team that was unnerved by her style, it didn't work so well anymore. When she saw in her 360 results that people had negative feelings about and resentment toward her, she was at first resentful herself. However, when we reviewed the situation, she saw the team dynamics and feedback in a different light. She understood that the team wanted more warmth, connection, and compassion from their leader, and that this simple adjustment would go a long way in building team morale and loyalty. Simone had previously unconsciously believed that being quick and to the point was showing respect for her colleagues' time. Once she identified that belief and came to understand the team's desire for a different communication approach from her, Simone easily adjusted her communication style and even had conversations simply to build connection and relationships. That's transformative learning theory in action.

Experiential Learning Theory

Experiential learning theory is grounded in John Dewey's research that learning occurs within a social environment—that knowledge should be organized into real-life experiences that provide a context for the information. The concept states that people, especially adults, learn by doing. This is core to coaching!

Coaching invites clients into experiments for new ways of doing, thinking, leading, and managing. These are new experiences that help the client apply concepts and theories to their work and life and then learn from those experiences; increase their self-awareness; and reflect on what worked, what didn't work, and how to adjust the experiment to try again. Anchored in the IDP, you want to invite your client to try something new and develop self-awareness to assess how it went, capture their reflections, and help them begin to build the muscle of adaptive behavior, choosing more functional behavior in the moment.

You see experiential learning beautifully illustrated by Simone's IDP and the key actions or experiences she was practicing in each competency area. She had a chance to reflect on how it went and adjust for the next phase of applied learning. She demonstrated keen insight about the root of some of her behaviors and how she sought continued improvement through new experiments. This is experiential learning theory in action.

Max's Multipurpose Competency Development

Situations have a way of arising that allow you to work on several competencies at the same time with your client, for the same situation. It's an excellent growth spurt!

I had a client named Max preparing to interview for a new job internally. We worked on his listening and presentation skills in preparation for his job interviews. At the same time, and as part of our coaching work, he was working on his boss relationship competency, because the policy in his company was to obtain manager approval to interview for another job. So he was forced to improve his confidence in managing his manager through this potential job change.

Max was taking on many skills and competency enhancements to gain positive results and get to where he wanted to go: his new job opportunity! These were real-life experiences that helped frame the learning in a relevant and timely manner, aiding in the application of key concepts and overall integration of the coaching practices. The competencies we focused on helped him in this transition and would serve him well in his future.

Competencies
Listening, presentation skills, boss relationship

Make It Relevant

In short, your client learns by doing. This is the basis of the practice exercises and experiments that you assign each coaching session. Make sure your client knows why they are learning something. They will learn best when the subject is of immediate use, hence the regular practices and reflection that you'll dive into later in the chapter. Your client will need to try and try again before they begin to really embody a new skill or ability. They'll learn especially through support and feedback, which is a core part of your role.

You might also explore whether your client has a strong learning preference for visual, auditory, or kinesthetic (tactile). Try to tune your practices and experiments to their preferred way to learn, while also exploring other modalities to help round out their learning abilities.

Laura Builds Competencies While Doing Something New

As she jumped in, the first two competencies she had to strengthen were project management and prioritization. She got to work addressing the priorities: tasks, timelines, engaging with legal, communication plans, and so on.

However, what got lost in this focus on project management was her compassion for what was happening—the impact on the people, both those being laid off and those staying. This was a new competency for Laura to build in a high-stakes, highly visible project. She realized that she needed to step back from the project details and get in touch with her compassion. Her role would include teaching others how to engage with this work and their employees with more kindness and caring; she was the role model.

In the end, the layoffs were done well across the company, there were no negative reviews or legal issues, and the company was able to hire back some of this great talent when the business improved.

Competencies
Compassion, communication skills, managing change

Resistance to Change

In addition to the learning models and theories that underpin an effective coaching program, it's helpful to have insight into why it's so hard for humans to change: We're hardwired to resist it. A part of our brain called the amygdala has one job: to protect us from harm. When we're faced with something new, the amygdala makes a quick decision about whether this new thing might harm us. Change of any kind, even good change, is seen as a threat, and our available responses in this reactive moment include fight, flight, or freeze. Those might not seem like the most advanced or insightful responses, but they're your body's way of protecting you from harm. Overcoming this amygdala hijack requires your executive function, your brain's prefrontal cortex, to override the biological reaction to change. As a coach, you are helping the client battle this biological hardwiring as well as a lifetime of habits. Keep this in mind when engaging with your client, especially when (not *if*) you face resistance or inaction from them.

Stay Centered on the IDP

The IDP is the foundation of the work in the implementation step. In this phase, your client fills in the second half of the IDP as they reflect on actions, observation, and tools. The IDP is the home base for all coaching conversations and a place to both reflect on what's happened since the last conversation and set goals and actions for the period before the next coaching conversation. It's the road map that keeps you and the client focused on and attending to the work of application and experimentation.

The IDP is not one event. It's your road map for the entire coaching program. As the coach, you need to keep a handle on the original goals and purpose of the coaching engagement, which are grounded in the 360 and the IDP. Although the first half of the IDP is static once established, your client should continue to record their actions and observations throughout the whole of implementation.

ON THAT NOTE
The Crisis du Jour

Keep your client focused on the competencies identified as most meaningful for their growth as a leader. Your client will always have a crisis du jour, and although it's important to help them release steam and get them through any crisis, that is not the most important part of the coaching work. You're going for deeper change. Clients can be quite creative about avoiding the work—because it can be hard! They might have spent their careers or lives avoiding some of the challenges and competencies they now want to conquer. And there is that pesky amygdala, keeping your client safe from change.

You must keep them engaged in this deep work, and the IDP provides the structure in a clear and mutually agreed upon fashion. Although it is necessary for you and your client to have a friendly relationship with sincere rapport, remember that you are not their friend. If your coaching conversations begin to feel like a chat with a good mate, you're no longer coaching. Strengthen the roles and relationship, and correct this quickly and compassionately. Bring forth why you're in this together in the first place, as well as the insights from the 360 and information from the profiles, and get back to coaching.

Recall Simone's IDP from the last chapter (Template 3-2). As part of goal setting, Simone identified three competencies as her priorities: maintaining composure, receiving feedback, and listening. In implementation, Simone and I built out the corresponding actions to begin developing or deepening these competencies. As you can see in Table 4-2, these priorities become the framework for the subsequent implementation.

Table 4-2. Simone's IDP During Implementation

Actions	Client Observations	Tools
Composure • "Count to 10"—hold back first response (verbal or nonverbal) and regain composure after emotional response is triggered • Visual cues • Detect and control triggers	• I've noticed that counting to 10 and employing a softer tone resulted in a non-situation (which is the ideal outcome). • Even though I was frustrated the tech had not reviewed the chart to understand the clinical question that prompted the workup, I was able to avoid conflict. • In other situations, rather than get irritated with technicians, I kept my composure and told myself to let it go. By taking a step back, I had time to understand the root cause, while not compromising excellent patient care.	• FYI: *For Your Improvement* • Sticky notes at my workstation reminding me to count to 10 • People giving me feedback about how I'm handling the situation • NADINE • Tom's support • Self-care
Receiving Feedback • Ask for concrete examples • Initial task at time of getting feedback is to accurately understand what people are trying to say; the decision to accept or reject criticism is made at a later point in time • Thank people for the constructive criticism • View constructive criticism as an important part of the path to cultivating a culture of excellent patient care • Start choosing different response mechanisms going forward	• I'm less defensive and more receptive to the content of constructive criticism. I'm less reactive when I hear the advice. • I ask myself more often about the "why" to constructive criticism, rather than viewing it as a criticism of my character or standards. • I viewed the feedback as support rather than criticism. • I've my own defensiveness and harsh tone reflected during in-person interactions I recently had with my mom and sister, both of whom I have not seen in person for years. It has been enlightening to "watch myself" in them—I now realize that I've learned some of these traits from them. I can "unlearn" this response mechanism and choose my own path.	
Listening • Don't interrupt • Ask for the "why" of their decisions to understand their viewpoint • Restate the problem in my own words to everyone's satisfaction	• After the person has finished sharing their perspective, I tell them "I hear you" and genuinely mean it. The priority is that I let them know they are heard. • I restate my understanding of the "why" to their words to make sure I have not misperceived the intention behind them. • If I catch myself in haste or not able to listen fully, I come back at a later time, apologize for not being fully present, and ask to have a more in-depth conversation.	

During implementation, the client should continue to update their IDP (Template 3-1). Under "Actions," they should record their three competencies of focus. These are concrete; they do not change over the course of the engagement. With your help during coaching sections, the client identifies a few key actions to experiment with to build their confidence in new competencies. Many of these actions are sourced from *FYI*, but they can also be self-created by either the client or the coach.

This column of the IDP also reflects the 360 feedback received during the assessment phase of the coaching engagement. You will get input from your client's colleagues and manager about what they would like to see from your client in terms of improved behaviors or actions (in response to the questions on the 360 about what potential improvement opportunities your client has, as well as what three things your client can do today to improve themselves, the team, or the organization). It's important to guide your client to include these in the actions section so you both have confidence that the direct behavior improvements requested from key stakeholders are being addressed throughout the coaching engagement.

Ask your client to document observations in the IDP as homework *before* every coaching session because they'll become the basis for your coaching conversations. These insights are robust sources of coaching moments. You will learn what worked for your client and what didn't work. Over time, they may gain a deeper awareness and self-observation, which is a positive and productive outcome of this regular practice of documenting observations. Capturing their observations before coaching also holds them accountable to come prepared to the conversation, having done the work assigned previously and reflected on the impacts they observed from these new competencies.

Your client may have a key aha moment, as Simone did in realizing that some of her behaviors were rooted in her upbringing and the lack of good social interaction skills modeled in her home and within her family. Her medical residency then further shaped similar behaviors. Aha moments create a powerful opening to help your client begin to separate from their habitual, sometimes unconscious behaviors and shift into a behavior that is better aligned to who they want to be in the workplace.

Finally, the tools section includes key assets useful in the coaching process (like the *FYI* book), as well as people and practices that support your client. It can be helpful to have your client identify at least one person (besides you) who supports their growth and will be present after the coaching program concludes to continue to encourage growth and learning. Ask your client to update this section regularly in the coaching conversations, continuing to call attention to the support available, personally and professionally. It's also important to help them identify self-care practices that can be supportive during times of stress.

The Logistics of Your Coaching Conversations

The implementation phase will consist of a series of coaching conversations. As you engage your client in the ongoing work of implementation, there are important steps to attend to for each conversation.

Determine Frequency

The frequency with which you meet can vary by client. In general, you should plan to meet weekly or every other week for one to two hours, depending on the client's schedule and their ability to engage in the work. The minimum amount of time to hold the relationship and accountability is one hour every other week. Meeting less frequently than that will not allow you and your client to maintain a close relationship, and remember that it's the relationship in part that motivates your client to engage in the work of coaching.

Be available between sessions for calls, emails, document review, role plays, and check-ins with your client. Build your response time into your contract so they know what to expect. I recommend you commit to responding to client requests within one business day.

I also recommend scheduling check-in time on your calendar, especially for clients on a biweekly schedule, to remind them of actions and their commitment to document observations in the IDP before your next session. This helps them remember the practices, the experiments, and their own commitments, while also keeping them engaged in the process.

Prepare for Each Coaching Session

Preparation is key to bringing you back into the client's frame of mind before you are with them in their coaching session. Review the IDP, go over your notes from prior sessions, and ensure you know how you want the coaching conversation to flow. You want to have a sense of your client before you enter the coaching session, which helps set the stage for open, honest, and transparent conversation.

If there is a competency you haven't spent much time on, it may be appropriate to focus on that competency for the next coaching session or two. If you know that your client tends to enter coaching with a situational drama that can consume a lot of time (see "On That Note: Crisis du Jour"), plan for setting appropriate context for the coaching session, including limiting the amount of time you'll spend on what's happening in their work environment that day.

After reviewing your notes from the previous session, you may want to ask your client a few questions in the next session, but it's important that you schedule time for the client to speak first, and for them to direct the subject matter of the session as much as possible. When the client is ready to approach a topic, they may also be ready to accept accountability.

Prepare on the relationship front. Recall the relationship competencies detailed in chapter 1. Several relationship skills are used during implementation because of the variability of how programs are implemented as well as the duration of this phase. Patience, handling negative emotions, relational capacity, handling mistakes, and humor are the amplified relationship skills built on the superpower foundations of beacon of hope, customer focus, and monitoring and building the relationship.

This is a good time to call on your relational capacity and reflect deeply on your client's presence. Are they invested in the relationship? Do they demonstrate early trust in you and the four-step process? Are they completing the practices and agreements, or do they already have excuses or reasons for incomplete action? Notice how they are showing up in the early stages of implementation. Are they presenting with armor and protection, trying to look too perfect? Are they humble and curious, interested in what they are learning? Do they bring their insights from experiments and ask you for your insights as well? As part of your preparation, take stock in your relationship to learn how to piece it all together and hold the container for learning grounded in strong relationship capacity.

Additional preparation also means preparing yourself, which will look different for each coach. Practices you employ might include preparing for sessions, reviewing your notes and your reactions to the client, and taking stock of where you both are in the four-step process. We'll discuss more about the practices recommended for you, as a coach and an entrepreneur, in chapter 10.

Manage the Flow of the Coaching Conversation

Most coaching conversations are an hour. Be sure to attend to the overall flow of that hour in service to your client and your best competency-developing work together. You will develop your own style and approach and may even have a specific method for each client based on what is most effective for their style or preferences. Table 4-3 presents a sample agenda that you can customize as you see fit. (It's also included as Template 4-1.)

Table 4-3. Sample Agenda for Coaching Session

5 min.	Warm up and reconnect
15 min.	Updates on the work-life front, what's been happening since we last spoke, and observations on homework
25 min.	Review IDP: competencies, experiments, observations, and feedback
10 min.	Refine or renew experiments and practices
5 min.	Top three things from today's conversation, logistics for next session (if needed), and new homework

Consistently ending the meeting by asking the client to give a short recap of their top three things from the session ends the conversation on a high note. This technique gives you tremendous insight into what your client finds most memorable. Don't comment on their three things—this is their own subjective recollection of the most salient parts of the session. This also builds positive reinforcement into each coaching conversation.

I am often surprised and humbled by what stands out to clients. I hear all kinds of things, ranging from sharp insights to how they are feeling deep down about themselves or their situation. There is usually some overlap with what stands out to me, showing alignment and integration of the shared experience.

Template for Success

> Template 4-1. Agenda for Coaching Conversation
> A suggested agenda to structure your coaching conversations. You will find your own pacing and template over time.

Take Notes on the Coaching Session

It's essential that you take effective notes during your coaching session. This discipline gives you a chance to summarize what you think is important and keep a thread of development consistent throughout the coaching program. You can use Template 4-2, "Meeting Notes Form," for this purpose. You'll also use your notes later as a reference when setting action steps for your client's goals. Taking detailed notes and referring to them helps the client feel seen and understood, thereby helping deepen the relationship.

Some coaches prefer to take notes in real time. Pay attention to your engagement and presence with your client. The priority is staying present, continuing to build the relationship and trust. If your note-taking diminishes this connection, it's ultimately not effective. Consider recording your sessions (with permission) so you can capture notes afterward. This is a particularly helpful idea for those new to coaching, because you have a chance to observe and assess yourself as well.

Luckily, I have a good memory and for the most part take very minimal notes in real time. I usually include IDP progress, three things that stand out, and homework. I keep the notes "neutral," focused on process and progress. In the back of my mind, I also imagine what it would look like to an outsider to read my notes, with the goal that it wouldn't make much sense to them and couldn't be used against my client or their company.

ON THAT NOTE
Confidential Note-Taking

A few times in my long career, clients have been involved in employee-relations, legal, or public-relations issues. When there's an investigation, the internal or external legal expert or the company's HR department might request to see the coaching session notes, which I refuse. If there is a threat of subpoena, I will have the client show their IDP, which is a fairly neutral document. Usually, the manager has already seen it, so it doesn't add that much information or value. If there is a direct subpoena for my notes, I'll comply; because of the way I write my notes, there really is no harm in sharing them. This information about notes is also good to keep in mind as you protect your business.

Others prefer to capture key thoughts, takeaways, and insights right after the coaching session. This requires adding a buffer to your calendar and can be cared for with attention to your scheduling. If this is your preference, learn to capture the moments and insights that will be most helpful in continuing development. For example, if your client is working on the competency of building strong teams and taking a new approach to hiring and developing, your review of actions, experiments, and observations will be key to both you and your client.

If your client is challenged with remembering content or homework or just needs more structure, it can be helpful to offer coaching notes that serve as a summary and memory prompt. In this situation, you can email your coaching notes along with the main themes of the session, reflections and observations, assigned homework, and three things that stand out about the coaching session. This is a tactic to align on key themes and actions that the client will take before you meet again. Template 4-3 presents an example of session notes you might share with your client.

Lastly, you can offer a journal to your client, such as the example in Template 4-4. Present it at the outset of the coaching program or at any point it seems supportive to recommend the practice of journaling, so your client can capture their insights.

Templates for Success

Template 4-2. Meeting Notes Form
A suggested note-taking form for keeping track of key points in the coaching sessions. It's for your own records and not typically shared with the client.

Template 4-3. Sample Session Summary for Client
A suggested format for summarizing your notes and insights for the purpose of sharing with your client. This helps ensure clear communications and improved engagement on experiments and practices agreed to in the coaching session.

Template 4-4. Client Session Journal Form
A handy tool your client can use to capture notes, insights, and action items. Particularly if it's clear your client doesn't have basic note-taking systems in place or would benefit from separating work and coaching notes, this can help keep them in process between sessions.

Assign Homework Between Coaching Sessions

We thought we were done with homework when we finished school, but we're never really done learning, are we? Assign homework each coaching session—through practices, exercises, and other assignments—to help your client engage more deeply in their learning process. You can assign reading, recommend a book for deep exploration of a topic, send articles or TED Talks, or use any other means that you think will help your client stay engaged in the process and see things, even themselves, from a different perspective. There are also numerous resources offered for every competency in *FYI*. Make sure your client is reviewing and updating their IDP between every session and returning it to you in advance of the next session.

The work between the sessions is almost more important than the coaching sessions themselves, so be thoughtful and specific about the homework. Share the purpose of the assignment so your client has a place to anchor their learning and understand why you are assigning a particular book, article, or practice. Check in with your clients on their homework, building it into the coaching session so they begin to treat you as an accountability partner. You are helping create the space during the sessions, and then hold that container between the sessions through homework.

ON THAT NOTE
Homework for the Executive With No Time

It's worth reiterating that you are working with very busy executives. They already have an overflowing plate with competing priorities. They may resist adding these actions to their schedule. It's important to set this expectation of engaging with the homework up front and then hold them accountable for their work throughout the coaching program. This is where your understanding of what motivates them can be useful. Ensure that you have a clear agreement to practice, experiment, and do homework assignments, then discuss how they will support themselves to complete these actions. If needed, spend the last five minutes of each coaching session helping your client build the work into their calendar—this can also help them with the time management competency. Getting your client to do their homework is also where your own key coaching skill of courage comes into play—to hold the standard for performance with this high-performing leader.

If you think it will be helpful, ask your client to fill out and return a pre-session form (Template 4-5) within 24 hours of every session, but not earlier, so their observations are fresh and reflect the work of the whole span between sessions. This can help get your client in the right frame of mind and gives them ideas for what they want to talk about in the next coaching session. You can also share Template 4-6, "How to Prepare for a Coaching Session Checklist," which gives your client a very specific and structured way to ensure engagement and accountability.

Templates for Success

Template 4-5. Pre-Session Form
If your client will benefit from more intentional structure and support, use this template to get them thinking and processing (and completing experiments!) ahead of each coaching session.

Template 4-6. How to Prepare for a Coaching Session Checklist
A checklist is another way to hold your client accountable and help them prepare for a coaching session. This is most useful at the beginning of an engagement or anytime you see your client struggling to come to your coaching session fully prepared.

Coaching Toolkit for Implementation

These techniques are the heart of your coaching conversations. Now that you have established the framework for the ongoing development, identified key focus areas, and assigned actions, coaching during implementation focuses on experimentation, practices, feedback, and other engagements aimed at your client's ongoing development. You will give assignments to coaching clients to help them meet the goals in their IDP. These may include reading, watching a TED Talk, practicing new competencies, running a meeting differently, or experimenting with new behaviors, as well as evaluating the response or results. Use your wisdom to piece together implementation practices that make sense for your client and their goals.

Experimenting and practicing can be challenging for your client. You will rely on the power of your relationship and the trust you have built to invite them into these practices, and then explore the insight and learning together. You will help them stay energized to try new things and help them extract the "so what" insights that keep them motivated. Your relationship skills continue to be paramount to the coaching program.

Encourage Experimentation

Encourage your client to experiment by intentionally trying new behaviors, actions, thoughts, or habits to "live into" a new way of being related to a competency. This requires some faith that your client can achieve a positive outcome. It's grounded in the trust created between you and the client.

Help your client identify experiments by asking questions like:

- What would it look like to be excellent in this competency?
- What gets in your way of a more favorable behavior related to this competency?
- Who around you demonstrates this skill exceptionally well? What do they do?
- Why is this important for you to improve or resolve?
- How can you help yourself remember your goal related to this experiment?
- How will you stay committed, even when facing challenges or adversity?

Remind the client that when they try something new or different, they're also retraining their team, colleagues, manager, or partner in how to interact with them. That's not always easy! Your client may be changing up the rules of engagement, and it will take some time for those in their circles to adjust. Remind them not to get discouraged if things don't go perfectly the first time they attempt a new behavior. Stay with the work and invite them to remember their motivation for engaging coaching. Remembering their *why* will help them stay committed and persevere during challenges or pushback. This also helps build their competency in conflict management, which can take more time and repetition to master than other competencies.

Remember to pull on their motivation to help them stay committed to their practices, even when things don't go as expected. Resistance to experimentation or to reporting back and reflecting on experiments could cause a covert or overt conflict with you, the coach. Ask for permission to highlight and name any interpersonal elements between them and you. For example, they might be embarrassed that they didn't follow through on something, but your relationship is much deeper than some missed homework. Call upon the relationship capacities detailed in chapter 1 and have the conversations necessary to get and keep the coaching engagement on track. Then, get to the bottom of the cause of their resistance, leaning on your relationship to help them through any reservations or resistance to following through on their IDP.

Agree on Practices

Collaborate with your client to brainstorm practices that could help them build or deepen a selected competency. Use *FYI* as a foundation in the conversation to explore what it looks like to be a role model in a particular competency. Review the remedies offered as inspiration for the potential experiments and practices. Guide them based on your perspective of the client, grounded in your experience and expertise. Remind them what success looks like, continuing in your role as beacon of hope and inspiring them to engage the selected practices or experiments with strong intention and a learning mind.

Practices—consistent activities or repetition of new behaviors that transform their experience—will help your client attain the behaviors outlined in the IDP. They can range from assignments that capture their learning to exercises that improve their presence. This chapter provides a sample of practices, and you will curate many others over your coaching career.

Many books have practices integrated into the text or in an appendix to help deepen the learning. Every chapter in *FYI* that focuses on a competency highlights numerous practices to help inspire development of that competency. I recommend you create a library of practices that are well crafted with clear instructions and build a discipline around evaluating the effectiveness of these practices over time.

Think about practices in two categories: competency development and personal development. Practices for competency or skill development are broad and varied. The 38 distinct competencies that *FYI* offers have been determined through research to be crucial for your executive. In practice, the following competencies especially bubble to the top for my executives:

- **Drives vision and purpose.** This is about painting a compelling vision for the future and creating a strategy that includes and motivates others to achieve the vision. People will look to their leaders to provide direction and clarity during times of uncertainty and change. They want something to aspire to and believe in, and to contribute to something larger than themselves. A leader's privilege is to create a vision that compels others to action. This can be a crucial competency for your executive to develop. Skilled leaders talk about future possibilities, create milestones to rally support, articulate the vision in a compelling way, generate organization-wide optimism for the future, and show personal commitment to the vision.

- **Directing work.** This involves providing clear direction, delegating, and removing obstacles to getting work done. It represents a shift from doing to leading and getting the work done through others. A leader needs to give up control, trust others, provide adequate resources, and empower their team. This is also a shift from being the technical or subject-matter expert to leading those experts. Skilled leaders provide clear direction, hold people accountable, delegate with resources, monitor and measure progress, and remove obstacles to the team's progress.

- **Communicating effectively.** This is the ability to develop and deliver communications in all modalities that convey a clear understanding of each audience. Leaders communicate all day to a wide variety of audiences using a vast array of tools and modalities. Being an excellent communicator is a core leadership competency. Good communication creates mutual understanding, harmony, and action. It saves time and resources, accelerates goal achievement, and keeps healthy relationships intact. The skilled leader communicates effectively in a variety of settings at all levels and with varying communication styles (such as one-on-one, small and large groups, and large keynotes). Skilled leaders attentively and skillfully listen to others, adjust their message to fit the audience, provide timely and transparent information, and encourage open expression of ideas.

- **Builds effective teams.** This one is about attracting top talent, creating a strong identity, and inviting your team to apply their diverse skills and perspectives to achieve shared goals. Teams are the primary way work gets done. To be a team (not just a group reporting to the same person), shared goals and interdependency are necessary. Great teams require attention and intention to create purpose, define tasks, build relationships, and establish supporting processes. Skilled leaders build diverse teams, establish common objectives and goals, create a feeling of belonging, share wins and rewards, and foster open dialogue.

- **Strategic mindset.** This competency is the ability to see future possibilities and translate them into compelling business strategies. This requires both long-view thinking and the ability to see how to tactically pursue the strategy. This includes decisions like mergers, investment strategy, build versus buy, organic growth versus inorganic growth, adjacent market opportunities, expansion, and reduction of product portfolio. Skilled leaders anticipate future trends, pose future scenarios, articulate credible possibilities, and create breakthrough strategies that connect vision and action.

Practices for personal development or self-care are also wide and varied. Most high-performing executives could use more focus on self-care, so thinking through practices in support of their balanced development will be critical for effective coaching. Many of these topics and corresponding practices are covered in excellent detail in my book *Stress-Less Leadership* (Entrepreneur Press 2019). There are, of course, many additional resources to build out these practices around self-care, and books on these topics should be an integral part of your bookshelf. I offer a few personal development ideas here to get your creative juices flowing, both for yourself and for your clients:

- **Journaling** is a powerful reflection and learning practice. You can invite your client into open-ended journaling or give them prompts to respond to on a regular cadence throughout the week. Substantial research underscores the value of journaling for executives. A terrific article in *Harvard Business Review* purports there is "strong evidence that replaying events in our brain is essential to learning. While the brain records and holds what takes place in the moment, the learning from what one has gone through—that is, determining what is important and what lessons should be learned—happens after the fact during periods of quiet reflections" (Ciampa 2017). You could offer your client the miracle diary exercise for a specific journal practice (Template 4-7). Have them journal in a different way from how they work day to day, which can help create a unique reflection experience. If they work on a computer all day, I'd recommend they keep a handwritten journal, and journal somewhere other than work. This can invite more in-depth insight and learning (and is potentially more private if they are a high-profile leader).

- **Meditation** can be life-changing for many executives. The pace of work and the tremendous demands put on leaders call for even more grounded calmness, which a regular meditation practice can help cultivate. It's become such a transformational practice that many companies offer meditation and mindfulness as part of their wellness programs. Smartphone apps such as Calm and Headspace are a great place to begin a meditation journey. Don't be surprised or deterred if your client dismisses this practice or jokes that they failed meditation. Invite clients to start small—five minutes of intentional practice per day can make a big difference.

- **Nature** is restorative. Research has amplified the need for people to be in nature more regularly. In fact, some healthcare providers prescribe walks in nature for physical and mental wellness. There are many ways to offer this practice of being in nature. For example, you could suggest that a client who runs marathons take a slow-paced, luxurious walk in nature and journal about what they notice. You could invite a client who would benefit from more strenuous, heart-pumping exercise to go for a hike and pay attention to how their body responds to being worked in this way. The point is to be outside, in fresh air; move in a different way; and notice what comes up. Of course, make sure your clients take care of their own safety. Sadly, threats against people in high power are increasing, against women and people of color in particular. While they are likely already paying attention to this trend, mentioning any risks involved in being alone indicates that you care for them and your relationship.

- **Exercise** is an essential practice in combating stress and being more resilient as a leader. Cognitive function is directly linked to physical fitness. Exercise helps support concentration, memory function, learning, mood, and creativity. Your client may need to add aerobic activities to their schedule. If they already have a practice of running, swimming, biking, kickboxing, or other means of intense physical fitness, consider recommending something to balance that, like yoga or qigong. This is an opportunity for them to experience balance in fitness routines and see what they might learn. Pay attention to their privacy by recommending in-home coaching, online training, or other options that will help them maintain anonymity and independence.

- **Social support** is more important than ever. Help your client create social structures and relationships that are in their best interest. At work and in life, we need one another to thrive, and with some intentionality, you can support your client in creating or recreating a social network that sustains them in times of experimentation and practice and beyond. Your client likely has a close group of friends and family, so encourage them to carefully select who should be part of this trusted inner circle. This can help them assess who's present already, whom to add to the group, and who might not be suited for this intimate engagement.

If you are coaching a high-profile leader or officer in a public company or government agency, be sensitive to possible adaptations to ensure privacy.

Template for Success

Template 4-7. Miracle Diary
A practice for recording positive events and happy moments for a client working on deepening gratitude and appreciation. Journaling can help your client process events and emotions to support learning.

Offer Feedback

A big part of your role is to offer continuous feedback for growth and development. You are in a front-row seat to your client's unfolding journey, and your job as a broker of hope is to continue to support and challenge them with their learning. Tackle barriers immediately—you have good instinct as a coach, so give that instinct a voice in sessions.

It's your role to ask that next question, to explore with deep curiosity what's becoming known to your client, and, with kindness and compassion, to invite them to explore with you. If they are taking the easy road—and you'll know when that happens—remind them of their development, career, or other goals and implore them to engage the coaching journey more deeply. Offer your perspective and insights, what you see in terms of development, and perhaps where they may still need further development. Continue to shape their growth through motivation and support, and sometimes with some challenges. Your ability to speak your truth, calling it as you see it, is a foundational coaching capability and responsibility.

Ask Skillful Questions

As a skillful listener, you will be prepared to always ask smart, necessary questions. Coaching is a personal engagement focused on your client's development goals. Talented coaches know how to ask skillful questions, helping the client identify options, define their own success criteria, think through solutions, and choose the best path forward. Coaches don't usually directly solve their clients' problems. Rather, they engage in dialogue to help the client solve the problems themselves. Coaching is built on asking skillful questions and avoiding solution mode (unless it's providing a resource or adding a solution option for a technical matter that would take them too long to get to alone). You never want to inhibit someone's learning by jumping in to rescue them or solve a problem for them. Exercise your humility by asking questions rather than telling or solving.

Hold Accountability

A prime responsibility for an executive coach is to act as an accountability partner, ensuring that your client is doing the work to help them achieve their goals. When your client seems lackluster about the coaching work—and that's likely to happen for a variety of valid (and not as valid) reasons—keep the purpose of the coaching program as a central focus. Remind them about the goals and aspirations that brought them to coaching in the first place. Make sure they know from the beginning that you will hold them accountable for the work, in service to their own competency development and dreams. As needed, you can always refer your client to the "Expectations of Coaching Engagement Agreement" and the "Accountability Form" (Templates 1-7 and 1-8).

Make Distinctions

Make important distinctions for your client to help them reframe. A distinction is when you contrast two or more things, concepts, or ideas and help your client learn from the new perspective. You can offer perspective and perhaps a different way of looking at a pervasive challenge by reframing it or showing it in a different light. You answer the question "What else might be true here?"

You make many distinctions throughout your day and in various conversations. They show you a different way to understand or relate to something. Making distinctions is an important element of coaching. Being able to offer another perspective, in your client's language and appropriate to their development stage, can awaken a new learning or insight.

For example, I had a client whose boss had scheduled a meeting with no agenda and on short notice. My client was concerned by this sudden meeting invite and had a tough time figuring out how to prepare for or engage in the meeting. I invited them to evaluate why they were stirred up by this meeting invite, calling their attention to the fact that it was different from the last time their boss had scheduled a last-minute meeting in which they'd learned they were being laid off. I helped them release this old narrative, so they entered the meeting with less trepidation and a more open mindset.

Defuse Breakdowns

It's possible your client will have a breakdown during a coaching session or a period of helplessness in the wake of any sort of stressor. This is an incredible opening for learning and growth. Develop an ear for detecting and addressing breakdowns. The client may be subtle about the issue that is emerging, and without some skill in noticing their verbal and nonverbal cues, you may miss it. Addressing breakdowns is a chance to build your client's competence, deepen their commitment, and improve the structure of your coaching practices.

A breakdown can be momentous, like "I've lost my job and I'm depressed." Or it could be a small hint at something much larger, like "I can't hear positive feedback, and I question myself when people recognize me for achievements." How you engage the next set of questions will vary widely based on what your client is offering you. A possible invitation for further exploration could be, "That is a significant disruption; how are you processing this information? What is the impact on your body, mood, emotion, or mindset?" Or, for the subtle opening, further exploration could be, "Tell me more about this insight. Why is it important to you? What could it mean that you reject positive feedback? Where does this pattern originate?"

A breakdown can also be a break in the practices, such as your client not attending to the work between sessions or not getting any insight from the assigned homework. Your skill in detecting the breakdown and addressing the concerns directly will help establish your position as trusted advisor and broker of hope for your client's growth. Questions to explore include "What about this practice is difficult for you? Is this a pattern (of not adhering to agreements) in your work? Where else does this show up in your life?"

If your client is experiencing a breakdown of not completing the practices or homework they decided on and agreed to, pay attention to your instructions and your skill at securing their agreement to complete the practices. You may be assigning practices that are too advanced for your client. If this is the case, dial back the intensity or the complexity. The instructions or work may be unclear or unspecific. In this instance, be disciplined about clear instructions, and the frequency and intention of assignments. You may be missing the crucial step of securing your client's agreement when assigning the practice. If this is the case, ensure you build in clear agreements and accountability language in your conversation, with written follow-up.

CLIENT SPOTLIGHT

The Client's Personal Circumstances

Filomenia, a vice president in a public-relations firm, had come to me for coaching to help her on her new assignment. She'd been tasked with leading the startup of a new office in another state. Despite the many activities involved in moving to another state and setting up a new office, Filomenia was always able to decide on and complete her coaching experiments . . . until she wasn't.

As we explored this shift, and what was happening in her life that would make it more difficult for her to engage in coaching, she revealed that her marriage had taken a hit with the move *and* she had lost her accounts director. Two big relationship changes were affecting her time as well as her ability to focus on work and coaching assignments during this intense professional and personal move.

We adjusted the homework to give her more time to complete it and more time to reflect on her learning and insights. Given the change in her circumstances, we agreed to update her IDP to add a personal disclosure to deepen skills in being more self-aware and self-disclosing. This addressed the fact that I'd had to figure out what was going on with her, rather than her offering these insights. We also added hiring and staffing as a focus area, which freed up more time for her to spend on her coaching engagement.

I am so glad that I noticed the lack of engagement and had built a strong relationship that allowed me to directly address this shift and face the breakdowns head-on. It took courage on her part to dig deeper and bring these things to light. In the end, it strengthened our relationship and the work as well. She has since opened three other offices and is dating again!

If this breakdown continues, I recommend you use the pre-session form (Template 4-5) and share the checklist for preparing for the coaching session (Template 4-6) to help create the structure and accountability necessary for your client's development.

Deploy Interventions

During implementation, your focus is on assisting your client in meeting the coaching goals. Over the years, I've found it best to do this in the regular coaching sessions as well as in the engagement between the sessions to help hold accountability and continue to build the relationship.

There are many interventions you can deploy when working with clients. You will develop your own that align to your voice and values, ones you have found effective in the situations you experience as a coach. I offer numerous standard engagement strategies here to help you begin to build this framework. You can also revisit this list if you aren't making the inroads you expect with your client, to ensure you're courageously engaging all the tools in your coaching toolkit.

Overall, these interventions will help your client celebrate their wins and feel supported, hold the tension of development, and sometimes confront their self-limiting beliefs or biases. Choose the right intervention for your client and their stage of development. If they're overwhelmed or unable to absorb at that moment, go back to more supportive interventions like *engage, build trust*, or *support*.

A client may take the position that there is nothing they can do about a situation. Perhaps they seem stuck or lost. They have resigned. Don't get hooked by learned helplessness that may show up in your coaching engagement. Build your client's competencies of critical thinking, problem solving, and a learning mindset. Support *and* challenge them to glean their own insights and harvest their learning. Remind them of times they solved similar issues. Ask skillful questions: "What are two choices you have at this moment? What would you advise your friend in a similar situation to do? What action can you take today toward your goal?" Connect their actions to their beliefs, use reframing, and challenge their thinking.

Always make sure you have a theoretical framework in mind behind an intervention. You need to stay highly engaged and 100 percent conscious about what you're doing and saying when you are working with someone's development. Each intervention is a careful choice. This overview of critical intervention skills serves as a foundation for your verbal exchanges with your coaching clients. It's also an invitation to learn more, develop your competencies as a coach, and continue to refine your approach with each individual who has entrusted you with their development.

The following three sections offer ideas that you can customize as you develop your own coaching interventions and best practices. I suggest keeping them close at hand and reviewing them periodically. (These interventions are also included as Template 4-8.)

Template for Success

Template 4-8. Coaching Interventions Aid
Reference these lists of coaching interventions as you work with a client. Add interventions or otherwise revise this tool to be most useful to you.

Supportive Interventions

Supportive interventions include strategies for supporting or celebrating your client, helping them release a block or be seen in this moment.

Anchor New Ways

When developing a new competency, it's powerful to tie that new skill to adjoining competencies or the role the client occupies. Over time, this helps the new competency become more automatic. This is likely more helpful as you get into the middle of implementation and can help to connect the dots of the overall program and outcomes so far, as well as anchor those outcomes in new competencies.

Coach's questions or statements:

- "This competency is linked to an overall executive skill area of X. How will improvement in this area improve X overall?"

Build Trust

This is core to relationship building and sets the foundation for the entire coaching program. Show that the relationship is grounded in integrity, showing up as your full self, and being trusting and trusted. Share information about the process; inform your client of what's happening along the way and how the process will work. You're always working to build trust with your client.

Coach's questions or statements:

- "How are you experiencing our time together and work?"
- "How are you feeling just now or these days?"
- "Do you have any questions about the process or how we'll work together?"

Camera Work

This can be significant for certain competencies, such as presentation skills or improving nonverbal communications. Recording, with permission, can illustrate tremendous opportunities for continued development. Use this intervention when your client has a challenge that self-observation would be especially helpful in overcoming.

Coach's questions or statements:

- "What do you observe about your nonverbal communication?"
- "Are your words aligned in tone and intent with what your face and body are expressing?"
- "How are your employees responding to you at this moment?"

Cathartic

Help the client release tension or come to terms with emotions that are blocking their progress. If the client is afraid of risk or failure, feels incompetent, or is frustrated, helping them release these unhelpful restrictions is powerful. This is used when you notice an emotional block or hesitancy to move forward with an action or a practice.

Coach's questions or statements:

- "In your heart of hearts, what are you feeling about this topic?"
- "What is the most intense part of this situation?"
- "What are you ready to let go of?"

Celebrate

Highlight progress, insights, and positive outcomes from the experiments the client is engaging. Use at any time to celebrate small wins and big wins to keep your client in process and reinforce desired new behaviors.

Coach's questions or statements:

- "Let's take a moment to celebrate this achievement."
- "That is a huge win. How does it feel to accomplish that?"
- "What a helpful insight. What does that tell you about your growth in this area?"

Connect the Dots

Show how experiences are connected. Highlight patterns you see in your client and their circumstances. Help them see the system within which they're operating and the powerful actions they can take to improve themselves in that system.

Coach's questions or statements:

- "Do you see how this is related to X?"
- "I see a pattern here, so zooming out, where else does this show up in your life?"

Encourage Experimentation

Engage your client to try a new behavior or language to create a different outcome. Present it as experimentation, trying something new, and piloting a concept. This is used in almost every coaching session as part of reviewing the IDP's actions and observations.

Coach's questions or statements:

- "I'm inviting you to practice X in the coming weeks. How does that sound? Will you commit to that experiment?"

Engage

Build real-time rapport with the client. Define the relationship and the expectations. Use this especially in the beginning, but remember that you're always in a process of reengaging, between sessions and at the start of each session.

Coach's questions or statements:

- "What is on your mind now?"
- "What have you been working on?"
- "What has occurred to you about our engagement?"

Inform

Give information and knowledge. If you know something your client needs to know, don't wait for them to discover it. Share your knowledge to help them learn from your experiences. This can be a helpful jump start to further exploration and study on the client's behalf.

Coach's questions or statements:

- "Let me share some research with you."
- "This book/article has been helpful with other clients."
- "I have experienced this before, and here are some ideas to address this challenge."

Monitoring

Used in session and very helpful in person, monitoring is the work of coaching. It's helpful to see how the client interacts with their team or customers and their office environment and how people respond to them. This is an action that a coach takes; they may offer observations afterward that could help in the "Actions" section of the IDP.

Coach's questions or statements:

- "How are you doing on your experiments? Let's review them."

Offer Support

Used in session, this can help clarify what support the client needs to make progress. Use this when your client could use some additional help and may not know how to ask for it. Build the client's self-esteem, self-confidence, and self-respect. Demonstrate empathy for their experiences while holding the tension of development and learning. Underscore that this is a safe space for deep emotions.

Coach's questions or statements:

- "How can I help you?"
- "What would be supportive?"

Prescribe

Give instructions, advice, or recommendations. This is helpful if the client lacks confidence or is unable to direct their own learning yet.

Coach's questions or statements:

- "I see you would like to work on X. Maybe you could give Y a try."

Reframe

Help the client see a situation in a different light. Show a new way of looking at a situation, person, or conflict. This is helpful if the client seems stuck in a certain perspective or is not able to see other sides of a situation. This helps them learn perspective taking, a key skill in building self-awareness.

Coach's questions or statements:

- "Let's look at this from another perspective."
- "Can you argue the other side?"
- "If you were the other person in this dynamic, how might you be feeling or what might you be thinking?"

Rehearse or Role Play

For difficult conversations or experiments, offering to role play the other person or even your client's role can be helpful to model the interaction. This is powerful for the client to see how it can be done (role model) and then practice in their own voice and style (rehearse) with your feedback and support.

Coach's questions or statements:

- "Would you like to practice this situation so you feel better prepared when it comes up?"

Reinforce

This is a version of celebration, focused on lessons learned, insights gained, and progress made. It helps the learning to stick. The three good things practice (found later in this chapter) is an example of this reinforcement intervention. This is especially helpful if the client is having success with some new actions. Reinforce the learning and the positive outcomes they've created.

Coach's questions or statements:

- "Do you see how your improvement in X has a knock-on effect in Y?"
- "What further insights can you share from this accomplishment?"

Round Back

Take good session notes and return to topics previously discussed. Revisit the IDP and key themes from prior conversations, and reflect on what is similar to prior episodes or experiences. This is a key intervention for coaching conversations and used regularly in sessions.

Coach's questions or statements:

- "Let's review the themes from last time."
- "This seems to come up in your relationships. Let's look at a few examples from our time together."
- "How is this related to the experience you shared last time?"

Shadow

Often leveraged at the outset of a coaching engagement, the opportunity to be with your client in their day-to-day work can be illuminating. You have a chance to observe and assess them in a variety of interactions and can use those insights to continue their learning.

Coach's questions or statements:

- "I'd like to shadow your interactions during X so we can identify experiments that can help you reach your goal."

Challenging Interventions

Challenging interventions include strategies for pushing your client to do more, dig deeper, challenge their biases or assumptions, or expose the core issue.

Assess

Foundational to coaching, assessment is about continually assessing your client's thinking, approach, engagement, and commitment. This also includes self-assessment. Continually assess in coaching conversations and spend some time after each session to self-assess as well.

Coach's questions or statements:

- "Am I being a good coach?"
- "Are they overcoming obstacles?"
- "How is the health of our relationship?"

Draw Out

A regular intervention used to engage the client in sharing more information or providing more context. This is helpful if you believe the client is holding back or hasn't made time to deeply reflect.

Coach's questions or statements:
- "Let's explore X more."
- "Tell me more about Y."

Increase Insight

Help your client deepen their awareness of a particular insight. You help them draw conclusions and shed some light on a topic so they can understand themselves and the situation more. Use this when a new insight is made or you have fresh observation from an action. You can help make the learning even deeper and broader by increasing insight.

Coach's questions or statements:
- "What conclusions can you draw from that?"

Stimulate Motivation

Part of your job as a coach is to keep the client engaged in the work of coaching. Leverage the 360 process and profiles to learn what motivates your client and tie their experiments and actions to these personal desired outcomes. This is important when your client seems stuck or isn't making the progress you expect to see.

Coach's questions or statements:
- "How does this help you achieve your goal of X?"
- "How is this related to your vision for yourself as a leader?"

Wonder Out Loud

A posture of curiosity is taken in session to explore alternative approaches and different possibilities to offer a new way of thinking. This can be used when you want to open your client up to another point of view or softly challenge their thinking and assumptions.

Coach's questions or statements:
- "I wonder if you've considered X?"
- "Have you thought about Y?"
- "What would research tell us about Z?"

Directly Challenging Interventions

Directly challenging interventions more assertively confront or challenge your client. Use them when your client seems stuck in a particular belief, bias, attitude, or assumption that isn't correct, complete, or helpful. Your client may be digging into a position or making conclusions based on something other than the facts you can see in the situation. Use these interventions selectively to directly confront your client and invite them to see another perspective. These interventions help you support your client in getting underneath what drives their beliefs more directly.

Catalyst

When your client needs to make a decision, sometimes you need to be the catalyst for that decision. When you're hearing the same thing and your client seems stuck, you can challenge them to action.

Coach's questions or statements:

- "What additional piece of information do you need to decide?"
- "What is going to light a fire under this?"
- "What are you waiting for?"
- "Why are you unwilling to make a decision?"

Challenge Thinking Process

Be courageous to directly confront your client and their thinking process.

Coach's questions or statements:

- "How did you get from A to B?"
- "What information did you use to make those conclusions?"
- "Upon what beliefs is that conclusion based?"

Confront

Challenge the client's assumptions. Stimulate their awareness of their own behaviors, attitudes, or beliefs.

Coach's questions or statements:

- "Is there an underlying belief you are aware of?"
- "In your heart of hearts, what do you believe about that?"

Connect Actions to Beliefs or Values

Understand if there is a belief system or value that underpins an action or a behavior. Question the underlying belief or bias that may be in play. Some of these may be long held and unconscious to your client.

Coach's questions or statements:

- "What belief system is driving this behavior?"
- "What value do you place in behavior X?"
- "What is important to you about this?"

Question

Challenge their logic, conclusions, and assumptions. Dig deeper into what they're truly feeling about a situation and what happened. Push back a bit.

Coach's questions or statements:
- "Can you explain your logic?"
- "What data did you use to draw that conclusion?"
- "Are you holding any assumptions that may no longer be true?"

Make Use of *FYI*

FYI is an anchor when implementing your client's IDP. Each competency chapter in the book details development tips or remedies that are grounded in research and highlight how to gain the experiences and learning to help develop a particular competency. You get a good sense of what the development tips look like in action. Each chapter offers many remedies, sometimes 15 or more, all focused on how a lower competency shows up in a work setting. This is a useful place to spend some time with your client to focus on their particular ways of doing (or not doing) something.

For example, returning to Simone and listening skills, two remedies may be strong development paths for her. If the core issue of poor listening is a desire to ensure she's heard, the remedy is to slow down and listen. If the core issue is not being open to others' ideas, the remedy is to solicit input and facilitate discussion. You can see how this same low skill in listening shows up differently. You need to explore what is right for your client and then review that deeper focus area together. These remedies give you excellent ideas for actions your client can take between coaching conversations as part of implementing their IDP.

Each competency chapter in *FYI* also includes suggested readings, job assignments, reflection questions, and additional search recommendations. These areas of deeper exploration and learning are terrific sources for homework assignments to give in many coaching conversations. Review these areas as part of your own learning and development, and to gain a deeper understanding of your client's behavior patterns. This will help you more capably recommend some research to support their learning. You can also use the reflection questions in a coaching conversation or as journaling assignments to help your client refine their self-observation and deepen their self-awareness.

Assorted Templates for Your Toolkit

I offer many templates for use in the implementation phase. Although extensive, this list is certainly not exhaustive. So, peruse them to decide if any of these templates will help your client and their particular situation or challenge. Let this list also inspire you to source or create other templates on topics that consistently emerge among your client base. You should also feel empowered to use any of these in your own development.

Templates for Success

Template 4-9. Active Listening
An overview of listening types as a skill builder and job aid for you or your client.

Template 4-10. Conflict Overview
An overview of conflict styles and unique strategies for responding to conflict. It's useful in coaching new ways to approach competencies in conflict management and in helping your client adapt their natural style to something more appropriate in a particular situation. It mirrors the feedback your client receives if you choose to use the Thomas-Kilmann Instrument during the assessment step.

Template 4-11. Difficult Conversation Outline
A practice for preparing for and conducting a difficult conversation.

Template 4-12. EQ Exercise: Finding Joy
A practice you can use working with your client as a way to increase their awareness of and access to joy in their life.

Template 4-13. EQ Exercise: Meditation
Help the client develop their emotional awareness through mindfulness meditation.

Template 4-14. EQ Exercise: Recognize Triggers
Increase the client's ability to identify their emotional triggers and reactions. It's especially helpful for clients who externalize circumstances and have a low ability to recognize internal reactions and narratives that may contribute to the situation.

Template 4-15. Personal Evolution Worksheet
A two-part process to guide your client through an exploration of their vision for their life, relationships, career, and more. Offer this to a client who is working through questions of identity.

Template 4-16. Self-Awareness Activity: Weighing Options
A classic T-chart to help a client who is weighing a decision with two competing options or paths. This template includes an example of a client considering closing their successful business near term or long term.

Template 4-17. SWOT Analysis Worksheet
Use the SWOT (strengths, weaknesses, opportunities, and threats) model for a client who needs to reflect on and identify focus areas for development. This can be helpful if they are struggling to identify competencies to develop or seem stuck with their assessment of a situation.

Template 4-18. Time Management Quadrant
An exercise for clients struggling with feeling overwhelmed or unable to extract themselves from their day-to-day tasks to operate more as a leader. It includes a summary of time management concepts in a model popularized by the Covey Leadership Institute. It walks the client through how they're really spending their time and what actions they can take to invest more time in nonurgent but important matters.

Templates for Success (Cont.)

> **Template 4-19. Tolerations Worksheet**
> A worksheet to help your client identify things they've been tolerating in their life and work to prioritize and change them.
>
> **Template 4-20. Trust Article and Practice Exercises**
> For clients struggling with keeping or building trust in an important relationship, this worksheet gives information in a consolidated form, and two worksheets for the client to work with trust. This also invites them to look at what they are doing to contribute to the situation and what actions they are willing to take to try to rebuild trust.
>
> **Template 4-21. Uncover Your Inner Wisdom Worksheet**
> An exercise for a client who needs to tap into their inner wisdom to make an important decision or decide to move forward. This is a directed journaling exercise with a specific topic to reflect on.
>
> **Template 4-22. Vision Board Exercise**
> An exercise for a client who needs help identifying what they want in work and life to serve as a road map for their development.

Five Simple Ideas for Life Coaching

During your executive coaching engagements, you will likely find yourself dipping into general life coaching with a client. That's OK; it happens sometimes, and it helps the executive in work and life. The following are effective life-coaching exercises that you can easily implement in your coaching practice.

Wheel of Life

The wheel of life allows clients to understand where they are currently and where they would like to be in the future. Through evaluating different life aspects and current goals, the wheel of life encourages self-reflection and helps your clients gain insight into their life balance and life satisfaction levels and identify their strengths and weaknesses.

You can use this exercise to help them delve into why their wheel of life looks the way it does, what they would like their wheel to look like, and how to make these changes happen (Template 4-23). The exercise measures life satisfaction in predefined life domains, which typically include finance, career, health and fitness, recreation, community, relationships, love, personal growth, spirituality, and physical environment. However, it can also be customized with whatever categories are significant to your client.

Once your client has identified their life domains, they rate them individually on a scale of 0 to 10 to reflect their level of satisfaction within that particular area. After the assessment is complete, you'll have a visual representation of their life satisfaction. From this, clients can learn what domains require the most attention to get them to their ideal future.

Three Good Things Gratitude Exercise

The expression of gratitude has been shown to contribute to positive emotions, and in turn to overall well-being (Emmons and McCullough 2003). The three good things exercise is an effective way to promote well-being through the regular practice of gratitude (Seligman et al. 2005). The basic premise of the exercise is simple: Think about and write down three positive things that happened that day and explanations for why they happened (Template 4-24).

The effectiveness of three good things hinges on reflection and repetition. The degree to which the client continues with the exercise mediates the long-term benefits. Seligman et al. (2005) found that completing the exercise regularly over a month resulted in increased happiness, with the positive effects enduring at three- and six-month follow-ups.

One Door Closes, Another Door Opens

Developed by Tayyab Rashid (2015), one door closes, another door opens is an effective way to develop optimism and reframe negative events more positively.

In this exercise, invite clients to think back over their life and identify an occasion when they were unsuccessful in achieving their objective. Then invite them to consider and write down the positive things that happened as a result of the first door closing, thus reframing negative outcomes in a positive manner (Template 4-25).

The client can also use this practice outside coaching. Rather than thinking back over an entire lifetime, clients can carry out the exercise regularly throughout their weekly routine, asking the question "What failure led to unforeseen positive consequences?"

Coping-Strategies Wheel

Effective coping strategies are an important mediator between negative life events and psychological well-being. Ellen Skinner and Melanie J. Zimmer-Gembeck (2007) identified 13 common hierarchical categories of coping: problem solving, support seeking, escape, distraction, cognitive restructuring, rumination, helplessness, social withdrawal, emotional regulation, information seeking, negotiation, opposition, and delegation.

Your client can use the coping-strategies wheel to detect adaptive or nonadaptive coping strategies—you can then draw upon this information to consider and introduce more effective strategies (Template 4-26). Customize this tool to include your client's coping strategies.

Using Strength in a New Way

Using strengths in new ways has long-term positive effects on happiness, well-being, stress, vitality, self-esteem, and positive affect (Seligman et al. 2005; Wood et al. 2010).

To begin this exercise, the client should select one of their top strengths, identify where it is already in action, and then endeavor to practice the strength in a novel way at work, home, or leisure. The client should commit to using this strength in new ways every day for one week.

You and your client can discuss areas in which this signature strength can be applied to improve or make the most of a given situation. For instance, how might a client use the strength of gratitude to center themselves in the face of public-speaking anxiety? Or use the strength of curiosity to engage with new people? Template 4-27 is an aid to implement this practice.

Template for Success

> **Template 4-23. Wheel of Life Exercise**
> This aid directs you through an assessment of your client's life and a short practice to evaluate balance in each area of importance. Use with a client who seems out of balance or generally dissatisfied with their life overall.
>
> **Template 4-24. Three Good Things Gratitude Exercise**
> A process that a client can use anytime more gratitude would be helpful. I use this process to close every coaching session, which helps ensure that each session ends on a high note and reflects the client's positive outcomes.
>
> **Template 4-25. One Door Closes, Another Door Opens Exercise**
> A self-awareness exercise for any client who is struggling to let go of something that has ended or is struggling to find the good in what is ahead. Examples include a job change, a relationship ending, a change in their family structure, or a reset of an important work relationship.
>
> **Template 4-26. Coping-Strategies Wheel Exercise**
> Use this with a client who needs reminders about their calming and self-care tactics.
>
> **Template 4-27. Using Strength in a New Way Exercise**
> A practice for any client looking to expand their effectiveness through new uses of existing strengths, as well as any client struggling to remember their own capabilities. Building on strengths has been proven to develop higher levels of happiness and help lower levels of depression.

Specific Coaching Situations

In my coaching practice, I sometimes find myself coaching a client through a job change or transition, or coaching to achieve a very specific competency, such as decision making or delegation. And I sometimes coach teams or organizations. You will likely face similar potential coaching situations and decide to take them on. These are unique circumstances, so I am calling each out specifically to help you with these opportunities. Ultimately, these situations will make you a stronger and more marketable coach.

Coaching Your Client Through a Job Change or Transition

At some point, you'll probably find yourself coaching someone through a job change: searching for a new job, landing a new job, integrating into a new company or team, or preparing to step into new leadership shoes at the next level.

The book *The First 90 Days*, by Michael D. Watkins, has become the standard playbook for beginning a new role and offers tremendous insights, tools, and templates. I highly recommend adding this book to your bookshelf. You may even find it valuable enough to send to your clients as they prepare for a new role.

Building a new leadership team brings a unique opportunity to intentionally form the team, establish norms and agreements, design decision-making and problem-solving structures, and build trust through deepening relationships and appreciation for individual styles. This competency helps the team accelerate through the four stages of development and more quickly achieve a high-performing environment together.

Your role is to help the client making this transition envision the leadership presence they want to have in this new role, intentionally create the brand they want to live out with their new team, and think through the steps to build a highly effective team. They will need to learn quickly, make some early decisions, and have a longer-term vision for the work, their direct team, and the overall organization. You are an essential partner to them in this process.

CLIENT SPOTLIGHT
Sharon's Executive Transition

Becky worked with a leader who had recently transitioned to a senior role at her company. As part of the early days in Sharon's new role, they discussed her leadership vision: What kind of leader did she want to be in this new role? This was assigned as an exercise for her to consider and complete between sessions. Sharon had a clear sense of what leadership brand she held and what she wanted to embody more fully. Her answers included trusted leader and colleague, delivers lasting results, builds strong relationships, creates positive stakeholder engagement, and credible technologist. This provided the platform for Sharon's vision board as well as the foundation for experiments, exercises, and practices to help her more fully develop and live into these leadership attributes.

Competencies
Approachability, stakeholder management, visioning

Template 4-28, "First 90 Days Agenda," is a checklist to help clients move into their new role successfully. Template 4-29, "Interview Questions for Meet-and-Greet Appointments, is a helpful framework your client can use when they first meet their new colleagues.

Templates for Success

Template 4-28. First 90 Days Agenda
A helpful checklist for a client who has experienced a job change and needs to navigate and assimilate quickly into a new role or organization.

Template 4-29. Interview Questions for Meet-and-Greet Appointments
A helpful guide for a client who is meeting colleagues, partners, and peers for the first time. This is a good supplement to the "First 90 Days Agenda" (Template 4-28).

Coaching a Client Through Decision Making and Delegation

The competencies of decision-making skills and proper delegation are likely to emerge with many of your executive clients. It's critical to coach them to lead at the right level for their role, position, and organization's complexity. Always coach your client up to extend their reach and become more expansive in their scope and influence.

Understanding where your leader is operating from and what is most appropriate given their organization's size is a key focus for coaching. I have found the following is handy to keep in mind for various organization sizes:

- For smaller teams and scope, your client is likely delegating tasks and using more decision-making authority. As the scope increases, so do the ambiguity and the leader's requirement to lean on those around them.
- For teams of 50 people, the leader will be delegating projects and processes. Their primary decision making is delegation and holding their leaders accountable for key results.
- At an organization of 500, the scope is expanded to platforms and systems. This is a decision-making model of influence. Many decisions are best done locally, and your leader will likely influence the ultimate direction for these systems.
- At 5,000 people, your leader is managing other leaders who are accountable for businesses, independent profit centers, and distinct clients, stakeholders, and partners. The decision making at this level is much more nuanced, strategic, and agile.

If you haven't operated at this level in the company, you have a magnificent learning opportunity. Watch CEO podcasts, study the governance of countries and large systems, and research what the C-suite leads, listens to, and talks about. You have the tried-and-true system of the 360, profiles, and IDP to support you in engaging with senior leadership, and it's your job to learn more about their environment.

CLIENT SPOTLIGHT
Teaching Trudy to Delegate

I worked with a senior leader who had a challenging new boss and a team that seemed stuck in mediocrity. Feeling the pressure, Trudy sought out coaching to help build trust with her new manager and develop her team to perform at a higher level. I learned from Trudy's 360 that she was a serious micromanager, and this was reflected in her profiles. The quality was great but only because she was so deeply involved in every aspect of the work. Her micromanaging resulted in her team being stuck, and Trudy being stuck too. This way of working was not sustainable and resulted in a negative work environment for her capable team, which wanted to grow and contribute at a higher level.

Learning to work with her new boss was a priority for Trudy, and that was solved with a few simple adjustments and a targeted onboarding plan to educate her new leader quickly and effectively. The real work of the coaching engagement was around developing others and delegating to her capable team. Once Trudy did this, she was able to let go of micromanaging, take on more strategic projects, and ultimately have a greater impact on the business (oh, and accelerate her career trajectory!).

Competencies
Managing up, executive presence, delegation

Team Coaching

Another model of coaching is team coaching, where you get to be the broker of hope for a whole group of people. This can come about during implementation with your executive client if you're getting positive exposure, or you may be contracted to do team facilitation and coaching as part of your engagement with a company. These opportunities include facilitating a retreat, guiding crucial conversations, or working with teams on their development goals. This is an exciting opportunity to work with a broader group of leaders, and, if applicable, see your primary client in action on a more routine basis.

Team coaching might be singularly focused, like facilitating a strategic-planning session. What makes this "coaching" is your skill and courage to ask the tough questions during the planning session. This can help your client's staff work through some long-held frustrations or challenges.

Team coaching could be more long term, like a one-year engagement focused on the leadership team's development needs. This allows you to engage an insightful diagnostic, like one of those covered in the assessment chapter, and explore that assessment's meaning for the whole team. You can work with the leader or a subset of the leadership team to design a yearlong program focused on the key capabilities team members need to improve in their quest to be high performing. Monthly or quarterly competency themes for the group can help them focus on the highlighted capability or capabilities, and additional practices can keep them engaged between sessions. Topics may include effective planning, prioritization, role clarity, measuring the work, healthy conflict, or decision making.

Team coaching is not for every coach. For coaches who don't feel as experienced or adept at managing group dynamics, team coaching could be something you work toward in the future as your business develops. However, those with a background in business and meeting facilitation might be suited for this environment. Those naturally tuned to group learning, like former teachers or professors, may find this type of coaching very satisfying. And a coach with a therapy background may bring a strength that can make a huge difference for the leaders.

Coaching in a group session requires excellent skill from the coach, strong alignment with the leadership team on purpose and intended outcomes, and commitment by all involved to stay the course on what may be a lengthy engagement. The coach will need to have courage to address what is happening in the moment, addressing the team's issues in real time.

Being effective in this group setting requires an up-front agreement and consent from all members to do "on the spot coaching" in front of, and with, colleagues. The ability to assess and diagnose on the spot requires you to have courage to address what is happening in the moment, a keen insight and appreciation for team dynamics, and the conviction to coach individually and collectively as issues arise. You have to be quick and unafraid to step in, make an observation, offer an intervention, and get the group back on topic, or even confront a particularly thorny topic or participant's behavior. Excellent memory to recall both the personal assessments as well as the team diagnostics is helpful in pinpointing the issue and offering a meaningful intervention. You can use or adapt Templates 4-30 to 4-34 if you find yourself coaching a team.

ON THAT NOTE

Setting an Expectation of Confidentiality Within a Program

Imagine you have the opportunity to work with a leadership program cohort, a group of leaders participating in a leadership accelerator where coaching is offered to all participants. The program is designed to improve specific competencies, including strategic thinking, mergers and acquisitions, board engagement, and leading global teams. All participants should have IDPs built against these leadership imperatives. In this case, the desired skills to deepen or develop have been identified.

Your sponsor for coaching is the program manager. It's important to contract with the program manager up front so you are aligned on the overall approach to development, how you'll work with each individual, and how you'll keep the program manager informed. Your coaching engagement remains strictly confidential, meaning you can share the overall coaching process, the stage you're currently working in, and the level of engagement and preparation your clients demonstrate. However, the clients strictly own their IDP and progress updates against those goals. Make sure to build this into the program design, so you don't find yourself in the position of being asked to report on each client's growth in the given competencies.

Templates for Success

Template 4-30. Group Coaching Overview
An overview of the pros and cons and best practices of group coaching. It outlines the many benefits and provides helpful tips on preparation and facilitation.

Template 4-31. Team Assessment Questionnaire
An assessment of team health and trust that can be used in team coaching and facilitation.

Template 4-32. Icebreaker Activities
Instructions for several easy-to-implement icebreaker activities for use in a group setting. A good icebreaker brings people into the room and helps them shift focus from whatever they just left so they can be fully present with the team. These activities help participants center on a shared activity and give them a sense of what the workshop will entail.

Template 4-33. Team Charter Template
A template to help a team develop a vision, values, and processes for team effectiveness.

Template 4-34. Feedback Survey for Team Retreat
A starting place to create a thoughtful evaluation to distribute to any team retreat participants.

Coaching in Organizations

You may have the opportunity to become a coach as part of a leadership program. The internal systems that precede these programs often include talent reviews or succession planning. Companies routinely take their top 10 to 15 percent of leaders through an accel-eration program, attempting to prepare them for the next job at an accelerated pace.

In this type of engagement, you will be told which competencies your executive client needs to develop to be prepared for a promotion or job expansion. Your role is to help them make sense of all the information provided in the academy, think strategically about how to best take advantage of this tremendous investment, learn how to apply the learn-ing to themselves, and keep them engaged through the whole process.

You also need to become a student of the company and learn the business, the industry, values, results, and key leadership competencies. This is an extra investment for you, but it's essential to be skillful in this type of high-stakes engagement.

Coaches may be asked to meet as a cohort themselves, to share themes and tools, and support one another in the shared effort to support the executive cohort. This would be coordinated by the company's HR or L&D team and conducted in partnership. Your role is to maintain absolute confidentiality about your client's specific learning and challenges, while skillfully contributing to the thematic challenges you observe about the cohort over-all, supporting your colleagues, and offering helpful insights, tools, and learning.

Summary

Anchored in the IDP, the implementation phase is about application, experimentation, practice, feedback, and homework. We reviewed some key coaching tools to have at your fingertips during your coaching sessions and coaching theories to ground your work in the research and academic insights about human development. We covered the overall coaching conversation and key elements to attend to in each conversation. We shared sev-eral real client stories and did a deeper dive into Simone's case study to give you a sense of how to nurture client development in the more common areas addressed by coaching.

Next up is the wrap-up step, the conclusion of your coaching program. This is where you bring together all the learning and growth set forth and achieved during your time together. You reflect on the IDP and what they've learned from the experiments and prac-tices. Then you set the stage for continued growth beyond your coaching engagement. You remind your client of their capability and capacity and help them have confidence to con-tinue to pursue their development goals and growth. You summarize the results so your client can share them with their sponsoring leader or HR partner, should they choose to do so. And you remind them that you are always there for them should they face a challenge better conquered with a coach by their side. Saying goodbye after such a long and mean-ingful partnership can be challenging, which is my focus for the next chapter.

Chapter 5
Wrap Up the Coaching Engagement

"Without courage we cannot practice any other virtue with consistency. We can't be kind, true, merciful, generous, or honest." —Maya Angelou

"Ends are not bad things, they just mean that something else is about to begin. And there are many things that don't really end, anyway, they just begin again in a new way. Ends are not bad, and many ends aren't really an ending; some things are never-ending." —C. JoyBell C.

In this chapter, I cover:

- Conducting a second 360: Interview the same people near the end of the coaching engagement to celebrate where your client has improved and to bring focus to the last few weeks of the engagement.

- Preparing for the final coaching conversations: Help your client bring the engagement to a satisfying and meaningful end, with strategies to continue their development.

- Retaining clients: Explore how you can or should keep in touch with your client to keep expanding your network.

You often come to the end of a coaching engagement with mixed emotions; like Maya Angelou said, it takes courage. You've made it through assessment, setting goals, and implementation, and now it's time to review and wrap up your coaching engagement. Having been through this many, many times, I can confidently say that each ending is a unique kind of bittersweet. After all, you've spent countless hours *with* your client, and even more time *thinking* about your client and their journey. They've become part of your life and you part of theirs.

Most people aren't awesome at endings. There can be a feeling of rushing to and through endings to get to the other side, to begin again, to get past what can be an uncomfortable experience. We may not have the skills to process or even recognize these deep feelings. But it's our job to bring the coaching process to a positive, productive, meaningful end. Role model for your client how you can end things without all the discomfort, learning to honor them and the process, and then let go with grace and kindness.

The conclusion of your coaching engagement is when you bring together all the lessons and growth set forth and achieved during your time with your client. You reflect on the individual development plan (IDP), capture knowledge gained from the experiments and practices, and set the stage for continued growth beyond your coaching engagement.

This step is grounded in your emotional capability to have an effective ending, which I'll walk you through in this chapter. As always, it's built on the foundation of beacon of hope, customer focus, and maintaining and building the relationship.

Common Limitations for Coaches During the Ending Step

I see several common mistakes or limitations during this final step in the coaching model. First, coaches often forget their key responsibility to mark progress and celebrate milestones along the way. As the client demonstrates new or deepened competencies, be sure to highlight this as part of your coaching sessions. And as you approach the ending of the coaching engagement, it's essential to recap success from their journey. Take the time to review the initial and updated 360 inputs—what a marked difference! Highlight feedback from their direct leader and others in their inner circle. The client may not always pay attention to their progress during coaching, so the coach needs to make sure to record their progress. This helps the client see where they have improved, and it also highlights the success of coaching.

Second, if coaches didn't experience good coaching themselves, they won't have a great role model to follow. Additionally, many haven't experienced coaching from the client side. This book should help fill that gap. You can also learn from other coaches to get the support you need in your professional development. You need to continuously develop your own competencies and use the language of the four coaching steps—marking progress and focusing on competencies throughout the coaching program—to the very end of the engagement. Learn the language of celebration so you can weave that into your final coaching sessions.

Third, like many people, coaches are not innately great at goodbyes. This super special work and relationship are both coming to an end, which can bring on real feelings of sadness, a sense of loss, and mourning. Follow the steps in this chapter to build your "healthy goodbye" muscles.

Prepare for Ending With a Final 360

The wrapping-up process includes several conversations toward the end of the contracted coaching program that are informed by a follow-up 360. When you reach about 75 percent completion overall, you want to have a plan in place to prepare for wrapping up the engagement.

In the final three to four coaching conversations, continue to reiterate the focus of the IDP based on the 360 and the profiles. If there are areas where your client hasn't achieved the shift they hoped for, this is the time to bring that forward so you and your client can agree on how they can actively improve this area during the final weeks of the coaching engagement.

At this stage, conduct a second and final round of 360 interviews. This is a robust way to demonstrate improvement, both for your client and their key stakeholders and sponsors. Re-interview the same individuals who provided 360 input at the outset of the program. Remind them of their feedback in the three key topic areas: strengths, opportunities for growth, and three things to improve. You are not with your client on a regular basis, so you need this kind of data from those who spend time with them daily or weekly to showcase progress and determine continued opportunities.

It's amazing what you can gather on behalf of your client at this stage. This feedback from all their most important people allows them to share in the success of their work. Here is just a small sampling of 360 input captured on behalf of several clients:

- "I am pleasantly surprised by his sense of humor. Who knew?"
- "She partners more, clarifies more, and helps and intervenes politely when needed."

- "The biggest change is intensity. When you get to know him, he is really down-to-earth and not stuck up at all. Now everybody can see that, now that he is showing his real side more."

Think about the impact on your client, who has been working hard to improve in these areas—connecting with the team, being more authentic at work, communicating more effectively, and smoothing pointed edges in interpersonal interactions. This feedback lets them know that they are making big improvements and that their colleagues have noticed. It's a moment of celebration!

CLIENT SPOTLIGHT
Shawn's Improvements Lead to Promotion

One of my clients was promoted from a field VP to a corporate VP. Although both VP level positions, they were very different leadership roles. Shawn needed to improve his competencies of informing and strategic agility because they were key skills for his corporate role, while also ramping up quickly in the first 90 days.

These areas were identified in initial 360 input and became the focus for coaching. Shawn was dedicated in his practices and observations and used coaching strategically in the early days of his new position to help him get focused and grounded.

Toward the end of our coaching engagement, the input from his peers and team was astounding. He received very positive 360 comments about his improvements in these areas and the positive impact on the team he was already having. He was highly motivated and got the reward he was after: strong, positive feedback from the most important people around him.

There was a great sense of accomplishment, recognition, and celebration as we reviewed the progress of his coaching program and the significant results he'd achieved. Following the ending steps detailed in this chapter helped us part ways on a positive, celebratory note, underscoring the value of the coaching program.

Competencies
Informing, strategic agility, partnering

Use Template 5-1 to invite those whom you interviewed for your client's first 360 to interview again; Template 5-2 provides an agenda to guide this second 360 conversation. You can use Template 5-3 to take notes. Don't forget to include your client's own assessment of their growth.

In the interview, remind each interviewee what they previously shared about your client's strengths. It's been several months, perhaps upward of six months, so they'll appreciate a brief recap. Then explore if they continue to see these areas of strength, if anything has changed, or if new strengths have presented themselves.

Then recap the areas they identified for potential improvement or growth. Be specific so they can recall exactly what they said and the examples they provided. Ask if they saw improvement in your client in the areas for growth. Actively engage them in reflecting on your client's actions and experiments, and capture any input that shows progress, status quo, or even a decline in the desired behavior. This feedback will help you refine the IDP and focus the final weeks of the coaching program to really get after the competency areas still showing up as opportunities for your client.

Lastly, review the three things question, which invites the interviewee to focus on the top three things your client could do to improve themselves, their relationships, the team, or the organization. Make note of any highlighted progress so you can share and celebrate with your client. Ask if anything new has emerged in the past months to be sure new learning is captured from this input process.

CLIENT SPOTLIGHT
Matthew's Three Things to Improve

One of my clients was working toward improving his communication skills, trusting others, and volunteering his expertise. Matthew was seen as withdrawn and not willing to help the team accomplish their projects, despite having deep expertise that would contribute enormously to the organization. His leader sent him to coaching to work on these three things.

Toward the end of the coaching program, Matthew and his leader met with me to review the progress and discuss feedback on the three competencies. To everyone's delight, the boss shared several comments from the team, his management, and others about how Matthew had really shifted in his team engagement and participation. He noted that their relationship had improved significantly. And he praised Matthew for the obvious hard work he had done in the coaching program. Matthew was assigned larger projects and promoted within six months. As we brought the coaching journey to a close, there was a deep sense of pride and celebration, recognizing the significant shifts Matthew had made in a few short months. It's always bittersweet to say goodbye (for now) to clients who are making such meaningful progress.

Competencies
Communication, trust, engagement

Remember that the IDP is directly anchored in the competency areas for growth and the prioritized actions to improve the team. Your client should have demonstrated progress in these areas through actions and experiments. These are the same topics you review every session, with observations from the client about the results of these experiments. Sometimes, however, those results are harder for third parties to observe. For example, if your client is working on not reacting to external circumstances and practicing internal exploration of what triggered their desire to react, this kind of inner work can be hard to see from the outside. If your interviewee is not seeing improvement, share some of the actions your client has taken to improve and ask for more examples from them on their experience with your client and their expectations.

Compile the results in a report like the one shown in Template 5-4. If feedback from the second 360 indicates your client missed the mark, you need to address this directly with them. Share the areas where their stakeholders are not seeing progress and facilitate a conversation about why that may be the case. If this is a career staller or continued concern from a sponsoring manager, encourage them to work on the topic with some urgency. Discuss the approach that will most support them growing in this competency area.

ON THAT NOTE
When You're Not the Right Coach for the Job

If your client hasn't grown in a particular area, explore the option to call in a second coach who specializes in that competency for continued development. Be open to the possibility that you may not be the right coach to take them to the next level in this competency area. After all, you've been working with them for months, and if the common feedback remains "missed the mark," perhaps they would be better served working with someone else. Review your network to see if you can make a recommendation. This demonstrates fantastic professional maturity and integrity to support your client in taking their development in another direction, even without you, if that is what most supports their growth.

Just as in the beginning of the program, you should set up a meeting with your client and the hiring manager or HR or L&D leader to review the results of the second 360. Template 5-5 provides an agenda you can use to guide this conversation. Remind the sponsor or your client's boss of the coaching process overall and allow your client to share key points of progress where they are continuing to focus. Seek any additional clarification or input from the hiring manager. This is an important alignment meeting for both you and your client. You can also confirm the method for closing out the engagement with this leader. Will there be a final meeting, or is a summary email sufficient for them to feel complete on this program?

Templates for Success

> **Template 5-1. Email Invitation to Second 360 Interviewees**
> An email for reconnecting with the client's first 360 interviewees and initiating a second interview.
>
> **Template 5-2. Second 360 Interview Meeting Invitation and Agenda**
> A meeting invitation and agenda to send to your interviewees for the second 360 interview to set the date and time, as well as to communicate the interview's structure.
>
> **Template 5-3. Second 360 Notes Form**
> A note-taking form to capture the updated feedback from the client's 360 inputs during the interview.
>
> **Template 5-4. Post-Coaching Results Example**
> An example of how I summarize the post-coaching feedback and results. In keeping with the confidentiality commitment, the results of coaching are the client's to share with their leader, teams, or colleagues.
>
> **Template 5-5. Final Meeting Agenda With Sponsor or Direct Leader**
> An agenda for the final meeting with your client's direct manager, sponsor, or program manager—the person who initiated coaching, if not your client. This agenda allows you to maximize your time with the leader while still allowing you to a build relationship and increase your understanding of your client.

The Final One or Two Conversations

Establish the agenda for the final coaching session during your penultimate session to make sure your client comes prepared for this special ending conversation. This is your opportunity to set the context for a helpful and reparative ending experience. It is a critical meeting, so do your preparation and support your client in doing the same. Send the agenda for the final session out in advance to set the stage for what the final coaching conversation will look like (Template 5-6). It's important to be clear that this ending conversation is intentionally treated differently.

Ask your client to reflect on their entire multimonth journey and come to that final conversation with their reflections on the coaching process. What stands out for them as highlights or breakthroughs? What growth have they seen in themselves? What impact is that growth having on them, their colleagues, and even friends and family?

This is an emotionally satisfying conversation for the client. They had work to do, sometimes quite serious work, and they did it. It's a chance for them to pause for a moment, reflect on their progress, and celebrate that progress with you to bring the process to completion.

Review all your coaching notes and prepare a few thoughts to share in your final meeting. Here are a few sample prompts for you to organize your thoughts:

- Where did you see a breakthrough with this client?
- What moments really stood out for you in the journey?
- What are *you* taking away in terms of key learning or a special moment that had an impact on you as a coach?
- What practices would you recommend they continue?
- What recommendations do you have for continued development?

Remember how pivotal your relationship with your client has been in their development—you're part of the reason your client was willing to go on the journey in the first place. You need to model a profound level of sincerity and support in these last conversations. Your authentic tone and cheerleading will help your client feel satisfied with the development path you trekked together and motivate them to stick to that trail. Because it's a loss on many levels, either of you might be tempted to continue your relationship under the guise of friendship or quick check-in sessions, but it's best for the client-coach relationship to come to an end.

Some clients want to become friends after a coaching engagement ends. You may get invitations to graduation parties, bar or bat mitzvahs, baby showers, quinceañeras, holiday parties, and more. This makes sense, given that you've been in an intense and possibly even vulnerable relationship for many months. You may be one of the only people in their life who really "gets them," and they may be afraid of losing that. However, I recommend that you keep the coaching relationship professional. This keeps you out of potential hot water with the sponsoring leader who hired you and helps you hold all your coaching engagements equally, as professional engagements.

ON THAT NOTE
Parting Words of Advice?

Sometimes a client will ask if you have any additional feedback for them. Because you've been monitoring, assessing, supporting, and challenging all along, they probably have a good sense of your feedback. But this is an invitation for you to celebrate the wins and underscore what you think will have the most impact for your client in terms of continued development. What did you observe from their journey? Did they have a particular breakthrough you're hopeful will serve them for years to come? What are the noticeable differences about your client today versus when you first met? Spend some time thinking about this so you're not caught off guard and miss the opportunity to share some highly meaningful feedback for your client and their continued growth.

In the final 10 minutes of your final coaching conversation, I recommend seeking feedback from your client about your performance as a coach. Be sure they know this is coming so they're not surprised that it's their turn to offer observations and assessments. Open this conversation by saying that you're continuously learning and would benefit from their perspective. Ask them, "What could I have done differently to help you even more? What were a few things particularly meaningful for you in terms of how I was as a coach?" Let them know you send an annual survey and, with their permission, they'll be included in that future outreach to provide more feedback.

Template for Success

Template 5-6. Agenda for Final Coaching Conversation
A coaching session agenda to ensure you cover all the important topics required for a healthy ending. Caring for this ending with great intention is essential. You have been on a lengthy and vulnerable journey with your client. This is where you bring all your work to a healthy and positive conclusion.

Wrap-Up and Follow-Up

The last stage is the work of wrapping up the engagement. Equip your client with notes from the final 360 (Template 5-3), summarized and confidential as the first one was, so they have all the inputs to help them continue to develop. You may also provide your summary notes from the last coaching session, which highlight their key learning and any additional reflection or input you provided. This is your final "farewell for now," with some guidance to keep going and growing.

You also want to formally end the engagement with the leader who hired you. This may be your client, or it may be a more senior leader in the company or an HR/L&D liaison. If the latter is the case, it's important that whoever is writing the check feels the care and attention of a positive and productive ending as well.

You already confirmed during your second alignment conversation to review the updated 360 input how this leader wants to be engaged at the end. If they want a meeting, be sure to book that before you conclude the alignment meeting. If an email is sufficient, which is often the case, remember to keep the summary high level; your client's improvements and knowledge gains are theirs to share with this leader. Let them that know the program is complete, that your client made significant progress, and that they were a joy to work with. Share your contact information and offer your support of others on the team who may benefit from executive coaching.

Client Retention

To stay connected with past coaching clients, I invite them to join my community. I add them to my customer list and website, where I post useful content and share relevant articles. You can do the same, because it works! Consider creating a private space for your past clients to network, share best practices, participate in discussion forums, and collaborate on key topics of interest, much like my "DrNadine salons," which I'll cover in chapter 9.

Other coaches offer additional training sessions or workshops to past coaching clients or even host reunions of former coaching clients as a networking opportunity.

Some coaches don't have a strategy to continue to nurture a community of clients. That is a totally acceptable and successful practice too. Whatever your practice, make sure it's right for you and that you have the capacity to do it sustainably. Please remember to get permission from your client to continue to be in contact with them professionally.

Summary

Before you close the file on this client, I invite you to take some time to reflect on your own engagement and results. What did or didn't work for them? What more could you have done to support their growth? Was there a breakdown for you? What did you learn about yourself as a coach that will be helpful to pay attention to in future client engagements? If you've been making note of these topics all along, you will have some good ideas already captured. This is your chance to summarize, wrap it up, and close the book on this engagement, for now.

We've now walked through and completed our deep dive on the four-step coaching process, including the final 360 and wrapping up the engagement. I have offered what I hope are many helpful and practical tips and templates to assist you in implementing these best practices.

The second half of the playbook focuses on the process to build your business—from creating your business plan to leveraging modern marketing tactics to recovering from setbacks. I'll share my hard-won lessons with you to help you thrive as an entrepreneur and a business owner. Let's jump to it!

PART 2

Building Your Business

Chapter 6
Are You Ready for Entrepreneurship?

"Fearlessness is like a muscle. I know from my own life that the more I exercise it, the more natural it becomes to not let my fears run me."
—Arianna Huffington

"I knew what I wanted in life and I worked day and night to achieve it, and here I am." —Tabitha Karanja

In this chapter, I cover:

- Exploring the many hats of an entrepreneur: Learn how to manage your time and prepare yourself for all the necessary work.

- Advantages of entrepreneurship: Think about all of the great benefits of owning your own business and use them as motivation to navigate the less exciting tasks.

- Challenges of entrepreneurship: Consider some of the downsides of being your own boss and assess your readiness to face them.

- Being a great entrepreneur: Explore whether you have the skills to run your own business, and make a plan for areas where you'll need to compensate.

- Setting yourself up for success: Start exploring the resources available to you as a small-business owner.

Part 2 of the playbook is all about entrepreneurship—what it takes to start and run a successful coaching practice. If you're moving from being an executive at a corporate job, what makes you want to build a business? As you invest your most precious resources—your time and talents—into achieving the work of the company that employs you, you probably find yourself reflecting on the return on that investment. Are your values aligned with your company's? Are you learning and growing in a meaningful way? Are the time, energy, and resources you pour into a corporate job bringing satisfaction and joy? The answers to these questions might tip you toward starting on an entrepreneurial journey.

As an entrepreneur, you can dedicate your time and talents to the work that matters most to you—building relationships and developing competencies in others—plus you get to set your own hours, work from anywhere, coach the most desirable clients (eventually!), and grow your own company through your dedication and hard work. In many ways, it's as fun and fulfilling as you might imagine. But good old-fashioned hard work and persistence are required to build a successful coaching business. Always carry this book with you; I have been in your shoes!

Before I jump into the mechanics of building or scaling your business, I want to reflect on you, the entrepreneur. I invite you to take an honest look in the mirror to evaluate if you have the stomach for entrepreneurship. There are some serious challenges and obstacles to being your own boss. Some are self-inflicted (*Can I even do this?*) and others are just the reality of the work involved in running a business (*How do I pay taxes?*).

It's also very helpful in the beginning to connect with your network and get their feedback. Talk with your friends, loved ones, colleagues, former bosses and mentors, and people you think might be your ideal clients. You will hear some really helpful insights about your strengths and gifts, and you may even hear some cautions or concerns. This gives you a way to get valuable feedback about areas where you may need to increase your capability or strength. It's just input at this stage and gives you good ideas for where to shore up your entrepreneurial skill set. Remember the Johari Window (chapter 3); they may be helping you see some things that were previously unknown to you.

The Work of an Entrepreneur

I think about the job of entrepreneurship in three buckets: doing the work (the fun stuff), managing the operations (the necessary back-office work), and building the client pipeline (the also super necessary, client-facing, network-building work; Figure 6-1).

Figure 6-1. The Buckets of Work

Do the Work
- Coach
- Consult
- Continuous development
- Collaborate

Business Operations
- Budget
- Invoicing
- IT
- Goal setting

Build the Pipeline
- Client meetings
- Proposals
- Networking
- Follow-ups

In which buckets do you see your strengths? What tasks make you feel the most fulfilled and energized? This is important to know about yourself. Notice where you spend most of your time, where you find yourself in "flow" most easily—that state of being fully immersed and focused, even losing track of time. Conversely, pay attention to what tasks you're setting aside or delaying. These simple observations may give you some hints about your strengths and competencies and where you may need to develop discipline to run your own business.

The work in all three buckets is essential, and over time, you may be able to outsource some of the tasks you find less engaging. And I definitely encourage you to do just that, especially for bookkeeping and taxes. At the beginning, though, it's all you, baby! So build the time into your schedule, use supportive technology as much as you can, and attend to all aspects of the business. Especially if you're an executive transitioning to entrepreneurship, don't underestimate the amount of work your executive assistant did for you. I'm sure you appreciate them and everything they did to make your life function as an executive, but now you're going to *really* appreciate them. Now you get to be your own executive assistant, or you could consider hiring a fractional executive assistant. It's going to take a lot of detail orientation and customer service to do this work well. Plan that into your schedule.

"Are You Built to Be an Executive Coach?" (Template 6-1) is a self-assessment to help determine your readiness. Template 6-2 is a weekly planning tool to help organize your priorities in light of everything you need to accomplish. Use the time management worksheet to help you evaluate where you're spending your time and adjust priorities as necessary (Template 6-3).

Templates for Success

Template 6-1. Are You Built to Be an Executive Coach?
A self-assessment to help you evaluate your readiness for entrepreneurship and build a development plan to increase your readiness and strengthen your resolve.

Template 6-2. Weekly Planner
A template to help you make progress toward your top priorities, and your wellness, throughout the week.

Template 6-3. Time Management Worksheet
A worksheet to help you evaluate where you spend your time in the main buckets of entrepreneurial work.

Advantages of Entrepreneurship

Let's start with the good stuff—the things that are great about being an entrepreneur. You get to work on the things that matter most to you, that you believe will contribute the most to your clients or the world at large. That's super motivating! The reading you do, the TED Talks you watch, the conversations you have, the training or certifications you may pursue, the networking groups you join—they're all aligned with and in support of what you're most passionate about. How cool is that?

It might take you some time to build your business to the point where you get to focus only on the things you want to do. In the meantime, you might need to take in "pay the bills" work so you can, well, pay the bills. You likely have talents that aren't your desired focus. For example, you might be known for strategic planning, supply chain management, or program management. Although you're most interested in executive coaching, these other talents are marketable skills that allow you to build the muscle of entrepreneurship, learn how to pitch work, write proposals, and appropriately price your services. Your vision for your coaching business may need to include a phase of other work to help you build your network and your brand as an entrepreneur. These successful projects may then parlay into coaching or consulting work in the areas you're most interested in. You might also equally enjoy the work of building your client base, and the variety and adventure of all the business-building tasks. That was the case for me and still is.

The operations side of setting up, growing, and maintaining your business can seem daunting as you develop your operational, marketing, and time management competencies on the fly. Remember the old adage "Building the plane while flying it"? That's kind of how it feels! You may need to learn new skills outside your historical areas of expertise, and quickly. In addition, you will develop perseverance and become a better problem solver in support of standing up your own business.

More good news: The scale of operations work can be "right-sized" to your company and done on your schedule. Perhaps your corporate role had a marketing team, and maybe you had an assistant to manage your time. You may be leaving a corporate job that had some significant support embedded in your role. In your new job as an entrepreneur, this is technically unpaid time, but it's necessary for managing the operations of your business. But because it's just you, for now, some of these tasks can be super simple: No more linked goals with several rounds of reviews up and down the management hierarchy. Budgets and incentives are much less complicated. Oh, and annual performance reviews? Those are a thing of the past (until you scale your business to include employees).

ON THAT NOTE
Work That Pays the Bills

When Becky first began to consider the idea of building her own business, she was fortunate that several former colleagues and managers hired her. The work was in her area of expertise: marketing, employer branding, and talent accelerator programs. It was interesting work, and it supported Becky's interest in learning how to become an entrepreneur and working for leaders she deeply respected.

Becky learned how to pitch ideas, write proposals, price her services, and deliver results for three different companies in her first month of entrepreneurship. Although none of this work was coaching or the kind of consulting she was most interested in, it allowed her to strengthen her entrepreneurial muscle, learn in low-risk situations with leaders who trusted her, and apply those insights to framing up her coaching and consulting business.

A few months later, one of those leaders asked her to work with his team to improve their communication and overall effectiveness. Now we're talking!

You also get to ditch corporate overhead. It's a special moment when you talk with former colleagues who are neck-deep in annual financial planning at their company. You may have been through it yourself: the hours of spreadsheets and debates among peers about how to divvy up the operational budget. I doubt you'll miss the conversations about what is most critical for the company at this time, what slipped from this year that needs to be funded next year, and what puts the company on the right path to meet the strategic goals it's committed to the board. Tough decisions get made, and inevitably no one is happy at the end.

Guess what? Your days of that are over! You'll still make decisions and priority calls, and you might have to wait for that next development workshop or delay the reward purchase of a new computer bag, but these are easy decisions that you alone get to make in service to your business. You will get to make your own decisions about how much to spend on marketing, or how to evaluate the success of your marketing campaigns, advertising strategy, and operational support, like bookkeeping or administration.

Last but not least, your hours are flexible (for the most part). You can work from anywhere with a strong Wi-Fi connection, and you can set your own travel schedule (or not), based on the kind of client work you're doing. This is a blessing and a curse. With that, let us turn to some of the challenges.

Challenges of Entrepreneurship

Of course there are also challenges to owning your own business. I offer a few here to encourage you to think through potential obstacles and build a plan to successfully overcome them. Call this your risk mitigation strategy.

You might sense a loss of authentic free time. Time taken to care for ailing parents or to enjoy a family vacation is unpaid time. In addition, you're not making progress on key deliverables, client deadlines, your next blog post . . . you get the idea. You may feel a sense of urgency to continue doing the work of an entrepreneur that keeps you mentally engaged, even when you're sitting poolside.

As satisfying as you find your work, it's important that you plan for these breaks from work and stay connected to your support system, even if it means your business sits idle for a few days or weeks. Set your boundaries: Do you own your business or does your business own you? You will want to negotiate your competencies of work-life balance and ambition. Remember how important the power of relationships is to being an effective coach? The relationships with your closest family and friends need to be tended to, especially in these times of shared leisure and relaxation.

Your client base may be uneven at first, which can be a double whammy if you are still working a "regular job" and starting this coaching business as a side gig. Sometimes it's just your luck that both need you more at the same time. You will have multiple clients at times and a changing client load. Whereas at a job, you might have had one manager and multiple stakeholders, here you will have multiple clients who require your time—sometimes at the same time. And sometimes the client volume comes in waves. Client management and measuring and managing your work are key. You need to learn your sweet spot—the number of executive coaching clients you can take at once. In the beginning, it might be three to five individuals at a time, giving you the mental energy to implement my four-step coaching model correctly while managing the overall flow of each individual's development journey. As you establish more confidence and capability, you may choose to increase this number.

Your income will likely be uneven too. If you're pivoting from a corporate job with a predictable paycheck, benefits, bonuses, and paid vacations, the shift to uneven income can be bumpy, especially at the beginning. It's important to know what you really need to manage your life and financial commitments and what a healthy cash flow looks for you. Plan for that by scheduling weekly or every other week distributions from your business account to your personal account.

ON THAT NOTE
A Savings Safety Net

I recommend you have six to 12 months of income saved before you launch into entrepreneurship. This will help you care for what is financially required and give you some runway to set up your business, build a client pipeline, and begin earning revenue. Consider establishing your coaching practice initially as a side hustle. This allows you to maintain your required income while starting up the business that will sustain you in the future. Personal and business financial planning are key competencies for any business owner to have, so consider attending a small-business seminar or taking an online class.

You're putting your services out there as you hang out your shingle, which takes courage and leaves you open to exposure. Doing your own thing is great, but it can open you up to criticism and setbacks. You're selling your skills and talents in a new way, and that can feel more vulnerable than you're comfortable with. Resilience is an important competency for you to carry with you. In the end, though, your clients are buying what you have to offer—in coaching, consulting, or other services—so learning how to talk about the skills and talents that you offer to clients is a critical part of becoming an executive coaching entrepreneur. It gets easier with experience and with successful client conversions.

Your customer conversion is uncertain as well. However, you learn over time what a reasonable "yield" might be from your business development efforts. It's rare to secure 100 percent of the potential clients you meet. Life happens for them. Business conditions change. Organization restructures delay development interests. High performers fall out of favor and are no longer options for coaching. For example, in just one year of Becky's consulting practice, two lucrative contracts with big-brand companies fell through at the last minute—one because of a massive restructuring that consumed leadership attention for months on end, and the other because of the sponsoring executive's exit from the company. These contracts, while "sure things" in Becky's mind, ended up being zeroed out of the budget.

COACH SPOTLIGHT
Powerful Networks

I worked with a client who was a coach and trainer with an outplacement firm who wanted to open her own business as a full-time executive coach. Jeel was a former executive, so she had all the capabilities you would expect from someone operating at the highest level of her company. Although she was an extrovert on the Myers-Briggs and had a keen interest in entrepreneurship and marketing on her Strong Inventory, it still took learning the competencies of self-confidence and communication to put herself and her services forward to others. She couldn't "let her work speak for her" in this open market. She had to learn how to identify, then effectively communicate, her strengths and value proposition.

We were able to start with smaller items, like creating social media posts (and rewards for efforts of course!), and worked up to moderating and speaking at events. She has since become a full-time coach, fulfilling her dream, and she is enjoying the coaching part as much as the marketing part.

You might feel isolated. Have you ever heard the phrase "It's lonely at the top"? Well, not only are you at the top, you may be the only member of your business for some time. It can feel like you're doing this all by yourself. Have a support system in place to help you during the roller coaster ahead. If you don't have a support system, try enlisting a friend or neighbor to be your sounding board. Perhaps re-engage a former mentor to support your progress as a leader in this new capacity. Let yourself lean on incredibly helpful and supportive family and friends. They're your cheerleaders, even if you think you don't need it. And remember your network—that group of people who know you, respect you, and trust you. They also believe in you! So have them be an intentional part of your outreach as you build your client pipeline. Lean on them to bolster your courage and confidence. Your network will help with referrals, new ideas, and making connections to support your new venture.

You'll have an overwhelming list of things to do. Remember the three buckets of work, all of which are necessary to run a successful business. There is a long list of things to do in each, especially at the beginning, and it's not always clear if there is a correct order or priority for the many tasks necessary to get checked off the list. Get out that *FYI* book and your own IDP, and work on your project and time management competencies. I also suggest you engage your local small business association or other similar organization. They support people just like you and have walked this path thousands of times. Find a local chapter and get engaged—I highly recommend their support for just about everything discussed in part 2. Other similar support organizations could be the Better Business Bureau and your local chamber of commerce. These associations are underused and can help with many things, including networking, brochures, seminars, and support systems. Don't stay isolated; get out there and use all the resources available to help you make your dream come true.

ON THAT NOTE
A Coach for a Coach

It's very helpful to have a coach of your own at this juncture, someone who has been at this for a while and can help you with capability building, both as a coach and an entrepreneur. Your coach can also be a huge time-saver and a source of referrals for professional support, like web design, bookkeeping, marketing, and other essential areas of running your business. This is a thrilling journey with deep learning and a tremendous sense of accomplishment. You got this!

Speaking of making dreams come true, here is a little about my personal journey. When I immigrated to the United States, I had $500 and one suitcase, which the airline lost. But, despite overt discrimination, and thanks to key people helping me at pivotal times and very hard work, I was fortunate to make a career of helping others. I was able to build a thriving business and work as an in-house executive. One of the good things about being an entrepreneur and an executive is that one role informed the other. And now I am happy to be able to give back to the field of coaching. Each country has a different approach to entrepreneurship, so be sure to find out what works best for you in your own situation.

Attributes of Entrepreneurial Savvy

Hundreds of books have been written about the rock stars of business—those college dropouts who created businesses that would ultimately change the landscape forever. You're probably thinking of some of their names while you read this. I am not going to attempt to summarize their amazing stories; instead, I'll focus on what attributes or attitudes have helped Becky and me start our small businesses. We may not change global industries forever, but we find honor in positively affecting the clients we get to work with in coaching and consulting. Let's look at some of the essential work you'll need to do.

Willingness to Do All the Work

In the beginning, some of the work can be tactical, operational, or administrative. Especially for people who have led teams for years, this can be quite a leap to do it all yourself. Across all three buckets of work, there is research and administration to care for: scoping the work, writing proposals, invoicing clients, keeping up with social media, researching new leadership models, and hiring and firing accountants, lawyers, bankers, and insurance brokers. The list can feel endless. I recommend you budget 10 to 20 percent of your time for this kind of tactical work. I also recommend outsourcing what you can. Bookkeepers, marketing consultants, and administrative assistants can be found on online platforms, complete with references and work samples.

A former colleague coined the acronym WIT—whatever it takes—as a mantra for the sales team he led for the company. Assuming you have proper guardrails around what is legal, ethical, and moral, the power of WIT makes a clear statement that you're willing to do whatever it takes to start and build your business. This might include working on weekends or holidays, taking online training to be more skilled at your bookkeeping program, researching small-business loans or grants, or doing the necessary operational work to manage your business. Let WIT be the motivation you need to keep at the work and stay dedicated to your dream.

Client-Centricity

It's time to get obsessed with your client. Who is the ideal client for your coaching business? What motivates them? What are their pain points? What are they coming to you to resolve? In marketing, we call these "character personas." These thorough pictures of your potential customers allow you to build more effective advertising campaigns that target their problems. (More on this in the next chapter.) This kind of work matters for your business. You should continue to listen to what your clients want and need. Have a plan for your ideal client and what you're offering to them, then adapt. Your business will change, sometimes in substantive ways. Be flexible and enterprising. If you do good work, your clients will do some of the business development for you through referrals.

Believe in Yourself!

While it's important to have a network of people around you who are your support structure and your cheerleaders, you also need to believe in yourself. Be your own rock. Build your stamina and resilience. Learn what amps up your anxiety and build self-care routines that help you manage your anxiety and insecurities. Be persistent in pursuing your dreams—you got this!

Real Business Savvy

Given that you possess the three essential experiences that make a great coach (executive experience, understanding of human motivation, and an effective coaching model), you likely also possess the foundational business skills of an entrepreneur, including planning, budgeting, selling, working with executive clients to clarify desired outcomes, managing the details of an engagement, estimating projects, hiring support, and outstanding communication. Remember to be clear on what you're good at and start to build your competencies in other areas. This is a chance for you to learn new skills and grow.

Set Yourself Up for Success

I explored at length the tools for assessing your client in chapter 2. As you consider your appetite and readiness for entrepreneurship, I recommend you complete your own set of self-assessments to help you take an honest look in the mirror.

Assess Your Entrepreneurship Readiness

A simple Google search will yield several entrepreneurial assessments aimed at helping you determine if you have the aptitude and drive to run your own business. I recommend completing a few of these to help identify your inherent strengths and potentially uncover areas for you to closely manage to become a successful entrepreneur.

For example, you may be very strong in client communications and developing a portfolio of solutions to offer to potential clients. These are valuable assets to have in building and running your business. Conversely, you may not be detail oriented or you may lack basic financial-forecasting competencies. These are important skills as an entrepreneur, and knowing these areas of weakness can help you attend to them more actively before you're able to outsource that type of work.

A small-business association is a great source of tools and support; I highly recommend you engage with one to help you assess and build necessary skills. Here are a few other free assessments:

- The BDC (Business Development Bank of Canada) Entrepreneurial Potential Self-Assessment
- Human Metrics Entrepreneur Quiz
- Psychometric Tests Entrepreneur Test

Take Your Psychological Profiles

I highly recommend taking the psychological assessments you're also administering to your clients. This gives you a deeper and more personal understanding of the assessment. In chapter 2, I mentioned some companies who administer and compile various psychological profiles. Engaging them for yourself could be a way to vet whether they'd be a good asset for your coaching toolkit while also imparting some insight into your own psychology.

Specifically, the Strong Interest Inventory can help you understand your work interests and the industries best suited for your preferences. This tool doesn't test abilities; rather, it inventories interests and showcases occupations, types of work, and industries that are aligned to those interests. Pay close attention to the summary of traditional versus entrepreneurial roles as a good indicator of your natural aptitude for entrepreneurship.

Other instruments, such as the FIRO-B, can give you insights into your approach to work and your ideal work environment. The Thomas-Kilmann Instrument (TKI) can give you insights into your approach to conflict, and the Myers-Briggs Type Indicator (MBTI) is always a good tool for your approach to planning and intrinsic need to complete projects. These are helpful tools to give you an objective perspective on your strengths and areas to carefully manage as you build your business.

Solidify Your Why

Whenever you make a big decision in life, it's helpful to have a clear vision of your "why." This is a chance to question your motivation in a way that perhaps you weren't able to when you were pursuing a new role, applying for an advanced degree program, or pivoting your career in a past stage of your life. This is a very personal, yet public, decision, and your ability to market to your client base about why they should choose you is anchored in your own "why." What is the deep reason this decision or change is important to you, that maybe you'd tell only your closest friends and family about? What does it represent? How do you imagine your future? What doors will your decision open that are meaningful for you? What will motivate someone to work with you over one of your competitors?

No matter how prepared you feel at this moment to begin your own business, you'll be challenged in ways you can't possibly predict. Perhaps the funding for your planned startup costs doesn't come through. Maybe a huge client that stabilizes your budget for the year cancels at the last minute. You might close out the program of numerous coaching clients without any potential clients immediately available in the pipeline. A recession could take center stage in the national news and your client prospects begin to retract. The list of possible setbacks is long and varied. Some of these challenges have happened for me, and without clarity on my "why," any one of them could have been a total knockout, game over.

As Simon Sinek (2009) popularized in his TED Talk "Start With Why," a "why" statement is "the compelling higher purpose that inspires us and acts as the source of all we do." Figure out your own "why," write it down, and start telling it to people so it gets some life and becomes integral to how you operate.

Summary

All right, you have faced yourself in the mirror. You understand the many buckets of work you'll be required to invest in outside coaching, but the reward of ditching a "normal job" and the excitement of building a business aligned with your values bolsters you against setbacks. You are ready to take the leap of faith into entrepreneurship. Awesome! I am excited for you and all the learning and growth ahead.

In the next chapter, I explore defining your business. What will you offer? How will you bring a unique perspective and approach to this work? What kinds of clients will find you and want to engage with your services? This is where your company begins to take real shape.

Chapter 7
Define Your Business

"Chase the vision, not the money; the money will end up following you."
—Tony Hsieh

"Don't limit yourself. Many people limit themselves to what they think they can do. You can go as far as your mind lets you. What you believe, you can achieve." —Mary Kay Ash

In this chapter, I cover:

- Defining your offer: Get specific with the coaching services you plan to sell.

- Understanding the ROI of coaching: Get confident in the ROI you offer through coaching to improve your ability to sell your work.

- Homing in on your ideal client: Paint a detailed picture of the types of executives you want to work with so you know exactly whom you're selling to.

- Establishing your pricing: Learn how to create a pricing model appropriate for your services and your income needs.

- Writing your business plan: This is an entrepreneurial best practice to bring focus to your strategies and next steps as an executive coach and small-business owner.

Shaping the vision for your company is the exciting first step in setting up your executive coaching business. Clearly defining your business and how it will operate sets the foundation for everything that follows. You get to decide what your products or services will be, who your ideal client is, and how you want to price your offerings. Your new venture will begin to take shape as you answer the key questions that await you.

Think of this as your getting-started plan, which will develop as you evolve as a coach and an entrepreneur. In this chapter, I walk you through creating a grand vision, then breaking that vision into multiple phases versus trying to do it all right out of the gate.

Define Your Offer

The first step is to define your offer: What are you in business to do or deliver? Friends, family, and, most important, potential clients will ask you, "What is your business?" You need to have a solid answer if you're going to succeed.

Consider the following:

- What are your product or service offerings?
- Will you have one line of service, such as individual executive coaching, or do you plan to offer other services, such as group coaching, development workshops, keynote speeches, life coaching, or growth-related book clubs?
- How will you change as the market needs change?
- What will you add, remove, or adapt from your current offerings?
- Does your idea fill your needs or does it serve the real needs of the market?
- Do you see others successfully running a similar business or service?
- Do you see a need in the market for what you have to offer?
- What does your unique value bring to the service you intend to offer? How are you differentiated from others offering something similar?
- Why do people need what you have to offer?

The answers to these questions help you figure out your "what," which brings to life your "why," which I discussed at the end of the previous chapter. These questions and more are covered in Template 7-1, a worksheet to help you hone your thinking and get specific about who you are and what you have to offer. Template 7-2, "Dr. Nadine's Suite of Services," is an example to inspire your own line of offerings—those you immediately offer and perhaps those you may choose to offer over time. In chapter 9, I share several coach bios, which tailor my offerings so they're specific to clients looking for an executive coach, a coach for coaches, or an HR and organization development consultant (Template 9-2).

Your business plan and essential marketing tactics are also covered in subsequent chapters. They are all interlinked and interrelated, so thinking through marketing at this stage is very helpful.

These are just a few questions to consider at this early ideation stage so you can build confidence that there is a need in the market and that you bring something uniquely valuable as a service. Others will likely ask you about some of these, so having well-formed answers to questions like "Why should I buy from you?" will be helpful when you get to the sales and business development stage.

Ways to go about defining your offer include considering what kind of coaching you want to provide. Perhaps you're most interested in coaching younger professionals who find themselves confronted with some executive responsibilities. Alternatively, you may be interested in coaching new parents who are juggling responsibilities at home in addition to executive responsibilities at the office. Perhaps you have C-suite experience and would like to target those at the head of their organizations. There are many niche markets available to coaches, so figuring out your specific focus will be critical.

When I first began one-on-one coaching, I focused on the senior leadership segment, working with leaders in the healthcare sector. I had experience as an executive in this sector and wanted to focus first where I had some credibility. This helped me grow my coaching business quickly and establish a reputation as an expert in the field. A few short years into coaching, I was asked to begin working with teams, mostly by the people I was coaching. They were getting so much out of their coaching engagement that they wanted support for their team's development and improvement as well. This led to speaking opportunities at several companies, writing my first book about coaching, and speaking at national conferences.

As you think about your offer, consider doing some light market testing. Talk with a few colleagues or trusted advisors about your idea. See what they think about the offer, the positioning, and the value in the market. If they happen to be your target client, ask them if they would buy this type of service and how much they would expect to pay. This is excellent insider information about the market need as well as possible price ranges that will be acceptable to your target audience.

Be sure to begin your investigation with a few "first believers" who tend toward being supportive and helpful versus those who tend toward pessimism. There is value in those more cautious perspectives, but seek them later, after you have more confidence in your initial concept. Right now, your idea is fragile and new, so your confidence may be a bit shaky. Engage those who will help you form this very new idea into something more solid through support, encouragement, and creativity. You can gather a broader set of input through a more systematic market scan once you have a product or service definition drafted.

COACH SPOTLIGHT
Differentiating Value Proposition

In my role mentoring and teaching emerging executive coaches, I worked with a client who wanted to offer a specific service to help get women on boards. Representation has been a huge gap since the beginning of industry in the United States, so the purpose and value were clear. My client's unique value proposition helped the executives she coached to get board seats and experience while also helping companies seeking to diversify their executive boards. Despite a crowded marketplace, Elizabeth built her niche practice and quickly gained a reputation for success, both with her executive coaching clients and with the companies that needed board members. She was able to create a deeply meaningful addition to her coaching practice by following my coaching method and guidance on defining a unique and significant value proposition for her new service offering.

Template for Success

Template 7-1. Business Feasibility Worksheet
A method to fill out your vision for your business—what makes you unique in the market and how you can become a viable operation—through inquiry and reflection.

Template 7-2. Dr. Nadine's Suite of Services
An example of how to define your work to potential clients. Perhaps your longer-term vision is to do more than coaching. This gives you a way to think about that progression of services.

Get Confident in Your ROI Pitch

The business impact of coaching is clear—for individuals, teams, and companies. Imagine a leader responsible for a large division of a company and a hefty portion of the company's revenue. The investment in coaching to make this individual as effective as possible, on an accelerated path to excellence, is a tiny fraction of that person's responsibilities. Even modest improvements from coaching can justify the cost of hiring you when the executive you're coaching is responsible for tens of millions of dollars—the cost of your service could be a rounding error!

If you are sought out for coaching, your client (or the sponsor of the coaching engagement) likely already understands—either intuitively or from firsthand experience—the value and return on investment (ROI) of coaching. However, you might be asked for ROI data to help justify the cost. It's helpful to have this information handy and have the confidence to describe the ROI to potential clients in these scenarios:

- A future client may ask for this information so they can pursue support from their leader to fund coaching.
- A new coaching program may be in development, and the HR or L&D leader needs some data to prove the efficacy of coaching as part of their program design.
- A former client is referring you to someone new and wants to illustrate the high ROI of coaching, beyond their direct experience.

When you're pitching your service to possible executives, you want to confidently show them the value they're getting. This is such an important topic that I delivered an entire presentation on the ROI of coaching at the ATD 2019 International Conference & EXPO held in Washington, DC.

You can look at ROI in four main categories: the employee life cycle, financial measures, competencies, and your capability. The "ROI of Coaching Worksheet" (Template 7-3) provides an overview of these four categories of measurement, as well as a template for you to complete while you consider each one.

Template for Success

Template 7-3. ROI of Coaching Worksheet
A guide to help you think through the financial benefits you have to offer a client or company based on four ROI measures.

Employee Life Cycle Measures of ROI

The employee life cycle shows the full employee journey, from hiring and onboarding through retirement and offboarding (Figure 7-1). There are several steps in between, of course, and coaching can have a profound impact on many phases of the employee journey. Let's review how coaching can help in each phase.

Figure 7-1. Employee Life Cycle and Corresponding ROI Measures

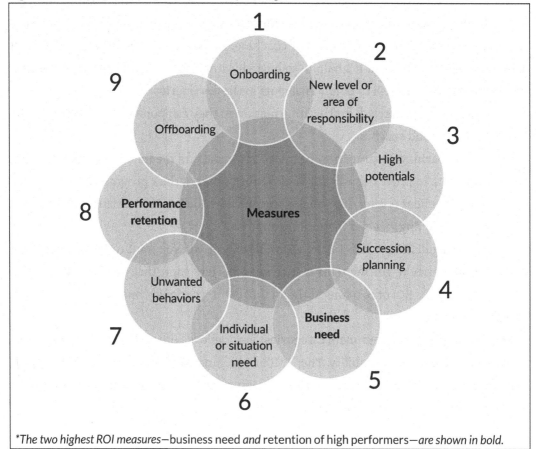

The two highest ROI measures—business need and retention of high performers—are shown in bold.

1. Onboarding

When onboarding a new executive, coaching can help the leader with a plan for the first 90 days by developing a strategy to meet key stakeholders, partners, and executives, and learn the industry and organization on an accelerated path.

2. New Level or Area of Responsibility

Coaching at the new level or area of responsibility phase involves helping an executive transition to a new functional area or take on significantly more scope in their existing job. This could also include helping a client move to a new level in the organization, which likely requires a different set of leadership competencies. Topics important here build on a 90-day plan (which is always helpful in transition) and include developing new relationships, refining business strategy, and communicating a vision.

3. High Potentials

High potentials are an emerging audience for coaching; these up-and-coming executives can be paired with a coach to accelerate their readiness for the next level or a strategic job rotation.

4. Succession Planning

Succession planning is a crucial part of a talent strategy, and more companies are paying closer attention to it as their employee base ages. Coaching in this phase includes conversations around readiness and preparing for what's next as a way to accelerate into that new level. It's also a signal to the next generation of leadership that they are looked at as future C-suite executives.

5. Business Need

Another powerful area for coaching to deliver real ROI is noted as business need, which could include rotating a product leader to marketing or a manufacturing rock star to sales as part of rounding out an executive's capability and broadening their mindset. These big functional changes are a great place for coaching to help that leader learn an entirely new area of the business and become productive as quickly as possible.

6. Individual or Situation Need

Individual or situation indicates a point in the journey where a particular situation might be challenging or an individual gets stuck in an unproductive pattern. Coaching helps target these situations and address the core issues quickly.

7. Unwanted Behaviors

Addressing unwanted behaviors delivers ROI to a business by directly working with patterns of bad behavior. Perhaps a brilliant engineer can't get along with key partners, or a physician leader is verbally abusive to their team. These are incredibly talented people who have one (kind of big) thing getting in their way, affecting the team and possibly the company. The business wants to retain them, but they need help getting after these conduct behaviors in a targeted way with someone the employee will respond to and respect.

ON THAT NOTE
High Performers With Unwanted Behaviors

Most coaches enjoy working with high-potential high performers who want to elevate their careers. I enjoyed building out a niche part of my coaching business working with elite and visible leaders who had unwanted behaviors (7 in Figure 7-1). The work was interesting and rewarding and had a very high ROI because these clients were critical to the business. Many of them became highly motivated as well, understanding that they were both essential to the business and getting in their own way with some unwanted behaviors. Their journeys were highly gratifying for both me and the client.

8. Performance Retention

Performance retention is about coaching the key leaders and technical experts the business really needs. It's an investment in their leadership development and signals their importance to the business. Helping companies retain these top-talent individuals delivers robust ROI.

9. Offboarding

Coaching through offboarding is a tremendous offer to employees who are affected through layoffs or other organizational decisions that decrease investment in one area of the business in order to increase investment elsewhere. Often this results in employees being terminated through no fault of their own. Businesses can maintain the relationship and goodwill through this challenging time by offering career coaches to help employees transition to a new job, company, or industry.

Financial Measures of ROI

When considering how to measure the financial return of coaching, consider this example from a previous client. A top-performing account executive at a large technology firm had recently been promoted to vice president of sales for the North American division. The executive had consistently exceeded his sales quota by 200 percent and had landed key marquee Fortune 500 customers in his previous role. However, he was underperforming in his new position. His direct reports were struggling to hit their individual quotas, the overall team morale had declined sharply, and engagement levels were plummeting.

Consequently, the CEO was considering replacing him. As a last attempt to rectify the situation, the CEO urged the VP to partake in executive coaching, to which he grudgingly agreed. After four months of twice-weekly intensive coaching sessions (at a total cost of $30,000), his performance increased markedly. Team members felt a much clearer sense of purpose. The VP had learned to be less prescriptive in his directions, affording team members a greater sense of authority and the ability to foster more genuine and authentic relationships with customers. After reviewing recent 360 assessments and performance metrics, the CEO was confident that a replacement would no longer be needed.

This story has themes of retaining top talent, improving outcomes, increasing customer satisfaction, improving team (and new VP) morale, and rebuilding confidence and sponsorship from the top. But how can you measure the ROI of all those benefits? You can calculate the ROI of executive coaching using the formula:

$$\% \, ROI = \frac{\text{Benefits Achieved} - \text{Executive Coaching Costs}}{\text{Executive Coaching Costs}} \times 100$$

Using the example of the new VP, the benefits achieved were the financial benefits from not having to replace him. These include search costs, internal-recruiting-team costs, time loss by the CEO and the new VP's peers, a dip in productivity from the team, customer costs, and more. To find the ROI, total all the costs and subtract the cost of executive coaching ($30,000), then divide by $30,000. Multiply that by 100 to get the percentage.

For illustration, we'll say the benefits achieved from coaching resulted in a $300,000 cost avoidance. When you then calculate the ROI, you get an ROI of 900 percent.

$$900\% \, ROI = \frac{300,000 - 30,000}{30,000} \times 100$$

This analysis only scratches the surface because it does not include other tangible and intangible benefits associated with coaching, including avoiding productivity loss among direct reports, increased rates of turnover, and strained customer relations.

Leadership Competency Measures of ROI

Research by Korn Ferry (2015) identified 10 leadership competencies that coaches most often focused on with clients. Based on their results, let's assume this tells us there are negative impacts of poor performance in these top 10 leadership competencies. With my approach to executive coaching being so deeply grounded in competencies, this provides a beautiful illustration of the benefits of my four-step model and competency-based approach to leadership development. The summary in Table 7-1 illustrates what more skilled capability looks like in each, giving a qualitative ROI for coaching.

Table 7-1. Top Leadership Competency Measures

Competency	Negative Impact	Positive Impact to Executive and Employees	Positive Impact to Business
Self-awareness	Distorted sense of self	Increased awareness of blind spots, enhanced leadership abilities	Increased ability to meet objectives, increased business performance
Interpersonal relationships, listening skills, and empathy	Inability to build and foster a collaborative work environment	Improved relationships with leadership, co-workers, and stakeholders	Increased employee satisfaction, increased retention rates
Influence	Inability to effect positive change	Increased levels of motivation, inspiration	Increased business performance
Leading during times of change	Lack of adaptability in times of transition, "change fatigue"	Increased sense of involvement, decreased sense of uncertainty	Increased competitive positioning, increased global positioning, increased financial performance
Communication skills	Confusion, unclear direction	Increased business transparency, reduced conflict	Improved brand image, improved internal and external communication
Motivation and engagement, leading with vision and purpose	Low levels of productivity	Increased felt responsibility, increased engagement levels, increased sense of purpose	Increased productivity
Building effective teams	Misaligned strategy, missed deadlines	Increased opportunities for career advancement, improved workplace culture	Improved product or service quality, shorter time to market
Strategy and strategic thinking	Short-term focus, inconsistent business results	Increased sense of pride	Enhanced long-term planning efforts, more consistent ability to deliver business results that meet or exceed forecasts
Working with uncertainty and ambiguity, decision skills	Low levels of engagement	Decreased levels of absenteeism, decreased stress levels, improved workplace culture	Improved innovation processes, improved risk management
Mentoring relationships, listening skills, empathy	Lack of leadership development opportunities, strained internal and external relations	Increased opportunities for personal and professional growth	Increased customer loyalty, increased customer service, improved diversity and inclusion efforts

Defining the ROI of Your Ability as a Coach

Last but not least in considering ROI is your ability to discuss coaching in an informed, confident, and convincing fashion, as well as your ability to be an excellent executive coach. Obviously the more capable you are as a coach, the more rigorously you can apply the four-step model, resulting in higher ROI for a coaching program. Do a little self-evaluation to see where you stand in terms of excellence in executive coaching.

- **How do you fare in the following abilities for discussing coaching?**
  - » How are your influence skills?
  - » Can you describe the coaching method and its ROI?
  - » Are you credible at the executive level?
  - » Do you understand the industry and the organization?
  - » Do you know why you're being hired as a coach? What is the client's motivation?
  - » Are you a great leader yourself?
  - » Do you have a rich personal journey with coaching as a client?
- **How do you fare in the following competencies for being a coach?**
  - » Do you have executive-level experience, whether in the role or in proximity to the type of client you are coaching?
  - » Do you have a solid understanding of human motivation and how to enlist your clients in their own development?
  - » Do you have an effective method? Can you apply the coaching method?
  - » Are you able to improve teamwork, problem solving, decision making, and conflict in teams?
  - » Do you have the ability to build your business?

Future clients want to know that you have a proven model, that you "get" them at their level and in their industry, and that you have a track record of success. Remember the numerous coaching competencies detailed throughout the first half of the book and reflect on your personal mastery of each one. The previous questions are just a litmus test to evaluate your effectiveness and offer ways to market your capability that will resonate with an executive seeking coaching.

ON THAT NOTE

I'm Just Starting Out! How Do I Get a Proven Track Record?

Good question! That is a key value of this book: to give you a proven method that has been battle-tested at the executive level for more than 30 years. You be confident that, when implementing my four-step coaching model and following all the recommendations and techniques outlined in the first half of the book, you are standing on the shoulders of people who have successfully walked this path ahead of you. You can have confidence in the method as a quick start to your track record of success!

Determine Your Ideal Client

It's best to start or develop your business with an idea about who your target client is. Who is your customer? Why would they want to buy from you? What do you have to offer them that is uniquely differentiated and valuable? Are you passionate about this client and helping to solve their needs?

This persona development helps you systematically define an ideal client or customer at a very deep level. It enables you to directly aim your marketing, messaging, branding, packaging, promotions, and pricing more intentionally at that individual—their wants, needs, and pain points. You can save time and money on marketing tactics and advertising if you know who you're trying to reach and where they "hang out" in the world and online.

There are many ways to think about your ideal client. I offer a few examples here, just to start your creative thinking. Many aspiring coaches ask me if I accept clients who fall outside my ideal pool. I will at least conduct a chemistry call to see if we're a good fit. Just because you may be focused on executive women, for example, doesn't mean you should turn down executive men. It just means your marketing, advertising, messaging, branding, and word-of-mouth efforts target this customer in a way that resonates with them and their needs.

Possible ideal clients for coaching:

- **Top executives.** As leaders ascend to higher positions of authority and responsibility, they can sometimes lose valuable feedback, critical support, or even encouragement. This is a powerful place to work with experienced leaders, who can have a crushing amount of responsibility in an increasingly challenging work world. Sometimes, a coach is one of just a few trusted confidants with whom a leader can take off their armor, refine competencies, and receive guidance for things deeply meaningful to their life and leading.

- **High potentials and fast trackers.** Many companies have programs for their high-potential individual contributors to accelerate competency development and management readiness, and many of these programs include coaching. At the top of the house, with an aging management community, there is also focus on succession planning and preparing the next generation of senior leaders for top jobs. This is an exciting and high-stakes place to work, with many highly motivated individuals in a structured program.

- **Situation specific.** There is a large category of situation-specific executive coaching clients. You could focus on parents who are returning to work and seeking support navigating their career while caring for their children. You could consider adults in the "sandwich generation," who are caring for their children and aging parents while also trying to maintain a successful career and their own health and happiness. You could work with veterans transitioning into the corporate world. This catchall category is a place where your passions might lead you down a very fulfilling career path with a client pool you care deeply about.

- **Skill or competency specific.** Many clients engage coaches for a specific competency or skill that is crucial for their leadership role. They're often required to accelerate their development in this key competency. Examples include presenting to the investment community, delivering a new strategy to the board of directors, or working across industries on a shared technology program. You can see in each of these examples that engaging a specialized coach would be useful for that executive.

- **Midlevel managers.** Many coaches target the middle of the management ranks, which is often where a lot of rich developmental coaching can happen. While there are great programs for early-career or high-potential future leaders, as well as senior leaders, many of those in the middle are left on their own to navigate and progress in their careers. An individual development plan can be a powerful accelerator, and as a coach, you have an opportunity to grow with them. This is the population of future executives, and focusing here could be quite strategic to build your future pipeline of executive clients.

As you review each of these examples, you might have a sense of those you are drawn to and those that don't hold much appeal or interest. There are plenty of opportunities in the world of coaching, and the more you clarify your focus, the more value you can provide to that client group and support other coaches with referrals for clients who don't fit your exact domain.

COACH SPOTLIGHT
Progressing With Your Clients

I helped develop the practice of a coach, Alex, who had a knack for working with midlevel managers. He had started out in the field of L&D, training first-time managers. He had stayed in touch with many of them, and they then turned to him for coaching as they grew to their next level of responsibility in their companies. This is an excellent example of growing with your client base and illustrates a potential strategic decision to initially focus on middle management, then grow with them into the executive ranks.

At one point, Alex was coaching about 20 midlevel managers with aspirations of attaining director-level seniority. He did an interesting blend of group coaching, team training, and individual coaching. To this day, I refer coaching clients to Alex. Over time, he was able to identify the five key competencies required to transition from middle manager to director, based on the experience of his client base.

In the beginning, you may choose to focus on clients who are easy to build rapport with. Perhaps they are in the same industry or operate at the same level or even in the same functional area that you did. This gives you a common language and shared experiences to build upon as you grow your client-coach relationship. Over time, you will develop more confidence and competence in coaching and as an entrepreneur, and I'd recommend you continue to expand your comfort zone when it comes to clients.

It's also important to consider your pricing model and revenue goals when choosing your ideal client. For example, although plenty of groups will be able to pay for your services, a client from a large publicly traded enterprise could be worlds apart in terms of their ability to pay a particular fee compared with a client at a nonprofit or startup.

Create a Pricing Model

As you enter the coaching world, you'll find many pricing models that work. Some coaches take an hourly rate, while others price a coaching package at a fixed rate. Corporate clients are often priced at a higher rate than individual clients. Most coaching programs have a defined timeframe, such as six months, although some are more open ended, based on the client's needs or preferences. With executive coaching, you can charge almost any reasonable rate and implement it in almost any way suitable to your work style and offering. That is both a blessing and a challenge—if you can charge almost anything reasonable, how do you know what to charge? And what is "reasonable"?

One way to think about pricing your service is to ask a few colleagues for their rates or a range for you to consider. Ask numerous people in different areas so you get a sense of the range and variability. If you have a close relationship with these colleagues, you can ask how they came up with their pricing strategy, what went into the price, what makes sense for someone new or someone with X years of experience, and so on. Consider offering specials for some future clients and build that into your pricing. For example, if you write a blog post on the value of coaching, you might offer a 20 percent discount to the first five people who book introductory meetings with you after reading that post. (More on these types of strategies when I cover business development and sales strategies.)

Another way to think about how to value your time is to do a little math. If you're coming out of a corporate or other paid position, perhaps with benefits, consider the total value of your compensation at the hourly rate. Table 7-2 is an example of an executive who left a corporate job and started a coaching business.

Table 7-2. Hourly Rate

	Cost
Base salary	$210,000
Benefits (30% of base salary)	$70,000
Annual bonuses (average of last 3 years)	$80,000
Total net compensation	**$360,000**
Hourly rate (divide net compensation by annual 2080 working hours)	$173

Now you have an idea of what your hourly rate might have been in your last job. This gives you a perspective on how to maintain your current earnings if you saw clients a full 40 hours per week.

This estimate provides a starting place for sorting out what seems reasonable for your skill set, experience, and capability, by the hour. It doesn't cover the costs of training you might pursue for your coaching certification, the time you spend preparing for and then reflecting on each coaching client, taxes or expenses, marketing and advertising, materials, travel, or any additional time outside the hours you spend with a client.

Now use the following two scenarios as examples for how you could build your own pricing strategy, depending on whether the client is a self-paying individual or a corporate client.

Example 1. Individual Self-Pay Client

To help you build confidence in asking for a coaching rate, Table 7-3 is an example of what a six-month coaching program might look like, using the hourly rate of $173.

Table 7-3. Self-Pay Client Pricing

	Time	Cost
Intake session	90 min.	$259
Coaching: 10 biweekly sessions	60 min./session	$1,730
Pre-work: 10 biweekly sessions	30 min./session	$865
Post-work (assignments, practices, check-ins): 10 sessions	30 min./session	$865
Materials (profiles, books, articles, etc.)	n/a	$100
Total Program	**21.5 hours**	**$3,819**

This approach helps you credit all your hours and effort, at your current pay rate, for one coaching client. The hourly rate spent with clients is essentially double your current pay rate to account for the pre-work, post-work, and materials. You might not show this level of detail to a potential client, but instead position your offer as a full-service, individualized, high-touch coaching program that includes biweekly meetings for 10 months, personalized coaching, individual assignments and practices, articles and materials, full access to you as their coach for the duration of the program, and so on. You can sell the package knowing it's priced to account for all your time.

Example 2. Corporate Client

Another way to think about pricing is from the client's perspective: What is the value of your client's time, and what is the total cost to the company in hiring and retaining them? This will give you a very different number to work with, and because of your experience as an executive working at this level, there is validity in this estimated rate structure (Table 7-4).

Again, there are many pricing models based on your individual experience, capability, client focus, network, brand, and more. Because this is one of the more ambiguous areas for any new entrepreneur, I wanted to give you a few ways to think about this for yourself and come to an answer that meets your revenue needs and feels right for you and your brand.

Table 7-4. Corporate Pay Client

	Cost
Annual executive pay	$900,000
Benefits (30% base for illustration purposes)	$300,000
Performance bonuses (20% base for illustration purposes)	$180,000
Total compensation	**$1,380,000**
Semiannual total compensation	$690,000
Executive recruiting and replacement costs	$50,000
6-month "value" of the executive leader	**$740,000**
5% of executive value	$37,000

Decide How Much You Need to Earn

You'll need to balance how much you can charge with how much you really need to earn to maintain a healthy and happy life. For some, your earnings in your corporate job may have exceeded your actual needs. If you're like most, however, you probably spent most of your regular earnings; that is, lifestyles typically expand to use growing incomes more fully. But if you work out what you really need for your lifestyle, it may be less than your current income. That's good news because you will likely earn less for your first year or two of coaching. So, it's important for you to determine what you really need. You may have to make some choices about your spending habits in the near future to ensure you maximize your savings and near-term earnings. Template 7-4 is a worksheet to help you calculate a personal budget that's funded by your earnings.

One way to decide how much money you need is to perform a break-even analysis. This financial calculation weighs the costs of your new executive coaching business against the price per "unit" (one coaching engagement, for example) to determine the point at which you will break even and can cover all your costs. This helps you determine when your company will be profitable. Divide your fixed costs by the result of your average price minus variable costs to determine your break-even point:

$$\text{Break-Even Point} = \frac{\text{Fixed Costs}}{(\text{Average Price} - \text{Variable Costs})}$$

Let's review each part of this formula in more detail:

- **Fixed costs.** The sum of your constant costs, regardless of your volume. Examples include office rent, utilities, internet service, and technology.
- **Average price.** The average price of your service. If you offer different prices for different coaching packages or customer types, take the average of these prices as the average price for your service.
- **Variable costs.** Costs that vary by volume. This could be materials, travel, credit card fees, and other costs that fluctuate with the volume of your coaching business. Take the sum of variable costs for producing one "unit" in your business. Over time, you will have data to estimate a forecast of variable costs based on actual costs from prior programs.
- **Break-even point.** The result of this algebra is the break-even point for your business, which illustrates when profits are equal to the costs.

According to the US Small Business Administration, most single-owner businesses cost around $3,000 to start, while most home-based franchises cost $2,000 to $5,000 (Caramela 2023). From my experience, you should plan on investing $7,500 to get started. This includes costs related to:

- Establishing your website
- Developing marketing materials
- Purchasing subscriptions needed to run your business (such as videoconferencing, marketing design, a customer relationship management system, and email and web services)
- Incorporating
- Paying ongoing legal, banking, and accounting fees

Template for Success

Template 7-4. Business and Personal Budget Worksheet
A worksheet to help determine how much money you'd need to earn to satisfy your personal budget.

Write Your Business Plan

At this point, you have enough information to build out your business plan. Some of you may be cheering (*finally, the fun stuff!*) and some may be groaning. Don't worry, you've done much of the work already. This is the integration of all your thinking and packaging of your business. Your business plan is the foundation. Should you pursue external funding sources, it will be a key asset requested by loan and grant officers. Plus, it's just good business discipline.

There are many templates for business plans. There are even "lean startup" templates that streamline much of a traditional business plan into the nuts and bolts necessary for a small, agile new business. You just need to pick a model that works for you and your vision for your business.

COACH SPOTLIGHT
Coaching New Entrepreneurs

I was coaching a coach, Mariah, who wanted to set up a business helping people identify, land, and get started in new jobs. She selected the Strong Interest Inventory/MBTI combination profile and the FIRO-B to help identify which fields and jobs were best suited for her clients. Then she coached clients in being an amazing candidate for their ideal job and honed their interviewing skills.

Mariah built on this typical career coach idea to then assist her clients in transitioning to their new role. She used the practices and guidance from the book *The First 90 Days*, by Michael D. Watkins, to get her clients fully onboarded and productive in their new job. She offered a full, end-to-end career transition coaching business.

However, before Mariah could realize her coaching dreams, she had to write her business plan and articulate a value proposition for the six-month program. She developed the tagline "It's time for a new job! How to identify, get offered, and thrive in your new job." That got the attention of her ideal client, a senior leader looking to transition to a new job or industry, a particularly tough move at more senior levels.

Mariah had fun using a template suite on Canva to develop her brand colors, logo, document templates, and overall look and feel. The market research showed that while the VP client market was crowded, nobody else was offering the whole program that she'd created. Mariah is super successful with coaching clients across many industries. They pay out of pocket for her services, and there is a waiting list to enter her program. A former client even gave the program as a birthday gift to a friend.

This is the power of clarity that comes from working on your business plan. Mariah had a clear "why," a picture of her ideal client, and a unique offer to make to this crowded market segment.

Let's review a few key sections of any business plan: executive summary, purpose, company name and background, product or service overview, market analysis, value proposition, client, goals, finances, and exit strategy.

Executive Summary

As in most business writing, your plan begins with a brief synopsis of what the remainder of the document will detail. In brief narrative, describe your executive coaching business, why it's needed, and why it'll be successful. Include basic information so if someone stops reading at this point, they have a good sense of your business, your offering, and how you plan to operate.

Purpose

What is the purpose of your particular coaching business, the value it will create, and the market need based on your research and informal focus groups? This is a place to tell the story of your "why" (your passion and purpose) and your "what" (your offering).

Company Name and Background

What do you call this thing you're launching? At the start, you might take the simple approach of using your given name and adding *Coaching* or *Consulting*. This is likely not trademarked by another company and, depending on the uniqueness of your name, might not be in use at all. This can even be your registered name, and if you choose to update it to a more fanciful name later, you can employ a "doing business as" solution. This section provides your ownership profile and company origins.

Product or Service Overview

Provide a summary of the service or services you intend to offer as a coach. Detail how this benefits your customer and how your coaching service is differentiated in the market.

An excellent way to summarize this is to create a coach bio as part of your overview (see Template 9-2). This is a marketing tool you will use often, so it's helpful to write it now, while all this other rich information is fresh in your mind. Also be thinking about website copy, which you'll need once you get to the stage of building out your marketing assets.

Market Analysis

Detail the market information you have, including competitive research, themes in the market, and emerging trends that inform your business strategy. Your light market research can help inform this section, as well as any additional market analysis you have subsequently completed.

Value Proposition

Describe what you sell or what service you offer. Explain the benefits to your customer and what a typical coaching life cycle looks like. Show how your business is differentiated in the marketplace. What is the unique value proposition that you bring to the executive coaching market? Perhaps you have dual-degree credentials, like me, or you have more than 30 years in leadership positions in corporate America, like Becky. What do you bring to this work that sets you apart, makes your offering unique, and therefore is valuable to the clients and market at large? This is also great content for your website, when you are ready to build that.

Client

This is the place where you explain your ideal client. Who is your target customer? How will you reach them? What are they seeking in terms of your offerings? This section defines the actual consumer of your work and gives a sense of the audience size available in the marketplace. Provide a detailed account of your client to give yourself (and your investors) a clear picture of who is seeking your offerings. The more you know your client, the more credible you will be when speaking about starting and scaling your business.

COACH SPOTLIGHT
Homing In on Your Ideal Client

One prospective coach I was working with was particularly interested in coaching physician leaders in a hospital system leadership academy. She happened to be married to a physician leader and had been a hospital administrator herself, so she felt she was uniquely positioned to understand and help develop the competencies to be a super successful physician leader. Among her key competencies were business acumen, finance management, working in a partnership, and straddling corporate culture versus provider culture. She used her experiences to detail her value proposition and differentiation as a coach, and she proceeded to build a successful coaching practice focused on emerging physician leaders.

Another coach client wanted to focus on veterans leaving the service and moving into all levels of leadership positions. This coach client had a deep understanding of the army culture through her own experience, as well as the corporate business she had navigated for more than a decade. She knew the challenges of moving from a military culture to a corporate culture, and she was highly motivated to help others following this same path find more ease and success in their journey. She was uniquely poised to help executives thrive in their careers in a corporate business structure, and she quickly established her expertise and brand in this niche market.

Goals

Every business needs to have goals. This helps the leaders and employees stay focused and aligns the work toward goal achievement for the health of the business. I recommend you have multiyear BHAGs (big, hairy, audacious goals) as well as annual goals broken down into quarterly milestones so you know if you're making progress (or not) as you go.

Depending on how your mind works, you can begin with the longer-term goals and work backward. What does your business look like in five years, three years, or the end of this first year? Or you can start near term and work out what the long-term results of this first year of accomplishments may yield.

Imagine what success looks like in your mind—what do you want to achieve at the end of the first year? You're enjoying the final days of this calendar year and looking back on a successful first year in business—what has happened? What kind of work have you delivered? Did you land a marquee customer or complete several coaching engagements? How many clients offered a testimonial for your work that can now be used in marketing?

Set SMART goals (which are specific, measurable, achievable, realistic, and time-bound). You might be motivated by a "stretch" goal—something a bit out of reach in terms of being realistic or achievable, but that you want to strive for. Perhaps you motivate yourself by attaching a meaningful reward to the achievement of that stretch goal.

Finances

If you're seeking funding, this is where you'll detail your funding requirements. Think long term and explain clearly how much funding you'll need over a specific period of time. Detail how you'll use that funding year over year. Make sure any liabilities or loans you are taking on as part of starting your business are clear in the financial plan.

This is also an opportunity to detail your revenue model and financial projections. What will you charge for your services at the beginning? Perhaps include a plan to scale that up over time. What is your customer mix? Are you planing for corporate clients at the higher end of the revenue scale as well as individuals? This is your opportunity to convince the reader you have a viable business and will be financially solvent in a reasonable timeframe.

Exit Strategy

Exit strategy? I know what you're thinking—*I'm just starting this thing, why would I plan to exit?* This is a good question, and there is a good answer! Your business will be successful, right? You need to have a plan for when it grows. (Will you hire, partner with a like-minded entrepreneur, or just work like mad until you fulfill all your clients' needs?) And you also need a plan for when you're ready to be done. The answers to these questions will likely change how you think about your business from the start. When you're ready to retire, will you sell your business and book of clients to someone else? Will you try to monetize what you have created? Or will you simply close up shop as your last client concludes their coaching engagement? Whom will you refer clients to if they return for additional support? Will you have a partner on board by that time with the intention of handing over the clients and business to them? Handling these types of transitions with intention and grace are important elements to running a successful enterprise. Think them through so you have some ideas about how the end will be, adhering to your vision, your purpose, and your brand.

COACH SPOTLIGHT
Planning for Acquisition From the Beginning

One of my coach clients ran an executive search practice. As she worked on building her coaching competency and confidence, using the four-step model of course, she also worked on the plan for her executive search business. She was able to sell her business to a larger consulting organization, which helped her exit that business while simultaneously ramping up her private coaching practice. Selling her business was the plan from the beginning. She had great business and strategic-planning competencies, which also helped her stand up her coaching practice.

Summary

You've completed the exciting first step in setting up your executive coaching business, and you have a great foundation to set up your marketing plan and go get those clients. Whether you found this work fun or tedious, it will pay off down the line when you're developing powerful client relationships and enjoying all the work-life benefits that will come from the smart business you created. You've defined your offer, created a detailed persona profile for the types of clients you're targeting, figured out your pricing strategy, and drafted a business plan.

In the next chapter, we'll explore some of the essential elements to finalizing and beginning to run your business.

Chapter 8
Set Up Your Business

"If you have a crazy idea, go for it! Don't be afraid to make mistakes."
—Bethlehem Tilahun Alemu

"I never dreamed about success. I worked for it." —Estée Lauder

"In all realms of life it takes courage to stretch your limits, express your power, and fulfill your potential. . . . It's no different in the financial realm."
—Suze Orman

In this chapter, I cover:

- Financing your business: Explore ways to fund your startup.

- Establishing your legal entity: Consider the various ways you can set up your company.

- Opening your small-business bank account.

- Setting up accounting.

- Choosing insurance: What's necessary and what's not?

- Creating a contract: Establish your terms.

As your company starts to take shape and you have a good sense of your offering, your ideal client for that offering, and how to charge for your time and expertise, it's time to turn your attention to some of the important business fundamentals you need to address at the outset of your new venture.

All of these topics are offered to prompt your thinking and invite you to make the right decisions for your business. I cover ways to finance your business, legal considerations, banking, accounting, and insurance. If you are groaning and about to skip ahead to the next chapter, wait! I implore you to consider these very important topics. Although the work of an executive coach—building your business, meeting new clients, and envisioning the next expansion of your services—is likely more appealing to you, these topics are the essential operations of running a productive, profitable business while protecting your personal assets and sanity.

Finance Your Enterprise

It's important to sort out a funding plan. To give your business time to take root and begin generating revenue, I recommend you either hold six to 12 months of basic household expenses in reserve or keep another gig with more predictable income. This allows you to focus on building the business, establishing a customer base, and earning an income with your new business, which may be less than your corporate earnings at first.

Having household expenses in reserve also allows you to focus on what you really want to do without getting immediately distracted by opportunities to earn revenue that might not be totally aligned to the vision for your business. Your time and energy are two of your most valuable resources, so be judicious about how you spend them.

The good news is that, as a coach, you can keep your expenses low. You don't need office space, expensive equipment, or loads of supplies. You might want or need some training to round out your skills (such as marketing or human motivation) and build your confidence as a coach. You might want books (like this one!) or other resources to build a library of helpful tools. Decide what is essential for you at the jump and spend as little as possible when you start. Luxuries can come later, when you're more established.

There are many routes to pursue when financing a new business, including:

- **Self-fund.** Depending on your circumstances, you might be able to self-fund your business. This means that you pay for anything you need to begin your business out of your savings, a home-equity line of credit, retirement accounts, or other sources of money privately held by you. Talk with your financial advisor about the assets you have available for funding your business. Consider this as a loan to your company so you can manage your books with an intention to repay it once you're more established.

- **Borrow.** There are many offerings for small-business loans. To secure a loan, you will need a business plan, including a financial forecast, so make sure you did your homework from the previous chapter. Check out the Small Business Administration or other similar organizations for more information. These resources offer informative workshops and other tools aimed at someone just like you.

- **Grants.** Federal and state grants are available to small businesses to promote and support entrepreneurship. Explore national and local grants through business associations or your chamber of commerce as another great source of funding options and opportunities.

- **Crowdsource.** There are many options to crowdsource funding through platforms such as GoFundMe, Kickstarter, or Spotfund. The models vary, so explore what is a good fit for how you want to secure funding to underwrite your business startup.

COACH SPOTLIGHT
Financing Your Own Business

I taught and mentored Duong, who was building his own coaching practice. Duong calculated that he needed $6,500 and 100 hours to start his business. The costs included a new website, a brochure, a coach's bio, business cards, a new camera for his laptop, and a tablecloth and signs for local events. The hours included the time he would need to invest to complete these marketing assets, as well as time needed to contact colleagues and friends announcing his business. Duong moved to working part time at his regular job so he could focus on growing his coaching business. He saved $1,000 by bringing his own food to work for six months, borrowed $1,000 from his brother, and put $3,500 of his personal savings into starting his own company.

Become a Legal Entity

One of your first expenses will be to establish your legal entity. In the US, you will need an Employer Identity Number (EIN) before you can open a bank account for your business, so get started on this early in the process.

There are a few paths to pursue, and I highly advise you to consult an attorney to determine the one that's best suited for you and your business. There are pros and cons to each entity formation decision. I am not a legal expert, so talk to an expert. LegalZoom is a good resource for you self-starters out there. Entities may vary by state, so it's important you do your own homework and set a plan that will work in your state of residence. And talk to an expert—did I mention that?

The following are the most common business entities:

- **Corporation.** A corporation is an entity that exists separate from its owners, which limits the owners from personal liability. There are some administrative requirements to uphold the designation of corporation, such as holding regular business officer meetings. You will likely need to engage an attorney for all the correct formation documents and national and state registrations.

- **LLC.** A limited liability corporation (LLC) offers similar liability protection to the corporation designation, but taxes are handled differently. If you're a single owner and plan to be for some time, most attorneys would recommend another entity registration for you as a sole owner.

- **S corporation.** An S corp is a tax classification that's available to some small businesses. It offers similar protection as an LLC for your personal and business liabilities. There are rules for business formation and structure (for example, a board of directors is required), as well as administration and record-keeping rules.

- **Sole proprietorship.** This entity choice allows an individual to own and operate a business. A sole proprietor has total control, receives all profits, and is responsible for taxes and liabilities of the business. This may sound like a great fit for your coaching practice. Talk with an attorney about the liabilities and how to protect your personal assets, such as your home and retirement accounts. There are some advantages to going with sole proprietorship at the beginning. For example, it's the easiest solution to start, it's inexpensive, and your risk level is likely quite low at the beginning. You might consider this entity formation at first, with separate bank accounts, until your business is really going strong.

Companies and high-net-worth individuals are increasingly requiring coaches to be incorporated and insured. Taking care of this up front removes any barriers to working with these kinds of clients.

I have worked with several high-net-worth individuals as coaching clients who paid me out-of-pocket or through their estate. In addition to ensuring I was incorporated, I also had to pass security levels and establish more robust contracts related to confidentiality and privacy. Corporations will also potentially ask you for other layers of protection, such as IP agreements in tech companies and HIPAA compliance in healthcare. I always run these by my own attorney to make sure that I'm not giving away a fundamental item I need to do business. That's one of the many benefits of having an attorney on retainer for your business.

In addition, forming an entity adds weight and credibility to your coaching brand and can serve as a key differentiator. There is a legitimacy to an official legal formation of your company that lends credibility and trust.

Other legal considerations include establishing a trust if you don't already have one. This will protect your personal assets in a more robust way and is highly recommended for any entrepreneur. I might go so far as to say it is a requirement. Also, consider privacy concerns when you are establishing your business. I recommend using a post office box for your business formation documents and establishing a business-only phone number. This gives you another layer of protection in an increasingly exposed world.

ON THAT NOTE
Privacy and Safety Concerns

On this topic of privacy, it's important to consider where you will offer coaching. There are pros and cons to every location and modality. From my experience, coaching in person is the most effective. Think about where your client will be most comfortable and what is most convenient for them (likely their office). Plan for a private space to maximize your client's comfort and safety. There are plenty of lookie-loos at the office!

If your client prefers to meet off-site, consider a park setting or a co-working location. Cafés and coffee shops are not ideal because of the noise, lack of privacy, and distractions. Your home office isn't ideal for one-on-one or team coaching either, due to concerns including insurance and personal safety.

Think about your brand, the quality of the coaching experience you want to co-create, and the support for your client to do their work. Be sure to build travel time and any additional insurance into your cost structure and contract.

Establish Your Banking

Now that you have some money secured to start your venture and you have registered your bank account with the necessary government entities, it's time to establish a separate banking account and credit card for your business. This may seem silly—after all, you *are* the business—but keeping a separation between business and personal expenses is good financial hygiene. Begin to think about the business as separate from you, as its own entity with you as the lone employee. You'll draw a salary from the business, and the business will pay rent to your household if you operate from your home. This intentional separation will help you orient yourself to the right thinking about money and earnings. Keeping a separate credit card also helps with your quarterly and annual accounting.

Think about what's important to you for your banking partnership. If you do all your business in a small community, and the local credit union is an important and valued community asset, you might consider it as a solution for your banking needs. If you travel a lot and may need reliable customer service around the clock, you might want to look at a big national bank instead. If you already have a bank and you're happy with their service, see if they offer a business banking solution. This might be easiest if you want to set up a weekly or biweekly payroll from your business account to your personal account. Look for banks that specialize in small businesses and offer special deals for opening an account with them. And if you're in the US, you want to make sure your bank is covered by the Federal Deposit Insurance Corporation (FDIC), which is the government agency that protects your deposits if the bank fails. Do some research, talk to two to three banks or credit unions, and go for it.

Create an Accounting Plan

In the beginning, it might seem unnecessary to have an accounting system or to hire an accountant. At some point, however, your business will be thriving, and you'll want to have your books in good order.

There are many accounting software solutions, as well as companies who will help you figure out the best solution for your small business. Some of them are free, and, depending on your comfort level with this type of work, they may be great solutions for you. Talk to some entrepreneur friends, seek advice from a local business association, and do some research. QuickBooks is a well-known standard for small-business accounting. Look for a platform that can grow with you as your business grows, as well as offer helpful tutorials embedded in the system or online. Choose a system that allows you to invoice clients, receive payments, issue checks, and accomplish many other financial transactions.

If you're an experienced finance professional or did bookkeeping in your past life, you may be able to run your company profits and losses (P&L) from Excel or another spreadsheet system. This option is a simple solution for those who know how to set up and manage a business P&L in Excel, scaled down to meet your startup business requirements.

Are you reading this and looking for an "Easy" button? Maybe this isn't your area of expertise or the space where you want to learn and grow skills as you begin your business. There's nothing wrong with that! Consider outsourcing your accounting to a CPA, an enrolled agent, or a bookkeeper. A CPA undergoes extensive training and testing and meets ethical and continuing education requirements. Many specialize in business tax preparation. In fact, the more complicated your finances are, the more you may want to employ a CPA. An enrolled agent also passes comprehensive examinations and may be a more affordable resource than a CPA. Lastly, a bookkeeper can handle a range of activities for your business and might be the most affordable partner in this space. There is support for you if you would rather outsource this type of work.

ON THAT NOTE
Bookkeeper Benefits

I hired a bookkeeper who is also familiar with taxes, which made it easy for me to do certain things throughout the year and saved a lot of time during year-end filing. She also educated me on all the deductions that were available to me as an executive coach. For example, training, travel, business development, meals, and entertainment were all deductible from my business taxes. Check with your tax professional because tax laws vary state to state and year to year!

Be sure to work with a tax professional who can help you with your tax planning and filing for your business. If someone already does your personal taxes, they might also be credentialed for business tax filings. It's most streamlined to have the same person or firm do your personal and business taxes. This allows for full disclosure of the income and tax implications for both your household and your business, gives the tax professional total transparency, and lets your tax partner identify and maximize business write-offs or write-downs to benefit your business and personal tax filings.

Keep in mind that receiving payment of more than a certain amount from a company or an individual has tax implications. As your company grows and the income from an individual entity grows, it's important to ensure compliance with tax laws. IRS and state penalties can run high, and audits take a lot of time. As a coach, time is money, so plan ahead.

Shop for Insurance

As a measure of protection, I recommend you procure business insurance. Many larger companies will require you to hold insurance before they'll book your services, so this is a good protection to put in place early in your formation.

Most home insurance does not automatically cover a home office or might have a nominal ceiling in terms of coverage. Investigate if your current insurance provider also offers a small business insurance solution. Be sure to maximize your coverage of equipment like computers and printers in case of theft or natural disaster. If they don't offer business insurance, look for companies that can offer this service.

How much insurance do you need? Well, that depends. If you plan to provide video-conference coaching with limited travel and no other services, you might not need much. You may also want insurance to protect your business assets in case of a lawsuit, as unlikely as that may seem. And if you choose to host clients in your home for coaching sessions, be sure to address this with your insurance provider so you're covered for any accidents that may happen.

If you plan to travel, you want to factor that into your insurance plan, including accidental death insurance and personal injury insurance to care for any potential risk factors assumed when traveling for work. If you offer more than individual coaching, such as in-house workshops or leadership seminars, many companies will require you as an external vendor to have some level of insurance. Your insurance provider should be able to guide you to the right level of coverage for your business and the services you offer.

For example, just before the COVID-19 pandemic, I booked a VRBO rental in Las Vegas, Nevada, for a planned corporate retreat. Overnight, all flights were canceled because of the pandemic and in-person gatherings were put on hold indefinitely. At the time, VRBO would not give me a refund. I contacted my insurance company, who took up the matter and was able to refund my $8,000 deposit!

Following is a short summary of the key types of insurance that are helpful to carry.

Professional Liability Insurance

Also referred to as errors and omissions or E&O insurance, professional liability insurance (PLI) provides several benefits, including coverage for personal injury (libel and slander, for example), defense costs, and claims against rendered services. PLI or E&O insurance also protects against claims of negligence.

For example, let's say a former client claims that following your advice led to them being fired, and they sue you for damages. E&O insurance could help defend your business, along with a contract that releases you from claims and holds the client accountable for their decisions and actions.

Though claims such as fraudulent acts, bodily injury, and property damage usually aren't covered by professional liability insurance, this type of insurance is very important for professionals who regularly provide services or advice to clients.

Here's another example of why insurance really helps: A coach was working with a client who had a high-pressure corporate job and was experiencing a lot of stress. After several sessions, the coach suggested that a major lifestyle change might be in order. The client resigned from his job, sold his house, and moved across the country, despite the coach's suggestion that they might proceed with a bit more caution. A few months later, the client found that he still wasn't happy in his work and personal life, so he sued the coach for "giving him bad advice." The coach's professional liability policy covered defense costs as well as a settlement. The insurance company was happy to see that the signed contract had stipulations on the client's decisions being their own and holding the coach faultless.

General Liability Insurance

Although coaches can benefit from having a professional liability insurance policy, general liability insurance helps cover scenarios that aren't usually covered under PLI or E&O insurance. General liability can cover coaches against client claims of bodily injury, associated medical costs, and property damage.

For example, say a coaching client trips and falls in your office, injuring their arm. A general liability insurance policy can cover many costs, including medical expenses and the coaching client's lost wages resulting from the injury. It's important to note that though your own property won't typically be covered under general liability insurance, damage sustained to third-party property would be.

Risk and insurance are different across countries, so I highly recommend you take the advice of colleagues and trustworthy insurance brokers. I recommend asking an attorney to look at your policy before you sign it. Coaching is a budding industry, and it is sometimes not immediately clear which path to take to protect your business. Arm yourself with as much knowledge as you can and protect yourself with detailed and all-encompassing policies, even if it might be a little costly compared with your revenue at first.

How much will this cost you? It depends! It's important to talk about deductibles. The higher the deductible amount, the lower the insurance cost. Conversely, the lower the deductible amount, the higher the insurance cost. In my experience, it is best to have a lower deductible to make sure that you are covered for small incidences as well. For insurance, you pay up front for the quarter or for the year, so make sure to budget for this and remember to write it off your taxes.

You will come across companies who require insurance, and some companies even dictate which insurance types and how much coverage you have. I have seen it range from $1 million to $5 million. In general, the more people you coach, the more risk you pick up, so it may be worth going for higher coverage.

Other Insurance Types

Depending on if you're incorporated and your size, you also might be required to have workers' compensation insurance. This varies by state and country, so please do your own research. Umbrella insurance kicks in when other insurance leaves off. It is often relatively affordable and may cover the gaps in your other insurance.

Create a Contract

It's important to have good contracts. Develop a standard contract that you can revise or modify based on an individual client's program design. Work with a colleague who has a good example or use the checklist offered in Template 8-1, and then have your lawyer review it for defensibility and completeness.

Contracts serve as a vehicle for clarity and accountability. Always have a contract in place, review it with your client, and get signatures as a statement of commitment to its terms. Always clarify expectations in contract form. At a minimum, list out what services will be provided, when they will be provided, and what the compensation and payment terms will be.

Good contracts should also define what your client should and should not expect. For example, add a simple clause stating that you don't take responsibility for the final decisions and outcomes of coaching, and specifying that your client should fully participate in the coaching process, including completing any agreed-on homework or assignments. You should also clarify that ultimately, the client is responsible for the outcomes of the coaching program.

It's also important to clarify that coaching is not therapy; if you as a coach believe your client would benefit from the deeper work of therapy, you will recommend that during the coaching engagement. This is a hard line for you to uphold as a coach. Unless you are trained as a therapist, like me, you should not cross over into topics where a therapist will be much more skilled and helpful.

It is best to have your attorney review your stock contract and any new contracts before you sign them. You'll want to balance legalese with accessible language for your client, always with an eye toward what is actually defensible and protects you in a court of law. Remember the psychological impact of including keywords or a full clause in a contract. It is much harder for a client to file a lawsuit requesting damages or payments for something that is clearly specified and protected against in a contract that they signed.

Use the checklist in Template 8-1 to start thinking about your contract terms. An enterprise client may have their own contract as well, so this will give you an idea of how to propose the outcomes, rates, timeline, and other relevant facts to contract the coaching program.

Template for Success

Template 8-1. Coaching Contract Checklist
A checklist to make sure you include the key elements of a contractual agreement in your client contracts.

Summary

For those of you who excel in operations, this was fun! For those who don't, all this business-y stuff may not be as exciting as envisioning your business or building your marketing plan. (That's the next chapter!) However, it's all very necessary. If handling the business side of running your business is not as engaging for you, be sure to prepare for your natural tendency to avoid it or delay working in this space. Schedule time to tick off one or more of these important tasks at the outset. Think of it as the "do your jumping jacks" (or other unappealing warm-up) of the business startup world—less fun, but healthy and good for you!

I recommend you also schedule weekly time to reconcile your books and keep your P&L updated. Build anything you're not naturally going to do as you begin your day into your routine so you take care of all the necessary items that allow for the more engaging and exciting parts of your work as an entrepreneur.

Chapter 9
Grow Your Business

"My advice to women all the time is: If you want a certain future, go out and create it. Conquer your fears as that is what enslaves most women."
—Dr. Divine Ndhlukula

"People don't buy what you do, they buy why you do it." —Simon Sinek

"Focus on the core problem your business solves and put out lots of content and enthusiasm and ideas about how to solve that problem." —Laura Fitton

In this chapter, I cover:

- Learning your customers and competition: Establish a clear picture of whom you're selling to and who else is selling to them.

- Creating a marketing plan: Set up your marketing efforts for success.

- Developing your brand: Think about how you'll present your company to the executive coaching world.

- Launching a website and social media: Learn what's necessary and what's not.

- Presenting your business: Develop a strategy for using speaking engagements to grow brand awareness.

- Blogging: Use blog posts to become a thought leader in the executive coaching space.

- Engaging your network: Learn how to use your network as your starting point for finding clients.

- Acquiring new clients: Outreach and pitch meetings will help you seal the deal.

- Retaining your old clients: Keep them engaged so your services remain on their radar.

Your company is ready to rock and roll, and it's time to put some of your creative energy into planning and executing your marketing strategy. This phase is ongoing and can be overwhelming. You could spend a lot of money on this part of your business operations, and while that may be tempting—go big or go home, right?—I recommend you stay focused, start small, test your tactics, and build organically.

For our purposes, we'll focus on the things you can do for your coaching business, as an entrepreneur and a business owner, and the subset of practices that are important to attend to out of the overall marketing domain. This should help you get started, and if you need or want more, a world of expert guidance is at your fingertips.

Learn Your Customer and Competition

Your customer is why you're in business, so knowing your ideal client helps you narrow your service offering and deliver messages to the market that have a higher chance of meeting your potential customer and compelling them to engage with you. Learn everything you can about your target audience through networking and research. Test your service offering to see if it appeals to them. Understand how you will fit into their work and life. Some due diligence here will help you start to understand whom you are trying to find in the market.

Many marketing experts will encourage you to draft your customers' psychographics. If you don't have a marketing background, you are probably wondering what this is. Simply put, it's a way to get inside the mind of your ideal client to understand their likes and dislikes, hobbies and interests, political affiliations, social conscience, lifestyle, and other characteristics. You can figure this out with some research, by interviewing a few people who are in your ideal client demographic, or by thinking about several people you know who meet your ideal client profile. Bring them to life by thinking through these topics. You'll be surprised how much you know.

Another part of this early strategic thinking is learning more about your competition. While my experience is that the coaches in the executive coaching industry support and help one another, it's business for all of us, and it's helpful to know a bit about who else is going after the same clients. Think about the other executive coaches you know in your geographic area or your niche focus:

- What is their company size and market share?
- How are they presenting their business and their unique value proposition?
- Are there any gaps or weaknesses in how they present their offer?

Based on what you learn about the competition, what opportunities do you have to differentiate your business? For example, one of Becky's colleagues, an executive coach, reviewed a competitor's website. The colleague offered her initial assessment of the competitor's company based on what she saw of their online presence: academic, heady, old-school, traditional, dense (content), and not very friendly. Conversely, this same colleague shared how she presents her own coaching business online—dynamic, trendy, modern, youthful, approachable, and personal—and how she would compete in a bid against the other company, highlighting the strengths in her approach when compared with the competition.

COACH SPOTLIGHT
Shared Experience With Your Ideal Client

I mentored an aspiring coach, Ariana, who chose to focus on helping executive women who were re-entering the workforce after an extended time away (maternity leave, planned extended time off, illness, caring for elderly parents) or sought to make a transition into a new field. She didn't think to do this until she reviewed her unique skills and evaluated the market. In her reflection, Ariana observed that she had personally experienced both types of transition and the unique challenges of each. She also looked at the market need, which was high, and other coaches offering a similar service, who did not appear to have her same experience. With these inputs, Ariana was able to create her candidate and client profile. She used these insights to target her marketing activities and outreach campaigns. She got creative about where her ideal client might "hang out" online, like when searching for doulas, doctors, schools, neighborhoods, psychologists, kindergartens, churches, and nannies. Over time, she branched out into other executive coaching areas, but her original inspiration remains the mainstay of her practice and passion.

Develop Your Marketing Plan

The ultimate goal of marketing is to match your services to the people who need and want them, and to do so profitably. Marketing efforts are most successful when they focus on what the consumer wants. It's important to understand your ideal customers and their desires for the services you offer. You also need to know your competitors and their strengths and weaknesses. From these two rich sources of information, you can build a successful marketing and brand strategy.

In addition to being strategic, marketing is also tactical—how can you get your message out, bring in and maintain customers, and continue to watch the market as you expand

and evolve your service offering? The marketing plan is developed, then reviewed and modified on a regular basis. Marketing is dynamic and responsive to the market, and you'll need to pay attention to what is working (*How can I get more of that?*) and what isn't (*I need less or none of that!*).

If you're new to marketing, building a full plan might be intimidating. Don't despair; there are loads of great templates online to help you get started, and you've done some of the pre-work already by completing your business plan. Use Template 9-1 to work out your own marketing strategies.

To complement the business plan you've already created, your marketing plan should include the following:

- **Executive summary.** In about five simple sentences, what is your business, whom does it serve, and why is it necessary in today's market?
- **Target customer.** Who is going to buy your services?
- **Unique selling (or value) proposition.** What is unique about your offering? How do you amplify your strengths and minimize your weaknesses? Describe your services in a way that will compel your client to engage you.
- **Pricing and positioning strategy.** How will you price your offering? How does that fit into the overall landscape of your service segment? How will you position yourself within this landscape?
- **Your offers.** What lines of service are you offering? Will you offer different packages? How will you bundle your services?
- **Marketing materials.** What platforms or media will you use to promote your brand—a website, LinkedIn, Instagram, TikTok, Pinterest? Understand where your target customer hangs out and where they are likely to come across your content or advertising. (Remember Ariana's story!) Don't assume that because they are an executive, they're not engaged with newer social media. Especially if your market segment is in the media or entertainment industry, your customers are likely current with all media platforms.
- **Promotions strategy.** With what messaging will you reach your target consumer? When, how, and how often? Will you have a blog? Will you host a podcast? Do you have a network that can help you get started?

COACH SPOTLIGHT
Basic Marketing Tactics Drive Success

One of my emerging coaching clients, someone I mentor and teach with my four-step method, was just getting her practice started. I helped her get a clear brand and a presence online that was easy to find. We optimized the search terms to ensure that if you search her name or "executive coach" in her geographic region, her website immediately comes up. She was also able to put in place several free measures to ensure the efficacy of her website and search terms.

Then she got busy! She gave interviews for free to various self-help, fashion, and health magazines and podcasts, which increased her exposure and activated her SEO. She wrote articles for free and got them published in relevant magazines or online, or she self-published them. She created a profile on all social media channels. All this also increased her presence and improved SEO. She is active on all her channels, posting even small items at least once a week and responding to genuine engagement.

Lastly, she speaks at events, whether online or in person. She is charismatic and tells a compelling story. She's built a highly successful coaching business in the type of coaching she wants to do.

From my experience, a good website and regular engagement on LinkedIn are great places to start and are mostly good enough unless you want your website to be featured in online searches, such as "Top 10 coaches in San Francisco." I also recommend creating a one-page bio sheet that outlines your service and approach. You can use my coach bio (Template 9-2) as a guide. What's important in this section of your plan is to be intentional about the platforms you choose, set a plan to experiment and measure results, and home in on whatever you find is yielding the desired results. It's a lot of work to be active on more than one or two platforms, so be sure sustainable engagement is part of your game plan.

The marketing plan helps crystallize your approach to selling your services. Once your friends, colleagues, and family know you're starting your own business, you'll be asked in almost every conversation thereafter one or more of these questions: "What is your business?" "Who is your client?" "How can I help?" This is how people make sense of what you are offering and can determine how to support you.

ON THAT NOTE

Engage Your Network to Grow Your Business

Friends and colleagues will often ask, "How can I help you?" Have an answer for this question! You might need some thought partnership or feedback on your marketing messaging. You may be stuck on pricing your service and could use some support sorting that out. You might be ready for new clients and could use some help with referrals. They might be a great guest on your podcast, a featured leader in an article you're writing, or someone who could refer you to a speaking opportunity. If nothing else seems like a good fit for your generous friend, you could ask them to write a recommendation on your business LinkedIn page or website.

We are blessed with so much information available at our fingertips. Depending on your learning preferences, you will find books, classes, college degrees, workshops, articles, and more on the topic of marketing. Check out TED Talks or workshops with local business associations. Courses on sites like General Assembly or Coursera may be more to your liking and offer the cutting edge in marketing strategy and social media execution. For reading material, a few favorites on my bookshelf include *The Lean Startup* by Eric Ries; *The Art of the Start* by Guy Kawasaki; and *Guerrilla Marketing* by Jay Conrad Levinson.

Template for Success

Template 9-1. Marketing Plan Worksheet A checklist for you to build out your marketing tactics and help you keep track of the deliverables for your marketing plan.
Template 9-2. Sample Coach Bio Sample coach bios for promoting your business.

Develop Your Brand and Identity

You are your brand. Your values, how you hold yourself, how you operate day to day—that is your brand. A brand is a promise of what your clients can expect from you and your business. It's the very beginning of your relationship and makes a statement about who you are and what you stand for. Are you communicating exactly what you want for your brand? If your clients said five things about you, what would they be? Are those the attributes you want to amplify as your brand?

Brand identity systems are sciences in themselves. And there is tremendous research that informs effective brand identity. What makes a brand believable to you? Do you notice the brands you habitually buy or engage with, or have they become unconscious preferences or purchases (maybe even upsells)?

Think about a time you sketched out your grocery list: oat milk, bread, coffee, tea. Every single one of these items has many brand options. Do you have a preference? For most of these items, you *definitely* have preferences. That is called brand loyalty and it drives repeat purchases and even customer advocacy. You likely wouldn't give your grocery list to a family member to pick up the items without also telling them exactly which brand items you want.

All of this is to say, it's important for you to think about your brand. What is important to you or about you in this business you're starting? Does that resonate with your target customer? Will it help you stand out from others in the competitive market? Clearly define the virtues and values you want to portray, and then consider how you can make them come through visually.

My brand identity, Dr. Nadine, calls forth several elements that tell you something about me before we even meet. *Dr.* tells you about my advanced education and commitment to the field of coaching. I also have a big smile, unique haircut, and personal look that have been designed into an illustration that I've put on my website and in several marketing assets. My website also includes many photos and videos so folks can easily get a sense of me, as well as important projects from my clients because I believe in community. Orange is a vibrant color and it's one of my favorites, so it's featured prominently on my website, social media, and videoconference background. These things form an experience and give people a sense of who I am and what I'm like—highly skilled, energetic, warm, and real.

An example of expressing your values through your brand identity is the logo for the World Wildlife Fund, which uses the iconic image of a panda bear as a visual representation of its core values of conservation and preservation. The nonprofit's simple and organic color palette also expresses its values. Another terrific example of brand identity expression is the Amazon logo. You find both a brown box and a smile, which is the basis of its business and the values it hopes to bring to consumers. Even if you knew nothing about Amazon, you would get an idea of its business just by examining its logo: They ship stuff and do it with a smile.

At the outset, your visual brand identity should be very simple: some nice pictures of you, a logo or brand mark, a color palette, and a specific typography. It may also include how you use imagery, iconography, or other graphics. You want all these design elements to work together and be consistent so you can build your identity in the mind of your customer. Begin with a vision board. What do you like from magazines or advertising, what messages resonate for you, and what colors feel right? Use your logo, fonts, and colors to create a stationery design, a business card, a word-processing template, and presentation templates to get started.

Stock artwork and graphic design sites such as Shutterstock and Canva can be very helpful to build out the look and feel of your company. Online tools like these provide templates and quick-start guides to help you think through each element. You could also outsource this work to a talented graphic designer. If you go this route, chemistry is key—they need to "get" you and your business. This should be a fun and creative phase of work, and having a partner who really understands you and wants to amplify your strengths and assets is crucial. Talk to three to five people, be sure to review their portfolios, interview their former clients if possible, and find a designer who can bring your business brand identity to life.

Aside from your design identity, the way you express your company's mission, vision, and values is also part of your brand. Marshall Goldsmith, one of the best-known coaches and thought leaders on organizations and leadership, has a simple mission: to help successful people achieve positive, lasting change for themselves, their people, and their teams (Goldsmith 2022). This mission tells you a lot about his brand, his values, and what it might be like to work with him. A global product company I work with has a company value of "handshake integrity," which says so much about how it operates, even with a global enterprise to manage. These are some simple examples of how to express your brand in your mission or values, consistently and continuously communicating what matters most to you as a business.

Launch a Website and Social Media Presence

Now that you have a strategy and a beautiful suite of brand identity assets, it's time to get out there on the internet. The reason you put together a website and engage with social media is to get referrals. Make sure your online properties reinforce your brand and services and are set up to help drive your business.

I recommend starting with a simple business website. It's a way to legitimize your small business and an asset that potential clients will expect. You don't have to overwhelm your audience or yourself with years' worth of awesome content at launch. Instead, provide a thoughtful representation of your brand with a few sections to share who you are, what you do, and how to get in contact. This is where potential customers will come to learn more about you and what you offer. You can include a short article or even a blogging section. Your website also gives you a place to publish information about upcoming workshops or specials, build a client contact list, and more. Make sure you have a clear call to action built into every website page and piece of content; know what you want a potential client to do next. Actions could include downloading a piece of content in exchange for a name and an email address or scheduling a brief introductory call through an online calendar.

Next, dig into social media. The good news is many platforms are available to you for marketing your burgeoning business. The bad news is . . . many platforms are available. It's hard to know which one is right. Start with where your target customer may be hanging out. If you think they'll be on Facebook then create a business page and go searching for those clients. Does your target customer use Instagram? Build your business page and start sharing. Many businesspeople hang out on LinkedIn, so you'll want to create a service business page to leverage that powerful platform.

I recommend you pick one platform and keep it simple at the beginning. Test the platform: Are you getting responses, do people interact with your content, and are they finding their way to your website to book a discovery call? Watch your metrics and see what is effective and what gets a response; then fine-tune your messaging. Once your first platform is performing for you, consider adding another and repeating the test-evaluate-refine process.

Another way to think about where to get started is thinking about where your network hangs out. If you want to engage your network of friends, colleagues, former managers, mentors, and so on, think about making it easy for them to support you. If your network is mostly on Facebook and LinkedIn, those would be the places to start building your business presence. This makes it easy for your network to support you by referring to your site, liking or commenting on your posts, or writing recommendations. If they aren't on TikTok, don't start there. That may be an example of a future platform to use for scale and to reach a new customer segment. Be ruthless in your focus in the beginning. Remember, this is not paid time; you are not earning revenue for this work (at least not yet), so keep it simple.

Seek Speaking Engagements

Becoming a speaker is another way to build your brand and your client pipeline. You're not likely to become an overnight phenomenon with your rock star speaking skills . . . but you might, and I would be in the front row applauding your success! However, most of us need a longer-term plan to get to the show, so to speak. This is how you can get started.

First, think about what expertise you have to share. Perhaps you're an HR professional with many years of experience and you love giving back to your community. That's a perfect combination for offering a workshop to budding HR leaders through a local non-profit or business association. Starting with smaller venues gives you a chance to refine your message, both the marketing messages that got your audience to attend as well as your actual presentation. You will get helpful feedback and continue to enhance your overall presentation.

Then you can reach out to local organizations to present at their member meetings. Your neighborhood business association or chamber may be an option. Local chapters of the Association for Talent Development (ATD) or Society for Human Resource Management (SHRM) are other terrific options to explore. Research your local community colleges to see if there is an opening for an adjunct professor or an option to be a guest lecturer in a relevant course. These are all slightly higher stakes and more opportunity for you to refine your message and continue to improve as a speaker.

Once you establish yourself in these venues, pursue larger speakership opportunities at the national conferences for ATD, SHRM, or another relevant association. Expand your workshops through the community college network. Seek in-house speaking opportunities for company sales conferences or leadership events. At this stage, you want your pitch to be professionally designed and delivered. It needs to be top level, and you'll soon find your client pipeline growing tremendously.

Template 9-3 provides an example of marketing collateral that can help you in your speaking pursuits.

Template for Success

Template 9-3. Speaker Information Brochure A sample marketing piece used in pitching for speaking slots at company meetings, conferences, or other venues where potential clients gather.

Start Blogging

Having a point of view on topics of interest in your field is a great way to get and stay relevant with your target audience. It also helps you stay in touch with current and prior clients. Plus it's an easy way for your network to refer potential new clients to you via sharing your compelling and insightful blog posts. You will find several coaches on LinkedIn who use blogging as a lead-generation activity.

Your first goal in writing is to stay on the radar of your current and prior clients. You don't want their awareness of you and the value you provided in their development journey to fade. Your second goal is to provide a turnkey way for your network to refer you to others. Lastly, you want to add some meaningful insight to the torrents of content out there already.

You can blog directly on LinkedIn or your website. Be sure to maintain your archives so clients can always find an interesting article you shared some months back. Consider if you want comments enabled. Reader discussions are a great way for people to feel more directly connected to you and engaged with your point of view. However, it requires you to monitor your postings and respond in a reasonable timeframe to preserve this sense of connection and engagement. Perhaps try a few posts with comments enabled, and then decide if that is time well spent in your overall mix of entrepreneurship.

How do you decide what's important to share? Start with what interests you and what you're reading or learning about today. Subscribe to publications in your relevant field. If you plan to coach people in real estate and construction, you should be on top of the most current research and trends in those fields. If you read business books, make note of interesting facts, content, or insights, and summarize them in a blog post.

Keep your content short—*really* short! It has been well established that we have a shrinking attention span, reportedly as low as eight seconds (McSpadden 2015). Yikes! Think about the many thousands of messages you're bombarded with every single day. This makes it difficult to consume and assimilate new content in a meaningful way. So make it easy on your reader and limit yourself to a maximum of three minutes of reading time. Three minutes (180 seconds) that's it. Make sure to make your most relevant and interesting points in that time. Make it easy to scan so your reader can get a first impression and decide if they want to continue reading. Consider a simple executive summary approach—list your top three to five points, then expand with more details under each one. You can also try a linked approach, where you share a few keen insights, then link to a longer reflection piece or the original article that inspired your insights.

Capitalize on and Grow Your Network

Don't underestimate the power of your network, and don't hesitate to call on colleagues and friends in this way. You are now a business owner and need to think like one. In this work especially, the power of your personal relationships and reputation is essential. Don't undersell yourself or the reputation you have worked so many years to build. You never know what kind of impressions you have made along the way.

First, think about all your connections. Start with family and map out all those connections: immediate family, extended family, and family-in-law. Then map out all your work connections: colleagues, former team members, peers, people you worked with on projects, former managers, mentors, vendors, and anyone you might have connected with or made an impression upon. Then think about your social network (the in-real-life one): hairdresser or barber, esthetician, Nordstrom personal shopper, landscape architect, pool service people, financial advisor, fellow PTA members, people you met volunteering, members of your bunco or book club, poker night friends, neighbors, other parents, people who share your hobbies, and anyone whose service you have employed. You get the picture—essentially every single person you have come into meaningful contact with in the last five to 10 years could help you get your name out there or offer valuable resources. You probably have a pretty big list!

You might consider using an online client management system to track your conversations and manage your client records. I have used a small-business Salesforce solution, and there are many other options too. Run a search for "small business CRM" to get evaluations from reputable third-party software evaluators, and schedule demo meetings with a few of them to get a feel for what they offer and their pricing. These customer relationship management (CRM) tools help with all things administration, like customer communications, email databases, drip campaigns (scheduled emails, newsletters, and blogs), client records, documents, contracts, and more.

Now think about how you will talk about your business venture with potential clients. What is your short summary of what you're up to? Make it simple so they can remember and repeat it. Be confident in what you're offering and courageous in speaking about the value you're creating. Then imagine how you might ask them for help. Can they think of anyone who could use a service like yours? Would they be willing to make a connection on your behalf? Or more generally, let them know you'd appreciate them keeping you in mind in case they cross paths with someone who might be a client or connection for you.

Lastly, think more strategically about your list. Are there people on that list who are your target customers? Find out who they know, where they hang out in life and online, and connect with them on platforms such as LinkedIn. Are they executives, current or former, who have a network of other executives who might be looking for coaching or to bring coaching services into their company? Perhaps they would be willing to make a connection for you. Are there people you can call when you're rolling off a big project or have room on your client books to help you fill that part of your card? These individuals are highly connected and highly willing to support you and your growth. Be strategic about when and how to engage them. Remember to show your appreciation for their support in memorable and personal ways.

Acquire New Clients

As a business owner, you're always in sales mode. If you bristle at the idea of becoming a full-time salesperson, think about the value you're offering to your clients. You're not the stereotypical "used car salesperson" most people resist. You're offering incredible value and helping people solve real pain points and achieve their biggest career goals.

The best referrals come from current or previous clients. Getting your first client can be a challenge, but once you have one, that client can easily lead to others and often does. Always let your clients know that you are looking to expand your business, and they will be sure to help you if they've benefited from your coaching services. Your clients may even start referring you before you ask. That is the power of a proven model and a highly competent coach.

This often happens within a single company, where coaching one executive can lead to coaching others. At one company, I ended up coaching the director of accounts payable, who got curious when he saw invoices the coming in. He checked out my website, and the rest is history. One of Becky's clients was so successful in her coaching program that peers wanted to know the secret to her success. She referred several clients to Becky to help them with their professional goals.

Another source of referrals can be friends, family, and community. People want to help other people, so let everybody know that you are open to new business. Let your neighbors know, your dog park people know, your gym know, your place of worship know, your book group know; let everybody know, and you will be surprised how many people will refer you. They know you, they trust you, and they want to help. Make your value proposition clear, and find ways to ask for help in referring business.

After securing permission from your clients, you can showcase company logos and client testimonials to communicate the value of your coaching. This helps build your business through credibility and experience from your client base.

Lastly, you can offer discounts for current clients to continue with coaching or return to coaching. This helps build loyalty and durability in your relationships with your clients.

Building Business From Personal and Professional Connections

Marc is a successful executive coach. He breaks some marketing rules, but he illustrates the power of a good network. Marc only has seven connections on LinkedIn and no social media, and yet is a fully booked executive coach. How did this happen?

I consulted with Marc to map out his closest colleagues from previous jobs and 10 of his friends and neighbors. Because of Marc's unique, caring, and grounded approach, his marketing competencies and outreach focused on how well these connections knew and appreciated him instead of whether they were connected to high personal earners or highly paid executives. The conviction of their referrals was so strong that Marc was a fully booked coach after just eight months of working together. It just took the first couple of clients that I referred to Marc; they then referred their colleagues and friends, and then Marc's network came in to help round out his client base. To boot, good karma pays off, and Marc is superbly supportive of his wife, who owns a small business. He even stands in for her occasionally, and some of his wife's clients have become clients of Marc's!

There are many lead-generation models and CRM systems. At the beginning, keep it simple: How do you reach your target customer with meaningful content that will get them to respond to you in a meaningful way?

First, you should always be building awareness. This is considered top-of-the-funnel marketing and is an ongoing effort to keep your name, brand, and value out in the market at large. You may offer a free piece of premium content like an article or recorded leadership module as a hook to pull in some interest from your target customer base. Or you may be a speaker at a local forum or blog on topics of interest. These are all ways to build awareness. Out of these efforts, you will get some interest, and potential clients will respond.

Marketing Rock Star!

Estella followed the marketing checklist and created tremendous success in a few short months. She has a military background and experience working at one of the big four consulting companies, a terrific base from which to differentiate herself in the market. Beginning with a single large contract, she wanted to build out her business to be larger and more diverse in offerings. Because of Estella's profiles and her unique personal story and media competencies, she and I embarked on a marketing plan that included a dynamic website and a host of different media appearances and platforms. Estella used the following tools in her marketing toolkit:

speaking, podcast guest, YouTube guest, contributing to articles and being interviewed for articles, and partnering with other consulting firms. Budget was a big consideration for her, but she was able to do all those things for free. Estella also learned how to build her technology and technical competencies to her advantage and created online classes and a closed community in her website. She also designed her own brand and made all her branded materials herself. Estella has a strong message and a unique point of view. She has successfully grown and diversified her client base and is leading a thriving coaching practice.

Once you have generated interest, have an initial discovery meeting to explore each potential client's needs and problems—let's call it the chemistry call. This gives you excellent insight into where and how you might be able to help them. Be prepared with helpful questions to learn as much as possible in your short time together. Discuss your offerings, packages, and any specials you may be running. Have a couple of examples of prior clients or work to illustrate your experience in the same or similar issues the potential client is bringing to the conversation. This is also a great time to share your ROI pitch to help highlight your value. Template 9-4 provides a sample agenda for this call. Follow up on this initial call with an email or letter to demonstrate your engagement with and awareness of your potential client's needs and challenges, such as the example in Template 9-5.

Now comes the big moment. You need a clear decision from the prospective client and a next step. They may have some objections or want to delay a decision. If you've done your homework, you should have reasonable and supportive answers to any objections. If there really is a need to delay, seek permission to follow up in two weeks or a month to keep the dialogue open. If they're ready to get started with a coaching program, have your contract and payment terms ready to quickly review and then send to your new client.

In an effort to build transparency and authenticity, I sometimes share a form with information on how to select the right executive coach (Template 9-6). Sharing this document with potential clients before they book with you tells them it's important that the chemistry is a two-way street. You want them to find the right coach, even if that coach isn't you. This is a tremendous trust builder and key to the start of a powerful relationship.

The contracting stage is a great place to confirm what your client should and should not expect. For example, include a simple clause stating that you don't take responsibility for the final outcomes of coaching and specifying that your client should fully participate in the coaching process, including doing any agreed-on homework or assignments in between coaching sessions. This helps set the stage for the coaching program and clearly defines who owns the work of and decisions from the coaching experience.

Templates for Success

Template 9-4. Chemistry Call With Potential Client
A sample 30-minute agenda for your introductory call with a potential client that helps you pitch your services in an engaging way.

Template 9-5. Chemistry Call Follow-Up Email
Follow up your chemistry call with this personalized email to your prospective client.

Template 9-6. How to Select the Right Executive Coach for You
A fillable form that helps future clients consider what is important to them in a coach.

Stay in Communication With Past Clients

It's easy to think often about client acquisition and sometimes forget about client retention. Before you conclude a client engagement, as discussed in chapter 5, be sure to get their approval to add them to your client contact list. This will keep them in the loop for any blogging, speaking, or podcasts you do in the future.

Particularly earlier in your coaching career, you may want to seek testimonials or new client leads from your current clients to help build your credibility and pipeline. I recommend asking for a testimonial or recommendation one to two months after your coaching engagement is completed. While you are in the coaching program, even in the ending conversation, the coach holds a lot of power—sometimes real, sometimes perceived. For some people, it can feel risky to say no to someone who was hired by their boss. I think it's important to let the power structure normalize before you ask for a professional recommendation. Keep the ending conversation focused on them—their experience, their learning, and their growth.

After 30 to 60 days, reach back out with a simple email, checking in and asking if they would provide a testimonial for you to use on your website and in social media. Get their permission in writing. It can be helpful to draft a testimonial to help them complete this ask. Remember, your clients are busy executives who don't have a lot of extra time, so honor the time they are giving you by making it as easy as possible for them to say yes and respond with a final quote. Keep testimonials short, one to three sentences, and confirm that you can use their full name, title, and, if possible, company name. If they cannot give permission for the company name (brand managers can be kind of prickly about how the company name is used in public!), you can note the industry. It's helpful to have their title so future clients can see the level of clientele you are accustomed to working with.

Offer a newsletter or blog to past clients. When you have specials, make sure they know about them first. If you are starting a new service line (such as a book club), invite prior clients to join first as a way to help them feel special and top of mind. Even though everyone's inbox at work and in their personal lives can be full, your content should put a smile on their face, ignite intrigue, or educate—or all three.

Create an email list to keep in touch with current and former clients. This provides an easy way to build email campaigns for relevant content, newsletters, blog posts, speaking announcements, special discounts, or packages you may promote, as well as any other relevant communication your customers want. If you keep the list current as you go, it's much easier to publish on an ongoing basis. If you are using a mail service, you can send branded emails to your client base and even set up a schedule of messages to go out automatically. Template 9-7 shows an example of an email I might send out to a past client a month after their coaching engagement has ended. I like sharing articles with easy-to-digest tidbits that are relevant to their development; this keeps the partnership productive, even though the engagement is formally over.

For your top-tier clients, think about special events that might help them and become a special memory you helped create. I host salons in my home for a small handful of healthcare executives every year. This helps me stay connected to my most important clients and helps them build their network of peers in the local area. Executives are often so busy with the demands of work and life that they can neglect professional associations or networking opportunities. Being a connector like this can be very helpful to them, professionally and personally, and it builds your brand with your clients in a unique way.

Template for Success

Template 9-7. Using Email to Engage Former Clients
An example of an email you could send to a former client on your email list.

Summary

Building your business is an ongoing effort to attend to your ideal client, find ways and places to connect with them, offer a valuable and differentiated service, engage your network for support, develop powerful assets to tell your story, and keep a vibrant connection to your client base.

Marketing is an area you can successfully outsource if this work doesn't excite you. A local association can be a helpful resource for finding local professionals who can pour their creativity and talent into your business.

Even if you aren't a marketing professional, there are many books, courses, TED Talks, articles, workshops, and more to help you. While several tasks of being an entrepreneur are only occasionally revisited or revised once completed (such as your business plan, hiring an accountant, and setting your goals), the work of marketing is ongoing. It becomes the lifeblood of your business and needs fairly constant attention to be done right. My hope is this chapter is a starting place for you to explore more and pour your own creativity, passion, and talents into marketing your business!

The next chapter covers a topic I'm personally passionate about: managing your stress as an entrepreneur.

Chapter 10
Take Care of Yourself

"An empty lantern provides no light. Self-care is the fuel that allows your light to shine brightly." —Unknown

"Rest and self-care are so important. When you take time to replenish your spirit, it allows you to serve others from the overflow. You cannot serve from an empty vessel." —Eleanor Brownn

"Nineteen people may love your work, but the twentieth one will hate it and will tell you so; you cannot allow that to affect you. That may sound trite, but there is huge risk in letting criticism get you down." —Carrol Boyes

In this chapter, I cover:

- Improving as a coach: Continue improving your coaching competencies as a lifelong learner.

- Improving as a business leader: Learn ways to stay up to speed in the executive landscape.

- Tending to the five domains of self-care: cognitive, emotional, interpersonal, physical, and spiritual; learn from several assessments that help you tune into your opportunities for improvement and develop a robust self-care plan.

To be an excellent executive coach, you need to practice the same level of self-care (or higher) that you wish for your clients. Take compassionate care of your full being—mind, body, and spirit—so you can be the very best partner for and have the best relationship with your client.

Be aware that you have biases and blind spots, and continuously make progress on your journey of personal development outside the realm of your coaching engagements. That means doing your best work with an intentional and durable practice of radical self-care. In addition, continuous improvement as a coach and an entrepreneur will help increase your impact for your clients and yourself.

This chapter aims to bring a no-nonsense, "seriously, this is important stuff" focus to this topic. If you're unwilling to attend to your health and wellness in a deep way, you should consider packing it all in now. I see bad coaching a lot, especially with the recent surge of coaches, and it's mostly well-intentioned people who simply have insufficient self-care and relationship skills. You cannot be excellent in a giving profession like coaching *and* run your own business if you don't take care of yourself—the foundation for both your service and your business. You got into coaching to help others. You must start by helping yourself.

Improve Your Coaching Skills

You've studied and prepared. You've read loads of books and articles, watched hours of expert videos, and maybe even completed an intensive coaching certification program. You're ready to launch your coaching practice. You're "done," right? Actually, you're just beginning.

The Japanese tradition of *kaizen* invites a disciplined approach to continuous improvement by making small, ongoing, positive changes to reap significant improvements over time. Being a coach means role-modeling the learning mindset and orientation toward continuous growth that you ask of your clients. Continuing to identify areas where you can improve in your own understanding of coaching models, development topics, and organizational psychology will help you stay on the edge of growth and learning. Never stop improving.

As you consider your IDP for your coaching practice, assess your own performance with clients so far. Is there an area that is more difficult for you than others? Do you feel equally confident in all stages and phases of the coaching engagement? Are there tools you can more deeply learn so as to better use them in the coaching process? Do the practices and exercises you assign invite your clients into deep exploration and understanding of their own opportunities for growth?

I encourage you to have an ongoing "coach's bookshelf" of resources to read and use in your coaching practice. Make sure you are thoughtful about having a diverse range of authors and topics so you continue to be challenged in your thinking and grow as a coach (and a human being). If you need more specific practices for a particular competency for yourself or your clients, look to the thought leaders in that domain to deepen your own understanding and practices. For example, if problem solving, managerial courage, or under-resourcing teams are recurring competencies in your coaching work, embrace the teachings of leaders in those domains.

Are there further psychometric assessments you can study to deepen your expertise and effectiveness? The assessment chapter detailed several, and there are others within companies like Hogan Assessments, Birkman International, and the Enneagram Institute. If any of these interest you, numerous certification programs are available to deepen your capacity to more confidently use these tools.

COACH SPOTLIGHT
Doing What You Love

A coach I was mentoring was frustrated with her coaching practice. She was starting to feel isolated, and even though she enjoyed her work and her clients, something was lacking. When I administered the Strong Interest Inventory and the MBTI, it became clear that she was extremely entrepreneurial with a strong interest in marketing and speaking. She was charismatic and creative, and enjoyed the limelight. But none of that was in her day-to-day work. Therefore, we devised an IDP where she started on the speaker's circuit. She ended up doing a local TEDx Talk and some presentations that were almost like stand-up comedy at conferences. Her unique perspective and sense of humor drew people to her. And she loved it! She enjoyed prestige and got some high-profile clients. She also offered a program where her clients would have a VIP day, spending the whole day with her at her house (at $35,000 a pop!). Yup, there are all kinds of coaches, and knowing yourself and what's important to you pays off.

Lastly, if there is a practice you personally struggle with or think, "Goodness, who would ever want to do that?" then it's likely that those practices will hold deep discovery for your own development. Sometimes the greatest growth comes from the greatest challenge.

Improve Your Business Skills

You're working with business leaders, so you need to stay current on business topics. Making sure to research the industries and companies in which your clients work is just the beginning. You also need to have a working knowledge of the current trends, research, and pain points for business broadly and for the industries you're supporting more specifically. Understanding the macro- and microeconomic trends affecting your clients and their companies helps you walk alongside them in some of their challenges. Lack of this basic information could affect your credibility.

Remember to talk with your friends, former colleagues, and clients. Ask about business trends and topics. Be curious about what is on their minds. Learn what leaders are talking about with their employees. Seek out their worries and concerns so you can better understand the dynamic nature of business and stay relevant in your insights and offerings with your clients.

ON THAT NOTE
Business Landscape Resources

Here are just a few content resources for you to explore to stay current on global business, industry research, and organization development:

- Association for Talent Development
- Farnam Street
- Gallup
- Gartner
- *The Guardian*
- *Harvard Business Review*
- *The Lancet*
- McKinsey & Company
- National Institutes of Health
- National Public Radio
- *The New York Times*
- TED
- Tim Ferriss
- *The Wall Street Journal*

You also need to hone your entrepreneurial skills. Evaluate where you're strong and where you could build some muscle based on the foundational business topics covered in the second half of this book. Explore best practices with some of the "basics" books (such as the For Dummies and Idiot's Guide to. . . series). So many basic knowledge books are written for people just like you and me: smart, self-motivated types who need to brush up on a single topic. They tend to have straightforward and simple language to help the non-expert build some competence in the topic. Perhaps you lack confidence in bookkeeping and finances; pick up a book to sharpen your know-how.

If you need to build your marketing skills, check out online courses from LinkedIn, Coursera, General Assembly, Udemy, Skillsoft, and more. Many community colleges and state universities offer workforce development training with talented professors and industry experts at an affordable price. You can pursue a full degree in marketing or a certification, or even just take a class. Remember the many great offerings from your local chamber of commerce or small business association.

The point is to invest time and even some money to build the competencies you need to run a successful business. At some point, maybe soon, you could be earning enough revenue to outsource areas that aren't your strengths or passions. But, you'll be better equipped to lead and direct that work if you know a bit about these entrepreneurial topics. Use Template 10-1 to create your coaching and business development goals.

Templates for Success

Template 10-1. My Entrepreneurial Development Plan
A handy template for you to create your entrepreneurial development plan. This is an annual plan with quarterly goals. It's important to continue to invest in yourself and your capabilities, both in the coaching practice and as an entrepreneur.

Improve Yourself

To effectively operate as a coach, you need to build a nonbiased, clear relationship with and for your client. This means any psychological or emotional baggage you may carry from your life and work experiences needs to be properly sorted and stowed before engaging with your client.

COACH SPOTLIGHT
A Coach's Unconscious Bias Can Negatively Affect Clients

I mentored an emerging coach, George, who had been laid off three years before he started his coaching practice. He had often wondered if the reason he was selected in the reduction in force was because he had spoken about some troublesome elements of the culture to his manager. He never quite resolved this question within himself. Therefore, every time his coaching client would mention approaching her boss with suggestions or complaints about the culture, George would directly and indirectly question whether that was a good idea. This was not what was best for the client. This was his own bias clouding the waters. He did some good work with this client, but they chose to move to another coach who specialized in women's empowerment and culture at work. In working with my coach clients, I dig deep into their interventions if I sense a bias or unresolved issues with their professional experience.

Working on yourself allows you to work effectively with your client. Working with a coach, engaging with a mental health professional, and doing the emotional, psychological, and sometimes physical work of your own development is foundational for your ability to be effective. This is the beginning of the radical self-care that is required to become excellent in this work.

Evaluating Your Stressors

The rest of this chapter focuses on evaluating the current stressors in your life and a plan for reducing them. Drawing on material contained in one of my previous books, *Stress-Less Leadership: How to Lead in Business and in Life*, I've outlined the five primary areas for stress: cognitive, emotional, interpersonal, physical, and spiritual. In addition to descriptions of each stressor, you'll find a short wellness self-assessment to evaluate your levels of stress and suggestions for overcoming them.

The stress status wheel (Figure 10-1) provides a great way to visually represent your wellness related to the five stressors outlined in this chapter. As you complete each self-assessment, you'll return to the blank wheel in Figure 10-1 to fill in the wedge for that stressor. Templates 10-2 and 10-3 replicate these exercises as worksheets for your future use.

These may be excellent practices or exercises for your clients too. Although that's not the focus of this chapter—really, this is about you—make note of these time-tested solutions to offer to clients who are experiencing the effects of stress in these five domains.

Figure 10-1. A Blank Stress Status Wheel

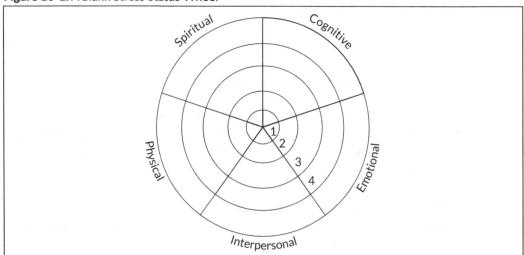

Templates for Success

Template 10-2. Wellness Self-Assessment Worksheet
A summary of the self-assessments offered in chapter 10, which you can use for ongoing evaluation and consideration of your well-being related to the five areas outlined in this chapter.

Template 10-3. Stress Status Worksheet
Complete this action plan to help you practice your way into healthier behaviors using the results of your self-assessment and the practices recommended in this chapter.

Cognitive Wellness

Stress can reduce cognitive flexibility. Like joints that you don't move on a regular basis, resulting in stiffness and even pain, you need to use your brain in new ways or it can become less active. Cognitive wellness can reduce stress and improve neuroplasticity—the nervous system's ability to change its activity by reorganizing its pathways in response to intrinsic or extrinsic stimuli. It means you can retrain your brain! When you try new activities, you introduce new neural pathways in your brain, which supports your overall cognitive function and creative thinking. Seeking out something new, taking a different route on your commute, learning a new skill, engaging in creative thought, or using puzzles to challenge your brain in new ways are all simple actions you can take to maintain and improve your cognitive wellness.

Use the assessment in Table 10-1 to evaluate your cognitive wellness.

Table 10-1. Simple Self-Assessment: Cognitive Wellness

	Yes or No
Do you forget meetings or other important commitments at work?	
Are you easily upset about work during your weekends?	
Is it hard for you to forget about working during your time off?	
Do you struggle to track projects?	

The more *yes* responses you have, the weaker your cognitive health. Give yourself one point for every yes, and mark your total by filling in the cognitive wedge in Figure 10-1.

Some of the more common effects of cognitive stress are mental slowdown, difficulty concentrating, feeling overwhelmed, and memory loss or impairment. Let's look at some suggestions for actions you can take to begin repairing the effects of cognitive stress and move toward cognitive well-being.

- **Difficulty concentrating:**
  - » Make a plan: Work backward from your deadline or desired result and stick to the work that is required to achieve your goals.
  - » Delegate: If there is work that isn't the highest priority or best use of your talents, find someone else who can help. Enlist partners or ask for support.
  - » Tune in: Pay attention to when and where your mind wanders. Notice and reflect on where your mind is preoccupied. Make some notes for yourself and get back on task. Review your notes later for themes.
  - » Do nothing: Dedicate some time to simply sit and be. Take breaks, practice metered breathing, and find a contemplative state of calm.
- **Feeling overwhelmed:**
  - » Attend to your goals: Review your annual goals and objectives to make sure you're dedicating your time and resources to achieving what matters most.
  - » Get help: Enlist the help of others who can support you. You don't have to work alone; there are many people who are your champions and want to help.
  - » Define the problem: Take some time to clearly define the problem that may seem overwhelming. What is and isn't in scope? What is yours to do and what can others do?
  - » Zoom out with a strategic view: The day-to-day tasks may be overwhelming, so take a moment to zoom out. Look backward to see how far you've come. Then, set your intention on what is required for next steps to move the most important work forward.
  - » Be creative: When the slide deck, business plan, and spreadsheet no longer inspire you, grab a paintbrush or block of clay. Invoke another part of your brain. Take a creative break and see what happens when you carve new pathways in your brain.
- **Memory loss or impairment:**
  - » Pause and take 10: It's easy to lose thoughts, to walk into a room and forget what you were after. Take 10 seconds to pause, breathe, and remember.
  - » Schedule important tasks in your calendar: Many of us are run by our calendars. If that rings true for you, be sure to schedule time to complete the important tasks and deliverables.
  - » Get some help: You might need some help from a time management expert. If you find yourself losing track of too many things and the other practices don't

seem to help, talk to someone you know who always seems to be on top of things and ask how they do it.

» Exercise your brain: There are mounds of research about the power of puzzles and games. Find ones you love and make time for them in your schedule. Crossword puzzles, jigsaw puzzles, sudoku, and brain teasers are all great examples of practices to keep your mind nimble and youthful!

- **Mental slowdown:**
  » Take time to think: Build thinking time into your schedule and commit to giving yourself this quality time.
  » Jump-start your thinking: Make lists, use novel brainstorming techniques to stimulate creativity, and practice visualization exercises.
  » Watch for the activity trap: Overcommitting can lead to spending a lot of time and energy on things that don't matter the most. Be ruthless about your time and manage your commitments. Activity doesn't necessarily equate to meaningful work or impactful results.
  » Turn off your need to have all the answers: Learn to invite others to solve problems and teach them that you aren't the only one who can think strategically and creatively.

COACH SPOTLIGHT
Overactive Planning Can Impede Coaching

An aspiring coach I was mentoring came to me initially to learn more about the assessment step and tools, thinking that was why she wasn't able to get past the initial interview with potential clients. It turns out, where Cassandra was really stuck was her perception that she had to be an "accountability coach" for her clients. An expert project manager, she was approaching her clients with a similar mindset—focusing on schedules, tasks, and duties versus the richer work of coaching the human being. She seemed to think that if clients just followed her program of tasks and timelines, they would gain the competencies they needed. She lacked nuance and understanding that it was a partnership, a relationship. In fact, she was scaring potential clients away by not letting them co-own or co-create the relationship and competency development.

Once we identified this, Cassandra was able to make the mental shift from command and control to more of a partnership, allowing her clients to be in the driver's seat of their own development. A big weight was lifted off her shoulders once she understood that. She also did some work on herself, learning to loosen the grip of control and increase her self-confidence and trust.

Emotional Wellness

Your emotions indicate the health of your body and mindset. If you have a strong capacity to know and manage your emotions, you tend to experience less anxiety, frustration, resignation, and resentment. Conversely, if you don't have a strong handle on your emotions, they can really run the show, sometimes without your awareness of the impact on yourself or others.

With some focus and attention, you can rewire your way of thinking and change your mind. Work on your self-awareness and deepen your compassion for others as you seek to understand how they see you and how you fit in the world. Your self-awareness is directly tied to the emotional effects of stress; when you're stressed, it's hard to be self-aware.

Emotional training includes learning compassion, practicing gratitude, managing emotions, and improving your emotional intelligence. All these capacities are rooted in self-awareness. In her excellent book *Insight*, Tasha Eurich (2018) defines self-awareness as "the ability and willingness to understand who we are, how others see us, and how we fit into the world." Thus, your three lenses of self-awareness are:

- Your understanding of self
- Your understanding of how others perceive you
- Your understanding of how you fit into the world

This is a much more meaningful definition for us to work with as we deepen our capability. Use the exercise in Table 10-2 to evaluate your emotional wellness.

Table 10-2. Simple Self-Assessment: Emotional Wellness

	Yes or No
It's difficult for me to recognize my emotions.	
People say I act before I think.	
When I'm mad, people around me know it.	
When I'm frustrated, I don't know how to calm myself down.	

The more *yes* responses you have, the weaker your emotional health. Give yourself one point for every yes, and mark your total in Figure 10-1.

Some of the more common effects of emotional stress are lower emotional intelligence, irritability, anxiety, lack of motivation, helplessness, and depression. Let's review some suggestions for actions you can take to begin to repair the effects of emotional stress and move toward emotional well-being:

- **Anxiety:**
  - » Make small changes: Anxiety can be brought on by too much change or turmoil. Take changes one step at a time, and don't rush to the conclusion.
  - » Focus on the present: Anxiety can be triggered by focusing on the future—what's coming and what's around the next corner. Focus on today and what you can do in this moment to move something forward or address a pointed worry.
  - » Find humor: Laughter releases all kinds of good hormones that ward off stress. Find humor in your life, keep it light, and learn to laugh at yourself.
- **Depression:**
  - » Avoid comparisons: Comparing yourself with others almost always results in feelings of inadequacy and reduced self-esteem. It's pointless. That's their path. You're on your path. Learn to love the shoes you're in.
  - » Connect with others: Relationships are the single most powerful antidote to isolation and depression. Schedule time with another leader or coach you admire. Share experiences and ask for advice.
  - » Mentor someone: Helping others can pop you out of rumination and gloom. Take time to mentor others and help them learn from your experience, accomplishments, and mistakes.
  - » Change your routine: We're back to rewiring your brain! Switching your routine can provide a welcome shake-up to help you get out of a slump.
- **Helplessness:**
  - » Get an outside perspective: If you're stuck and none of the usual tricks are working, it can be helpful to get a second perspective.
  - » Persist: Organize your work into buckets and schedule your time to dive into each with energy and commitment to see the tasks to completion.
  - » Increase your expertise: Look for ways to broaden your lens on your business or your clients' industry. Join a national association. Plug into your local small business association. Go to local events to share knowledge and network.
- **Irritability:**
  - » Count to 10: Slow down your decision making. Move from reactive to thoughtful and poised. Consider the power in the pause between stimulus and response.
  - » Know your triggers: What sets off a stress response? Get more curious about what's happening within and for you, and less curious about that jerk who just cut you off in traffic. Look inward.

» Downsize the conflict: Find points of agreement or synergy. Stay focused on the facts and the desired outcome. Spend your energy on the most important issues.

» Rebalance: Sometimes we can get out of balance with our work and life commitments, which can cause irritability. If this rings true for you, regroup and rebalance. Assess how important work is in your overall life, sense of self, and identity.

- **Lack of motivation:**

  » Partner up: When you're losing steam, it's great to have a buddy who can help you through a rough patch or even carry that proverbial bucket of water for a while.

  » Track progress: Look back to see how far you've come. Celebrate small wins.

  » Just say no: We can often overcommit ourselves and find it hard to get or stay motivated for the wide variety of assignments we have taken on. Learn to say "no" or "not yet" when you're being asked to take on something new. Be disciplined about your time and energy.

- **Low emotional intelligence (EQ):**

  » Apply your IQ to your EQ: EQ is a powerful predictor of professional success, so make sure you're being thoughtful and intelligent about your emotions.

  » Practice patience and openness to feedback: Learn to see another's perspective. Take the gift of feedback, and if you're triggered by it, get curious about why that is and what the feedback represents for you and your identity.

  » Stay calm and operate from a place of emotional stability, not reactivity: When you feel yourself reacting emotionally, take a breath and regroup, responding instead of reacting.

CLIENT SPOTLIGHT
Creating Safe Spaces for Coaching

My coach client Markus was just starting up his coaching practice, and while he was mostly excited, he was also a little nervous about it. He compensated by being overenthusiastic without knowing it—to the point that he put potential and current clients a little ill at ease. Once we got to the bottom of what was going on (his anxiety), he was able to see his true worth and relax, thank goodness. Because anxiety stops us from being present in the moment, he was creating a barrier to the coaching relationship without even realizing. He learned to become a partner for his client rather than worry about his skill as a coach or his budding business. This one adjustment made a huge difference in his coaching relationships and the effectiveness of his coaching skills.

Interpersonal Wellness

Stress can affect how you relate to others and yourself. Increased stress causes you to turn inward and withdraw from those around you. Just when relationships are most needed, stress can cause you to create distance from even your most important relationships. This can lead to wounded relationships, alienation, and even broken friendships.

Use Table 10-3 to evaluate your interpersonal wellness.

Table 10-3. Simple Self-Assessment: Interpersonal Wellness

	Yes or No
I only have one or two important relationships in my work and life.	
When I'm busy, people around me know not to bother me.	
I can go weeks without talking to my close friends.	
I have experienced broken friendships because of my busy life.	

The more *yes* responses, the weaker your interpersonal health. Give yourself one point for every yes, and mark your total in Figure 10-1.

According to Martin Seligman, one of the promoters of positive psychology, relationships are fundamental to well-being (Positive Psychology Center n.d.). There are many influences on relationships or interpersonal well-being, including motivation, the health of your primary relationships, and belonging, as well as steps you can take to improve the health of each.

- **Belonging:**
  - » Build strong teams around you: Help every individual feel included in the work of the team.
  - » Resist the urge to withdraw to the familiar: Reach out to include all with equal opportunity to contribute to the team and make a difference.
  - » Attend to your own unconscious bias: Make talking about topics of inclusion, belonging, equity, and fairness a regular part of your friend and family network. Be an ally.
- **Motivation:**
  - » First impressions matter: Manage the first few minutes of every interaction. Set the tone right away and be clear with yourself about your intention for this interaction.

» Show care for your team and colleagues: Get to know those you work with and around. What are their interests? How do they like to be included and recognized? What motivates them?

» Develop those around you: Like the other recommended interventions, investing your time and experience to help others grow is incredibly rewarding and motivating.

- **Relationships:**

  » Improve your listening skills: Practice deep listening, showing those you communicate with how much you value them and what they have to share through your verbal and nonverbal cues.

  » Be curious about others: Learn to ask questions and be genuinely interested in the answers. As the famous saying goes, "You have two ears and one mouth; use them proportionately."

  » Know yourself: Ask for feedback from people you respect. Use their insights to expand and deepen your understanding. Be authentically you, in work and life.

Robust relationship skills are crucial for effective coaching. I've talked about that throughout the book, and here is another way to care for essential relationship skills: build interpersonal capacities in your life and work as a coach. These are the foundation of trust, help you create a safe space for development, motivate your clients to complete exercises and practices, and give you leverage for powerful, courageous conversations. The biggest predictor of successful outcomes in a coach-client relationship is the relationship capacity of the coach. If you want to be amazing as a coach, develop amazing relationship skills.

COACH SPOTLIGHT
Progress Over Perfection

Ming was a coach who came to me because she didn't think her clients were progressing enough. She wondered where I got my referrals, and more urgently, she wondered if she was cut out to be a coach. I knew of her good work before we met, through reputation, so I was surprised by her uncertainty.

Going through her profiles, I didn't see much that gave me insight into her concerns. Then I interviewed her sister as part of the 360 process. I learned that their father and Ming's first manager were very demanding; that's how she became a perfectionist herself. She had rarely felt good enough, even when she got promoted over her first manager! Not surprisingly, she took this perfectionist tendency into her coaching relationship with clients.

By learning about her unconscious goal of perfection, we were able to develop Ming's competencies around self-understanding, self-motivation, and allowing others to set their own goals and standards without it being a reflection on her. This work softened her perfectionist tendencies and allowed her clients to demonstrate success with a more realistic goal of what "progress" looked like.

Ming worked hard to develop her coaching and relationship skills, and to this day, she has a great practice with all kinds of clients. I often refer clients to her, knowing that they are in good hands. I would take an overinvested coach client over a detached one any day!

Physical Wellness

We can't talk about well-being without talking about the most important factor in well-being—our bodies. It's a glaring statement of the obvious, but your body carries you everywhere you go. It's your vessel for navigating this world and is a magical being of great insight and healing.

Most of us abuse our bodies day in and day out. It doesn't take much to do the right things for your physical well-being, but so few of us pay attention until our bodies make some decisions for us. You might work and grind and hustle until you are sick and find yourself sleeping for an entire week. You might ignore the subtle warning signs in your gut and lower back until you have a raging migraine that takes you out for two days. Your body will always even the score to get the sustenance and rest it needs.

The exercise in Table 10-4 can help you evaluate your physical wellness.

Table 10-4. Simple Self-Assessment: Physical Wellness

	Yes or No
I regularly enjoy physical exercise that gets my heart beating.	
I eat a healthy diet that is balanced in nutrients and vitamins.	
I sleep at least seven hours, uninterrupted, every night.	
I drink enough water for my weight, physique, and geography.	

The more *no* responses, the weaker your physical health. Give yourself one point for every no, and mark your total in Figure 10-1.

There are many ways you increase stress on your body, including lack of exercise, poor diet, lack of adequate sleep, and substance abuse. Let's explore some solutions to mitigate these common physical stressors.

- **Diet:**
  - » Bump up the good stuff and eat well: A healthy diet is the second foundational element of physical wellness. Eat whole, nutrient-dense foods! Easy, right? If you're not sure how to make a healthy and balanced meal with all the good stuff and less of the bad stuff, cook with color. Make sure there are greens, reds, oranges, and yellows on your plate.
  - » Reduce the stuff that harms your body: You might be surprised by the ingredients in the foods you buy, so read your labels and limit additives, such as refined sugars, fats, and preservatives that can wreak havoc. Minimize white foods (simple starches like bread and white rice) in favor of brightly colored foods. And if you can't pronounce something listed in the top five ingredients, maybe skip that food.
  - » Experiment with a new lifestyle of eating: I have found that a vegan lifestyle has tremendous benefits for animals, the planet, and myself. Do some research, pay attention to your body, and adopt a way of eating that aligns with your values and makes you feel great.
- **Exercise:**
  - » Get moving: You know this. Exercise is one of the three most crucial things you can do for a healthy body and mind. Include aerobic activity and get your heart pumping for at least 20 minutes three times a week. That's your baseline.
  - » Find something you really enjoy: This will help you stick to a routine. Running, swimming, cycling, tennis, pickleball, walking, hiking—the list of enjoyable options is nearly endless.
  - » Lift weights: Work on your bone density and muscle structure. Muscle helps with so many things and can mitigate numerous chronic conditions, including diabetes. Try doing 20 minutes of weight training two to three times a week.
  - » Stretch yourself: Literally. Be sure to include some stretching in your exercise, such as yin, Kaiut yoga, or Pilates. Mobility work lengthens and strengthens your muscles and helps you avoid injury.
- **Sleep:**
  - » Get some rest: Lack of sleep wreaks havoc on our minds and overall wellness. If you aren't sleeping, you're missing out on all the goodness that happens in your brain and body while you sleep.

» Shoot for seven to nine hours of sleep: Don't convince yourself you can thrive on less. Try to get adequate sleep and see what a total rock star you can be.

» Have a consistent bedtime and go-to-sleep ritual: A routine signals to the brain that you're closing up shop and it's time to wrap up all your beautiful thinking and planning for the day.

» Avoid screens for at least an hour before bedtime: This includes your phone and your treasured e-reader. Step away from your computer and your television. This is part of what is called good sleep hygiene.

- **Substance abuse:**

» Make good choices: This is something we say to our kids and it holds value for us too. Inappropriate use of nicotine, alcohol, drugs, or medications can harm our bodies.

» Avoid other addictive activities: These could include gambling, social media, video games, pornography, work, food, and any other destructive behavior that is hard to give up or practice in moderation. Many groups and programs can help you better manage addictive patterns and improve your life and relationships.

Spiritual Wellness

You don't need to believe in God or another deity to reduce your stress through a spiritual practice. And if you're someone who prescribes to a traditional religion, lean into it. There is ample research that mindfulness, meditation, and belief in a higher power help you stay calm in the face of great tragedy and manage through challenges with greater ease and comfort. Spirituality has been found to promote well-being, and it's an essential part of your overall health and vitality. It is also associated with increased levels of happiness, lower risk of depression and suicide, longer life expectancy, higher resiliency, and greater life satisfaction overall (Seppälä 2016).

The exercise in Table 10-5 can help you evaluate your spiritual wellness.

Table 10-5. Simple Self-Assessment: Spiritual Wellness

	Yes or No
I believe that miracles happen.	
Being in nature gives me joy and a sense of the bigness of our world.	
I practice meditation, mindfulness, or prayer daily.	
I would enjoy a silent retreat.	

The more *no* responses, the weaker your spiritual health. Give yourself one point for every no, and mark your total on Figure 10-1.

There are many paths to creating or increasing a spiritual practice, including meditation, yoga, silence, and spending time in nature:

- **Meditation:**
  - » Take time for a meditation practice: There are loads of free apps, books, and other special meditation workshops with global thought leaders in this space. Start small. Even five minutes can be restorative as you build up to a more intensive daily practice.

- **Nature:**
  - » Nature is your playground: It can be incredibly restorative and help boost your connection to your community, the planet, and even the universe.
  - » Walk to work or make time for a peaceful and observant walk through a park: Book a weekend hiking adventure with friends or schedule time for a long, quiet walk alone.
  - » Observe nature and observe yourself in nature: See how it heals you from the inside out. Notice what you notice, in and around you.

- **Silence:**
  - » Make time for silent sitting: Our world is so busy and so loud—we're constantly distracted by and inundated with noise, demands, advertisements, and more. Find a quiet place to enjoy three minutes of silence. Attend to your breathing, notice when your mind wanders off, and bring it back without judgment. Just be still in the stillness.

- **Yoga:**
  - » Find a style of yoga that suits you: There are many kinds of yoga for all body and fitness types. Yoga combines the physical challenge with a state of emotional calm to generate a calm parasympathetic nervous system (your rest and digest state). The ability to be calm even when challenged is a powerful experience you can take off the mat and into your world.

Your Action Plan

Once you complete the self-assessments, build an action plan to address the two areas of highest need. For example, the two areas with highest level of stress or most out of balance in the completed status wheel in Figure 10-2 are physical wellness and cognitive wellness.

Figure 10-2. A Completed Stress Status Wheel

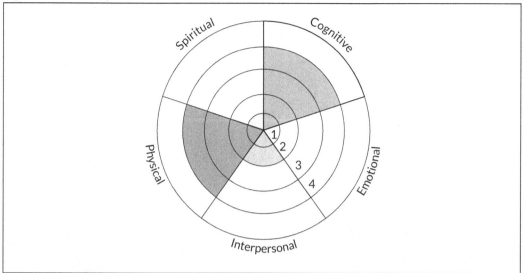

This person needs some quiet time for thinking and reflecting. They would also benefit from moving their body and perhaps attending to their sleep. To support them with better self-care, I might recommend quiet sitting each morning and evening as a meditative practice, along with good sleep hygiene to begin to get more restorative rest each night. In addition, time on the yoga mat feels supportive and could benefit their physical and cognitive health.

Summary

This chapter reviewed the elements of a healthy lifestyle that I have found crucial for being a successful coach and entrepreneur. Although this was the final chapter, self-care is really the first-order priority for you as a new entrepreneur. If you don't fill your tank, what resources will you have to support your clients and build your business?

Regularly reassess your stress status to continue identifying your stress patterns and developing durable practices in self-care. However, these simple self-assessments don't and shouldn't replace a more in-depth evaluation of any areas of stress or anxiety. If you're experiencing stress at level four in more than two areas, I strongly recommend you seek support from a qualified mental health professional.

Conclusion

"Celebrate endings, for they precede new beginnings."
—Jonathan Lockwood Huie

"The beginning is the most important part of the work." —Plato

"True success is about a passion to create a better world, live a life that you can look back on and be truly proud of." —Dr. Ola Orekunrin

---

Whether you're an experienced executive coach seeking new tools to refresh your approach or a novice coach beginning a business that serves the growth of others, I celebrate your journey and the exciting path ahead. I hope this playbook is a helpful resource for you to embody the essence of coaching, to breathe new life into your practice, and to solidify your business with strong entrepreneurial actions.

As I mentioned, high-performing executive coaches have a strong "why" for entering this profession. They love the work, and they leverage their high EQ to connect with and care about their clients. If this describes you, then you are a gift to the profession and this book is in service to you living more fully into your dreams through applying the proven model and best practices. As we all make improvements with our clients, bit by bit, we extend that to their teams, organizations, and communities, ultimately influencing thousands of people through the work of coaching.

Future of Executive Coaching

I see a promising future for executive coaching. The return on investment is clear, and organizations, agencies, and individuals around the world have experienced many personal and professional gains from coaching. Many top business executives, political leaders, and media moguls have benefited from coaching, and the more they talk about it, the more normalized coaching becomes. The days of coaching being a well-kept secret seem to be over, with more people proudly seeking the support of an executive coach and sharing the benefits they experienced from their coaching relationship. The view of coaching seems to have shifted from one of remedial course correction to reflect more accurately what coaching often is: an investment in high-potential leaders to become the best they can be in their role and in life.

I'm confident that the specialized areas of coaching I reviewed will continue growing in earnest. Executive coaching for leaders in new jobs helps them learn the ropes as quickly as possible and step into their leadership presence with confidence and conviction. This includes a focus on the first 90 days, stakeholder mapping and networking, meeting the team and partners, and identifying important strategic decisions early in their tenure.

Coaching for performance improvement will also continue. The return on investment for coaching senior leaders who are struggling is probably the clearest. The leader makes a significant salary, has responsibility for a large part of the business, may be customer facing, and certainly has a role in establishing and delivering strategic priorities. This is a high-leverage, high-cost, high-risk position. Excellence in this role has a profound positive impact on the business, and the converse is often true as well. A relatively minor investment in coaching will help this leader become more effective in every responsibility. And that makes for easy math.

I also envision that more organizations will invest in one-on-one coaching for the next generation of leaders. I am seeing big movement toward investing in tomorrow's leaders through various leadership development or leadership accelerator programs. High-potential middle managers and individual contributors are good prospects for coaching so they can take their enhanced capabilities into future roles. Offering coaching as part of the support structure for employees who have completed intensive leadership accelerators is a unique and affordable way to keep alumni focused on their leadership capability. As employees seek employers who are willing to make personalized investments in them as humans, not just as worker bees, coaching becomes a powerful way for companies and talent recruiters to differentiate their development offerings to current and future employees.

All Executive Coaches Are Not Created Equal

Not everyone who sets out to be a coach makes it. You probably already know that, but I think it's important to mention. Like the percentage of successful restaurants, I believe that the the success rate of coaches sits in the single digits.

That observation was a big motivator for me to write this book: to empower you with a proven model and many templates to help you get started right away. Coaches who make it are the best positioned, luckiest in some ways, and the best equipped to do this work. May the playbook be a powerful piece of your coaching equipment for many years to come.

Continuing Development

In part because of the popularity and normalization of coaching, there are a growing number of coaching certification programs and schools. As with anything, the quality and value of these programs vary widely, and they are largely unregulated—who certified them? I believe the model and methods presented in this book give you the framework for success.

If you truly feel you need to attend one of these schools or programs, be a wise consumer. Evaluate the curricula. Talk to colleagues who have completed them. Calculate the return on investment of your time, talent, and resources in what is often a lengthy, expensive, and intense program. And as I discussed here, be clear on your "why" so you have a more direct chance of achieving what you want and need out of the coaching certification.

Facing Your Own Breakdown

Let's take a moment to reflect on what could be your own breakdown as a coach. It can be nerve-racking to work with leaders in a coaching capacity. Questions your inner critic may be asking include "What could I possibly teach this person?" "What if I don't have the chops for this?" and "What if they bring up something I'm not equipped to help them with?" Every beginner coach experiences doubt, and sometimes it can be crippling. Even experienced coaches can find themselves flummoxed by a client.

So what do you do to get rid of this doubt and have a successful coaching business? While the only real cure for the voices in your head is some actual experience being a coach, here are some things you can do to bring your doubts down to a manageable level:

- **Offer free beta sessions.** Offer free sessions for a few clients so that you can get some coaching experience. You will be able to coach them without feeling guilty that they are paying you, and those feelings of doubt will slowly disappear as you see that you actually are making a difference.
- **Do shorter sessions at first.** You can charge less for shorter sessions and get your feet wet without having to jump in with a full-fledged, hour-long session.
- **Practice with friends or family.** If you have some friends or family members who need help with their problems, try coaching them first. It can be intimidating to

coach strangers, and a few full-length sessions with people you know might allow you to become more comfortable with yourself and your coaching position. This is also a great way to get feedback from a trusted friend or family member.

- **Keep up with your own coaching.** It's just as important, perhaps more important, that you continue your own development and coaching practices as a client. This will give you a safe space to explore your discomfort and unpack what may be holding you back from being the highly skilled executive coach that you desire to be.

- **Maintain the integrity of the coach-client relationship.** It can be tempting to slide into more of a personal relationship with your client. You'll know if this is happening if your coaching sessions begin to feel more like a conversation between friends. Your client is sharing, you're empathizing, but this is all about building the relationship, right? Yes, and . . . your role is to challenge your client respectfully and compassionately, ask the next question, help them unfold in their development, and deepen their own capacity. If you are a compassionate listener in a "gripe session," you are not coaching. Check in with yourself and ensure that you have continuous engagement as a coach, in support of your client and their development journey.

- **Remind yourself that you're supposed to be doing this.** This is your calling! Remember why you started coaching in the first place—you felt that you truly had something to offer. You'll eventually see that you were right the whole time. You got this!

Future Tools

Like the rise in coaching schools or certifications, I have also seen a huge increase in automation and digital coaching applications. These solutions are attractive to sponsoring organizations because of their simplicity and easy access. Time will tell if these solutions are effective and can yield the results that a personalized, intensive, one-on-one coaching relationship can achieve. I have a theory that they'll be much like employee assistance programs: They're offered, but not a lot of people use them for a variety of reasons, including their lack of depth or specialization.

The coach-client relationship is pivotal for client success. Often we know the answers to our questions, but only that close, trusting, powerful relationship will move the needle into competency development and behavior change. I don't hold much hope for automation. Most folks don't even like chatbots or texts for car repairs, let alone career matters!

There has also been a massive explosion in digital meditation and mindfulness applications. I think these solutions could be a helpful addition to your coaching toolkit to support your client in learning how to center, find calm in chaos, and build more self-care practices.

People often ask me if the now-mainstream use of videoconferencing applications (such as Zoom, Microsoft Teams, and BlueJeans) has changed coaching. As with most things, there are positive and negative consequences to the proliferation and standardization of videoconferencing. First, the good news: It helps erase geographic distance, makes logistics much simpler, and allows you and your clients to integrate coaching sessions more seamlessly into a busy workday.

Conversely, you miss out on a lot by removing or reducing in-person contact. Particularly with the approach I recommend in the playbook, not being able to see your client in action and in person means that you lose the chance to deepen the coach-client relationship, experience what it's like to be in their presence, and to talk face-to-face with their colleagues and staff. You don't get to observe their working environment and what happens between meetings and presentations, which is often just as crucial for their growth. When possible, I recommend at least taking a hybrid approach where you balance some in-person sessions with the utility of videoconferencing.

Far Future Tools

Looking much further out in time and considering the dramatic increase in artificial intelligence for solutions to business operations such as customer service, I wonder if AI or "bots" will have a place in coaching. Can a bot really be an executive coach? Well, maybe. It wasn't that long ago that using your face, fingerprint, or voice as your password seemed like science fiction, and yet these solutions are now well established in technology and still evolving.

How many of us talk to Siri or Alexa as if they're people, even arguing with them or making snarky comments back to them? They're programmed to respond to you in more and more natural ways. Someone had to predict what you were going to say to your household robot, then program context-appropriate responses. Think about that for a minute!

So back to the question at hand, can a bot be an effective executive coach? It's hard to be totally precise about what the next 10, 20, or 50 years will hold, but it seems clear that the use of smart technology that gets smarter the more we interact with it will be a big part of our future and how we operate in the world.

If you're not convinced of the possibility, use your favorite search engine to find "America's Got Talent AI." You'll see what is possible today through a company called Metaphysic that specializes in deepfake technology. It's easy to imagine what's possible in the future as technology gets more advanced through brilliant programmers and through our day-to-day interactions with this smart, adaptive technology. Envisioning building a coach-client relationship with AI is amazing, exciting, and a bit terrifying all at the same time!

Beacon of Hope

I began this journey talking about coaches as the beacon of hope for our clients and for the greater society. Our clients learn how to master advanced competencies and grow as leaders. They deepen their appreciation for their role in some of these challenging dynamics. They develop skills that help them achieve their professional goals. We each, in small and large ways, become better humans through this work, which can have tremendous positive results for companies around the world. And it's worth noting that this work often has a positive knock-on effect for the client's teams, communities, and families too.

Now more than ever we need hope, kindness, compassion, support, caring, healing, well-being, and connection. We're all teachers, in our own ways. I believe things are different, that humans are changing, and that progress is visible. As executive coaches, we are work, cultural, social, and psychological change agents in the most micro-sense: one person at a time. By supporting these leaders to be the best version of themselves, we help them achieve their dreams for themselves, their teams, and their organizations. We help create long-term, sustained change that has an immeasurable impact on our clients, their businesses, their colleagues and loved ones, and the world.

And with each client, we change too. We bring fresh eyes and a learning mindset to everything we do, and we evolve in small and large ways through our work. Our clients affect us and help us grow in our capacity as coaches. My wish for you is that you move forward in the world, with this work, with a curious and confident mind and an open and compassionate heart.

Acknowledgments

I am deeply grateful to the coaches who help leaders and organizations grow every day. Through your efforts, you are beacons of hope ushering in a new era of growth, peace, and prosperity.

I am personally very thankful for my loved ones, who continue to support me (including with this third book), and to my Zumba family around the world.

I'm also thankful for the animals and natural wonders of our planet, which keep me inspired and bring joy into my life. In acknowledgment of the global climate crisis and the suffering of animals, all proceeds of this book go to the protection and love of animals.

—Nadine Greiner
February 2024

My deepest gratitude to the teachers, mentors, leaders, and coaches who have poured into me, believed in, inspired, and encouraged me. You were my "first believers" and set the foundation for the work I am honored to do today.

To my husband, children, family, and friends, you have provided an enduring support system for the celebrations and consternations called life. You are my champions and I'm better for knowing each of you.

To my fellow coaches and teachers, you do such meaningful work that makes a difference in people's lives and leading. I'm inspired by you and honored to work alongside you in this incredible profession.

—Becky Davis
February 2024

Templates for Success

Template 1-1. Overview of the Coaching Process

Purpose: An overview of the four-step executive coaching process for you to share with your potential client, 360 interviewees, sponsors, and so on, or to use as a marketing piece.

How to use: This is an optional form to use in whole or in part. Put it in your own words and brand it to your business. Send in marketing outreach and initial meetings with your client and sponsor of coaching (if different from the client). You can also use this as a checklist for completing the components of each step of your coaching process.

Overview of the Coaching Process

1. Assess
- Self-assessment
  - ☐ Understand the executive's perspective
  - ☐ Areas of strength
  - ☐ Areas to develop
- 360 feedback
  - ☐ Understand how the executive is perceived and evaluated
  - ☐ What to do more of, less of, start, or stop
- Surveys and profiles
  - ☐ Personality, psychological, and performance assessments
- Other sources
  - ☐ Strategic plan
  - ☐ Performance review
  - ☐ Employee engagement data

2. Define Goals
- Individual development plan (IDP)
  - ☐ Agree on competencies, skills, behaviors, and measures of success
  - ☐ Agree on timelines and processes
  - ☐ Identify resources
- Plan for obstacles
  - ☐ Plan for eventual barriers or events that could derail progress
- Obstacles and challenges
  - ☐ Identify what can get in the way of success
- Share
  - ☐ With manager
  - ☐ With supportive colleagues

3. Implement Plan
- Experiment
  - ☐ Try new ways of leading
  - ☐ Start new behaviors
  - ☐ Strengthen skills
- Practice
  - ☐ Standard executive work
  - ☐ Engrain new executive competencies
  - ☐ New ways of thinking and behaving
- Feedback
  - ☐ Provide ample feedback and support
  - ☐ Tackle barriers immediately
  - ☐ Continuously shape motivation
- Homework
  - ☐ Regular cadence of new and enforcing behaviors

4. Review, Recommend, and Say Goodbye
- Post 360
  - ☐ Assess change in competencies, skills, behaviors, and measures of success
  - ☐ Interview key people
- Plan for slips
  - ☐ Continue to enlist colleagues
  - ☐ Identify support
- Document and celebrate
  - ☐ Addendum to original assessment
  - ☐ Include recommendations
  - ☐ Share with manager
- Say goodbye
  - ☐ Reminisce
  - ☐ Reflect
  - ☐ Separate thoughtfully

Template 1-2. Sponsor Outreach Email

Purpose: An email to arrange a meeting with your client's direct leader and the leadership program manager before the coaching engagement begins. You'll use this meeting to ensure that the sponsors are engaged in the coaching process and you understand their goals for sending their employee to coaching as part of the leadership development program. Your client should be present as well.

How to use: This is an optional email template to use in whole or in part. Adapt it to your client's culture and work style. Put it in your own words and brand it to your business. Send this email to the sponsors of new coaching clients.

Hello <*name*>,

Thank you for supporting <*client's name*> in their development and growth as a leader. I'm honored to be working with them and with you to improve their capability as a leader in your organization.

I am requesting 45 minutes with you and <*client's name*> to review the coaching program and align on your desired outcomes from this coaching engagement. Can you please connect me with your administrative assistant or provide several dates and times you can be available? I would like to meet <*in person/over video conference*>.

If you have any questions in the meantime, please reach out!

Sincerely,
<*Your name*>

Template 1-3. Sponsor Interview

Purpose: When someone other than your client has hired you, use this interview format to collect initial information about your client, the company, and leadership expectations.

How to use: This is an optional form to use in whole or in part. Put it in your own words and brand it to your business. Customize it to fit the person and conversation. Over time, you'll learn which questions have the highest impact and build your interview around those.

About the Client
1. Tell me about <*client*>. What are the company's goals for them in coaching?
2. What are their strengths as a leader?
3. What are areas they need to develop to be successful in their current job?
4. What are areas they need to develop to be successful in the next job or promotion?
5. Are there any areas that they are not fully aware of that need to improve?
6. What kind of development have they pursued?
7. Have they worked with a coach in the past? What were the outcomes?

About the Company
(Do your own research first. Use these questions to learn from an insider about the company culture.)
1. Tell me about your company. What do you do? What is your industry? What is the competitive landscape in which you operate?
2. What are the mission and vision for the company?
3. What are the leadership expectations for someone at <*client name's*> level? How do they know these are the expectations?
4. How would you describe the culture of this company?
5. What makes this a great place to work? What makes it challenging?
6. Are you facing any challenges as a business over the next few years?
7. What kind of leadership does your company need to be successful in the future?

Template 1-4. Client Interview

Purpose: A conversation guide to learn all you can about a new client, their life as a leader, and their company and industry. This agenda is the framework for your first one to two conversations, depending on how much time you initially secure with your client.

How to use: This is an optional form to use in whole or in part. Put it in your own words and brand it to your business. Customize it to fit the person and conversation. Over time, you'll learn which questions have the highest impact and build your initial interview around those.

About the Client
1. Tell me about yourself. What is your background? What brought you to this point?
2. What are your goals for coaching? Why am I here?
3. What are your strengths as a leader?
4. What areas do you need to develop to be successful in your current job?
5. Thinking about the next role in your leadership progression, what areas do you need to develop to be successful in that job or promotion?
6. If you could do three things to make an immediate positive impact on your team, organization, or company, what would those things be?
7. What kind of feedback do you get from your direct manager? Colleagues and peers? Customers? Staff?
8. What kind of development have you pursued? What is your approach to learning and development?
9. Have you worked with a coach in the past? What were the outcomes? What was that experience like for you?

About the Company
(Do your own research first. Use these questions to learn from your client about the company culture. Bring insights from the sponsor or leader into this part of the conversation.)
1. Tell me about your company. What do you do? What is your industry? What is the competitive landscape in which you operate?
2. What are the company's mission and vision?
3. What are the leadership expectations for someone at your level? How do you know these are the expectations? (For example, feedback, built into performance reviews, unspoken.)
4. How would you describe the culture of this company?
5. What makes this a great place to work? What makes it challenging?
6. Are you facing any challenges as a business over the next few years?
7. What kind of leadership do you need to be successful in your future?

Gathering 360 Input
- Set the expectation that you'll gather 360 input to get a full view of them as a leader, and set the foundation for their development plan.
- Ask them to identify a few people you can interview to help get a good sense of them as a leader. Get a balanced team of people.
- Describe how you'd like to engage their network for this input. (For example, you could say "I'll send you an email asking you to introduce me to these people, then I will schedule one-on-one interviews in the next two weeks.")

What's Next

- This is a great time to set some expectations early.
- Share a bit about your background if they don't already know you.
- Talk about your approach to coaching, that they'll learn and practice new behaviors, and that the coaching program is focused on them as a leader.
- Set the tone for accountability and engagement.
- Request that they begin working on their assessments (including self-evaluations and psych profiles).
- Schedule the next coaching session to review the consolidated 360 input—usually three to four weeks out.

Template 1-5. Client Intake Form

Purpose: An intake form to learn a few basics about your client.

How to use: This is an optional form to use in whole or in part. Adapt it to your client's culture and work style. Put it in your own words and brand it to your business. You may choose to send this to your client ahead of the initial intake sessions to get them thinking about key topics and for you to learn more about them. Alternatively, you can use this to take notes in your initial conversations.

Client Information

Title _____ First name_____ Last name_____

Nickname (if applicable) _____

Address_____

Contact Details

Phone_____

Email_____

How may I contact you?   ☐ Cell   ☐ Email

Employment Information

Occupation _____

Employer _____

Personal Information

Important relationships _____

Important dates in your life _____

Other relevant information _____

Expectations
What do you expect to get out of these coaching sessions? _____

_____

_____

_____

_____

Tell me something about yourself that you think I should know to coach you better: _____

_____

_____

_____

_____

Briefly share your overall business and life goals. Where do you see yourself in:

1 year _____

_____

5 years _____

_____

10 years _____

_____

Template 1-6. Coaching History Form

Purpose: A form that summarizes a client's history and results with prior coaches. This additional insight helps you understand their experience and engagement with other coaches. It also gives you perspective on how they think about a coach, and early and helpful hints about the topic of relationships.

How to use: This is an optional form to use in whole or in part. Adapt it to your client's culture and work style. Put it in your own words and brand it to your business. You can fill it out yourself based on conversations with the client, or you can ask the client to do so if you think it'll be well received. Consider sending it after the first or second coaching session.

Coaching History Form

Knowing your history with coaching helps me serve you better and tailor my coaching to meet your needs. Please answer the following questions about your past coaching experiences.

- I have worked with _____ business coaches in the past. (List dates and durations. Names aren't necessary.)

_____

_____

_____

_____

- Tell me why you chose the coaches you worked with. What made them appealing to you?

_____

_____

_____

_____

- List the three biggest accomplishments that directly resulted from your previous coaching experiences.

_____

_____

_____

_____

- Tell me what you wish your past coaches had done or said differently.

  _____

  _____

  _____

  _____

- Why did you end the relationships with your past coaches?

  _____

  _____

  _____

  _____

- If you were in the same place and time again, knowing what you know now, would you work with those coaches again? Why or why not?

  _____

  _____

  _____

  _____

Template 1-7. Expectations of Coaching Engagement Agreement

Purpose: This sets the stage for accountability and initial agreements between the coach and client. A C-suite client is unlikely to want or need this, so adjust accordingly! Use this agreement with clients who need a lot of structure and accountability.

How to use: This is an optional form to use in whole or in part. Adapt it to your client's culture and work style. Put it in your own words, brand it to your business, and add anything that's useful for you and your working style. You can cover this in a coaching session and send it as follow-up for your client to complete and send back.

Let's review some mutual accountability. This will enable us to work together more efficiently and for you to achieve the greatest success.

1. We will meet <*weekly/biweekly/monthly*> at <*time/day/date*>.
2. Before each coaching session, you will complete the ongoing pre-session form and return it to me no later than 24 hours before our scheduled appointment.
3. To prepare for our session, you will decide which area you'd like to focus on. If you are unsure, I will help you determine where I can be the most effective.
4. You will take the time to do the work necessary to further develop your competencies and career. Coaching is not a "done for you" relationship. You must commit to the work, or you will not have satisfactory results.
5. If, at the time of our meeting, you are unprepared, we will reschedule to give you time to complete the work necessary to move forward.

_____

Signature

Template 1-8. Accountability Form

Purpose: A form for the client who needs support outlining how they'd like to be held accountable.

How to use: This is an optional form to use in whole or in part. Adapt it to your client's culture and work style. Put it in your own words and brand it to your business. You can fill it out yourself based on early conversations with the client, or you can ask the client to complete this form early in the coaching engagement. Consider sending after the first or second coaching session.

How do you want to be held accountable?

One of the most challenging aspects of coaching is knowing what to do when the person I'm working with is not completing the work we've agreed upon.

Because everyone's motivations are different, I'd like you to tell me how I should respond in the following situations:

- If you aren't prepared for a scheduled meeting (first time), would you like me to:
  - ☐ Immediately request to reschedule
  - ☐ Spend the meeting discussing why you were unprepared and how to better manage your time

- If you aren't prepared for a scheduled meeting (repeated offense), would you like me to:
  - ☐ Immediately request to reschedule
  - ☐ Pause our coaching relationship while you reprioritize your tasks
  - ☐ Suggest a time management coach to help you

- If you don't complete the work required to move toward your goals (first time), would you like me to:
  - ☐ Help you explore potential roadblocks and solutions
  - ☐ Revise our plan to include smaller subgoals

- If you don't complete the work required to move toward your goals (repeated offense), would you like me to:
  - ☐ Revise our plan to include smaller subgoals
  - ☐ Impose a monetary fine
  - ☐ Pause our coaching relationship while you reprioritize your tasks

- If, after _____ days of coaching, you have not achieved the goals we outlined at the beginning of our relationship, would you like me to:
  - ☐ Suggest a different coach whom you might work better with
  - ☐ End our coaching relationship
  - ☐ Revisit our initial agreement and revise accordingly

_____

Signature

Template 1-9. Sponsor Status Update Email

Purpose: An email to contact your client's manager or the sponsor of the coaching engagement, suggesting a short meeting to share progress or provide a high-level written update via email.

How to use: This is an optional email template to use in whole or in part. Adapt it to your client's culture and work style. Adjust it as appropriate to the step you're on before sending it to the client's manager or the sponsor of the coaching engagement. Be sure your client is aware that you are connecting with their manager or sponsor and supports the message.

Hello <*sponsor name*>,

I hope all is well with you.

Things are progressing well over here. <*Client name*> and I meet regularly, and I am happy to report that they are always punctual, complete their assignments, and seem engaged.

If you'd like, I can arrange a 20- to 30-minute meeting, along with <*client name*>, to bring you up to speed.

We are midway through the implementation phase. <*Client name*> and I are making progress, and we are on the third of four steps:
1. Assessment (360 and profiles)
2. Set goals
3. **Implement**
4. Review and finish

<*Client name*> and I recommend another two to three months of coaching to achieve all our goals consistently. *(Note: Only include this line if it's necessary and agreed to by your client!)*

Sincerely,
<*Your name*>

Template 1-10. Sponsor Check-In Meeting Agenda

Purpose: An agenda to follow with your client's manager or the sponsor of the coaching engagement to keep them apprised of the coaching program's progress.

How to use: This optional agenda should be updated based on the culture and work style of the person you are meeting with. Note the suggestion to also attach the four-step model (Template 1-1) as a visual (and branded!) reminder of the coaching process.

Agenda for the Sponsor Check-In Meeting

5 min.	Introductions
3 min.	Purpose of this meeting, desired outcomes from our conversation
10 min.	Review the four phases of coaching program, highlight the leader's role in the overall process
20 min.	Discuss the leadership model, leader expectations, and goals for your employee from the coaching program
5 min.	Questions, concerns, and other topics to cover
2 min.	Close and next steps

Attachment: Overview of the Coaching Process

Template 1-11. Program Completion Sponsor Email

Purpose: A sample email to use as you near completion of the program, securing time with the client's direct leader or the HR/L&D program leader to review the outcome of the coaching engagement.

How to use: This is an optional email template to use in whole or in part. Adapt it to your client's culture and work style. Put it in your own words and brand it to your business. Send it to the client's manager or the sponsor of the coaching engagement to secure an end-of-program review. Be sure to include your client so you can review the progress of the overall coaching program and enlist the manager's or sponsor's ongoing support if appropriate. You may also want to attach the agenda (Template 1-12) to this email.

Hello <*name*>,

Thank you for supporting <*client's name*> in their development and growth as a leader. <*Client name*> has made significant progress in several areas, including <*list of three competencies*>.

At the outset of the coaching program, we met to discuss your goals and desired outcomes for <*client's name*> coaching program. In summary, you outlined the following goals:
1.   <*Goal 1*>
2.   <*Goal 2*>
3.   <*Goal 3*>

As we near the conclusion of this coaching engagement, we'd like to regroup with you to review how you believe <*client's name*> is performing relative to these goals. We'd love to hear what you've seen that is positive and productive and what remains in terms of development.

I am requesting 45 minutes with you and <*client's name*> to review the coaching outcomes. Can you provide several dates and times you can be available? I'd like to meet <*in person/over videoconference*>.

If you have any questions in the meantime, please reach out!

Sincerely,
<*Your name*>

Attachment: Program Completion Meeting Agenda

Template 1-12. Program Completion Sponsor Meeting Agenda

Purpose: A sample agenda to use with either the client's direct leader or the HR/L&D program leader to review the outcome of your client's coaching engagement.

How to use: This optional agenda should be updated based on the culture and work style of the person you are meeting with. Send it to the client's manager or the sponsor of the coaching engagement to set the agenda for the end-of-program review. You can include it in the outreach email from Template 1-11 or add it to the calendar invitation (or both).

Agenda for the Program Completion Meeting

5 min.	Greetings
25 min.	Client reviews the outcomes and their key learnings, where they have experienced growth, and what development or growth opportunities remain
10 min.	Leader feedback and input
5 min.	Gratitude and conclusions, next steps

Template 2-1. Self-Assessment Worksheet

Purpose: This self-assessment is an alternative way to jump-start the process to get to know your client. This invites your client to think about their goals for coaching and to evaluate their performance as a leader. Note that there is some overlap with this worksheet and the client interview. (Template 1-4)

How to use: This is an optional form to use in whole or in part. Adapt it to your client's culture and work style. Put it in your own words and brand it to your business. Reach out to your client before the coaching engagement begins to get to know them better and to get them thinking about their development goals, what they're seeking from coaching, and other "getting started" topics. Alternatively, you can use these questions as an interview guide during a session.

Self-Assessment Worksheet

1. What are your main goals for the coaching sessions, in priority order? What do you hope to get out of them?

   _____

   _____

2. What challenges do you face? What is most difficult for you right now?

   _____

   _____

3. What are your three biggest strengths?
   o
   o
   o

4. What are your three main weaknesses?
   o
   o
   o

5. What three things could you do right now to help yourself and/or the organization?
   o
   o
   o

6. What ideas do you have for moving forward? *(Your coach will review these and offer suggestions.)*
   o
   o
   o

7. What is your preferred learning style? That is, do you prefer to see, hear, or read when you're learning?
   o
   o
   o

8. Do you have any ideas of how you'd like coaching sessions to be conducted? Describe your ideal coaching session.

_____

_____

_____

_____

9. Please share any questions or concerns you have.

_____

_____

_____

_____

_____

_____

_____

_____

Template 2-2. Leadership Competencies Self-Assessment

Purpose: A detailed review of 12 key leadership competencies, highlighting several core skills within each competency. If your client seeks more detailed development aligned with leadership competencies, you can use this in both their self-assessment and the 360 interviews to gain a very detailed view of your client's strengths and areas for development.

How to use: This is an optional form to use in whole or in part. Adapt it to your client's culture and work style. Put it in your own words and brand it to your business. Customize this to include the company's leadership competencies to gain a thorough assessment of your client's strengths and areas for development.

Leadership Competencies Self-Assessment
Rate each item in the self-assessment on a scale of 1 to 5.
(*1=Strongly Disagree, 3=Neutral, and 5=Strongly Agree*)

Leadership Skills					
Communicates a clear and inspiring vision to their subordinates.	1	2	3	4	5
States clearly their expectations for performance.	1	2	3	4	5
Recognizes the efforts of others with appreciation and praise.	1	2	3	4	5
Is willing to let go of the reins and trust others.	1	2	3	4	5
Delegates responsibility.	1	2	3	4	5
Inspires others and promotes a sense of innovation.	1	2	3	4	5
Development of Others					
Is a willing mentor in the career development of others.	1	2	3	4	5
Provides others with opportunities to learn and grow.	1	2	3	4	5
Appraises the performance of others in a timely manner.	1	2	3	4	5
Coaches and counsels staff over rough spots and during difficult times.	1	2	3	4	5
Influence					
Supports their positions with solid evidence.	1	2	3	4	5
Successfully influences the thinking of subordinates.	1	2	3	4	5
Successfully influences the thinking of peers.	1	2	3	4	5
Successfully influences the thinking of superiors.	1	2	3	4	5
Interpersonal Skills					
Creates a positive working environment with others.	1	2	3	4	5
Treats others with respect.	1	2	3	4	5
Deals fairly with everyone and doesn't play favorites.	1	2	3	4	5
Demonstrates tact and sensitivity in dealings with others.	1	2	3	4	5

Communication Skills					
Listens well.	1	2	3	4	5
Keeps others informed; gives them the information they need to do a good job.	1	2	3	4	5
Speaks clearly, correctly, and to the point.	1	2	3	4	5
Writes clearly, correctly, and to the point.	1	2	3	4	5
Conflict Management					
Expresses disagreement constructively.	1	2	3	4	5
Resolves conflict with others effectively.	1	2	3	4	5
Resolves conflict between others effectively.	1	2	3	4	5
Is a decisive and effective disciplinarian without being offensive or antagonistic.	1	2	3	4	5
Creates an environment where conflict can be discussed openly and facilitates solutions.	1	2	3	4	5
Action Orientation					
Monitors projects closely; takes action to resolve problems before they're out of hand.	1	2	3	4	5
Brings new ideas and opportunities to the attention of the company.	1	2	3	4	5
Is a self-starter; makes things happen.	1	2	3	4	5
Follows through on tasks and fulfills promises; achieves goals for job performance.	1	2	3	4	5
Seeks partnerships and is an active member in promoting HR to the community.	1	2	3	4	5
Organization Skills					
Makes good use of time; avoids wasting time.	1	2	3	4	5
Sets personal goals for job performance.	1	2	3	4	5
Establishes realistic budgets and timelines for assigned projects.	1	2	3	4	5
Organizes their own work in an efficient manner.	1	2	3	4	5
Distributes projects to staff accordingly.	1	2	3	4	5
Professional Growth					
Learns from their mistakes.	1	2	3	4	5
Seeks out opportunities to learn, grow, and improve.	1	2	3	4	5
Asks for feedback on their performance.	1	2	3	4	5
Responds well to feedback received on their performance.	1	2	3	4	5
Character					
Has the courage of their convictions.	1	2	3	4	5
Says what they mean and means what they say.	1	2	3	4	5
Willingly shares the spotlight with others.	1	2	3	4	5
Maintains the highest ethics and moral code; demonstrates integrity and honesty.	1	2	3	4	5

Customer Service					
Is recognized by customers as a leading service provider in the company.	1	2	3	4	5
Anticipates, identifies, and resolves problems in customer relationships.	1	2	3	4	5
Provides distinctive customer service; adds value to customer businesses.	1	2	3	4	5
Provides subordinates with the resources they need to serve customers exceptionally.	1	2	3	4	5
Entrepreneurialism					
Evaluates new opportunities and shares them with the team for implementation.	1	2	3	4	5
Serves as a spokesperson for the team or agency in the larger community.	1	2	3	4	5
Is a key contributor to the organization's vision.	1	2	3	4	5
Has a high degree of technical expertise in their field.	1	2	3	4	5

Comments:

Template 2-3. Initial 360 Interview Outreach Emails

Purpose: An email template for you to send to your client to jump-start the interview process. It also contains a pass-through template for your client to send to their selected 360 interviewees.

How to use: This is an optional email template to use in whole or in part. Adapt it to your client's culture and work style. Put it in your own words and brand it to your business. After discussing the four-step coaching process and the importance of 360 input, gain agreement from your client to reach out to several interviewees and connect with them to schedule the input sessions.

Email From You to the Client

Hello *<client name>*,

It was good to start working with you this afternoon.

Please find the below email for you to send individually to the people you would like to participate in the 360. Please modify as you see fit.

Remember to cc me on each note to them so we are in direct contact and can begin the scheduling process immediately.

Thanks,
<Your name>

Email From the Client to Their Selected 360 Interviewees

Dear *<colleague name>*,

Because you are a valued and trusted colleague, I am inviting you to participate in my executive development. I am embarking on the next step of ongoing introspection and leadership development by engaging an experienced executive coach. I am looking for confidential 360 feedback and would benefit greatly from your thoughts on my strengths and areas for development. Thank you in advance for considering this request.

You will be hearing from my coach, *<your name>*, to schedule the interview. Thank you in advance for your time and candid feedback.

Thanks,
<Client name>

Template 2-4. Email Invitation to 360 Interviewees

Purpose: An email template for you to send to your client's 360 interviewees to begin scheduling the 360 feedback interviews.

How to use: This is an optional email template to use in whole or in part. Adapt it to your client's culture and work style. Put it in your own words and brand it to your business. After your client has made the introduction to you and each interviewee, quickly follow up to book the interview sessions with them.

Hello <*name*>,

As <*client name*> mentioned to you, we are working together to strengthen their leadership capabilities and help them grow as a leader. I am an executive coach with <*number*> years of experience working with leaders just like <*client first name*> to help them improve and increase their impact.

A crucial part of this engagement is collecting input from the people who work most closely with my client. You are one of a select few I'll be meeting with to get your perspective on <*client name*>'s strengths, areas to grow, and opportunities to influence the business.

Please select three of the dates and times below that can work for you. If you have an administrative assistant whom you'd prefer I work with, please copy them into this email thread so we can get this meeting booked.

<*Insert several dates and one-hour blocks of time that are available in your calendar. Provide up to twice the number of slots you will book. For example, if you have five people to interview, offer 10 slots, and ask the interviewee to pick three. That way, if anyone chooses the same slot you have back-up options and can minimize the number of back-and-forth emails required to book the time.*>

I look forward to meeting you in support of <*client name*>'s coaching program. Please note that all input is anonymized and confidential. We will talk more about how your input will be used when we meet. Please reach out if you have any questions or concerns in the meantime.

Sincerely,
<*Your name*>

Template 2-5. 360 Interview Meeting Invitation, Agenda, and Attachments for Interviewees

Purpose: A template for booking the meeting time with your client's 360 interviewees. It includes the agenda and recommended attachments for the interviewee to prepare.

How to use: This is an optional email template to use in whole or in part. Adapt it to your client's culture and work style. Put it in your own words and brand it to your business. When you have secured time with the 360 interviewee, send this with the calendar invitation and include the video-conference link, meeting location, or telephone instructions, as appropriate. If the interviewee prefers to book their own meetings on their calendar, you can send this as an email confirming the time and logistics. Either way, attach Template 2-6 to the email.

Hello <*name*>,

In advance of our meeting, I'm including here the agenda and interview template.

Meeting agenda:

5 min.	Introductions
5 min.	Purpose of this interview, how your input will be shared, questions
25 min.	Your feedback on strengths, areas for improvement or growth, and highest-leverage actions to take to improve the team, organization, or company
5 min.	Questions and clarifications
5 min.	Next steps, approximate time for second interview, and close

All input is anonymized and confidential. The feedback is reviewed in summary, without attribution, to set the framework for the coaching development plan.

We will meet again toward the end of the coaching program to review what changes, if any, you have observed in <*client name*>.

Thank you for your candid input in support of your colleague's growth as a leader.

Sincerely,
<*Your name*>

Attachment: 360 Interview Notes Form

Template 2-6. 360 Interview Notes Form

Purpose: A form to collect feedback from your 360 interviewees. You can include the responses from your client's self-assessment in this template as well.

How to use: This is an optional form to use in whole or in part. Adapt it to your client's culture and work style. Put it in your own words and brand it to your business. As you are interviewing each of the client's colleagues for 360 input, make short notes and summarize key themes. Capture as much as you can in detail, tone, and context to be of maximum use in the 360 consolidation. You will save a second copy that is anonymized.

Client name: _____

	What are the client's strengths?	What are the client's areas of potential opportunity, growth, and improvement?	What are three things the client could do right now to improve themselves and/or the organization?
Coaching client			
Interview 1 / role			
Interview 2 / role			
Interview 3 / role			
Interview 4 / role			
Interview 5 / role			
Interview 6 / role			

Template 2-7. 360 Interview Notes Completed

Purpose: A sample 360 notes template completed for Simone, whom we used as a case study throughout the book.

How to use: This gives you a good idea of what a completed 360 should look like.

Client name: Simone

	What are the client's strengths?	What are the client's areas of potential opportunity, growth, and improvement?	What are three things the client could do right now to improve themselves and/ or the organization?
Coaching client	• Technical skills. • High accountability. • Dedication to quality and doing a good job for the company and team.	• Learning the new company. • Prioritization and learning to say "no" or "not yet." • Delegation.	• Prioritize the highest and most important things. • Make sure the team's time and talent are being invested in the highest-yield activities. • Build strong partnerships.
Interview 1	• Simone is very accountable, and her follow-through is terrific. She is personally accountable as well. • She cares about quality and service, and is able to get the stakeholders' trust. • She has great communication, especially with her customers. They are in the loop with the weekly touchpoints. Incremental progress, not too early or too late. • Simone never says, "That's not my job."	• Sometimes when she commits, she has a hard time reprioritizing as other things pop up. She can turn to her stakeholders, manager, and team more for that. • She can learn that the culture is more forgiving than maybe before. • Simone should sometimes say "no" or "this is not priority," or perhaps allocate to a manager or someone else. Otherwise, the team gets squeezed. • Learning to trust moving deadlines: I will talk to the VP and maybe they won't be happy, but it will be OK.	• Simone could spend more time with the team, getting to know them as individuals. • Simone should actively reprioritize when she receives new assignments. It's OK not to do everything, and it can be stressful for her and the team when it's maybe not as critical for the clients. • Simone should assume good intent from people. She is in a good place in the eyes of leaders.

	What are the client's strengths?	What are the client's areas of potential opportunity, growth, and improvement?	What are three things the client could do right now to improve themselves and/ or the organization?
Interview 2	• Great at assessing situations, gathering the right information, connecting the pieces, and summarizing them to get to the bottom of things. I always go straight to her, not her staff. • Communication is a big strength. On phone and on email, she is fantastic at putting things concisely and bulleted and to the point. • She has learned how to say "no" the <company> way, and to temper her positive and negative passions. • Simone takes feedback well, both good and bad, and adapts to take it into consideration.	• Only been at <company> about a year, and understands that we are busy, and she is too. Her list used to be too long and she was too enthusiastic. • Very passionate about what she does, but sometimes fails to realize not everybody is that committed or passionate or has the time to review lengthy processes and policies. She is trying to engage people and we're remote, which makes it hard.	• Simone has already adapted quite a bit, despite coming into a team that was not high performing, yet had high expectations. She should hire the right staff sooner rather than later so she can delegate and not burn out. • She can also stand her ground more, and defend her task list and time better. She needs to prioritize and manage expectations.
Interview 3	• Simone wants to do the right thing, always. • She comes to partner. • She takes bigger picture view, and also deep in technical—rare. • She is inclusive, wants to grow, and wants to develop her team. • I love Simone, and see her potential and her talents.	• Is it her or her culture? But the silos and territorial aspects how to navigate without becoming territorial herself. • Does Kyle realize that this is going on with his team, just like all others . . . the territorial and protection?	• Create closer relationships with her peers and leaders higher than herself. This will help with adjusting to the territorial way of <company>. Also with her career. • Is she forthcoming with Kyle about her experience and how he can help? She could probably get more support from him. • Appearance (dress and presence) needs a little more adjustment to present to executives.

	What are the client's strengths?	What are the client's areas of potential opportunity, growth, and improvement?	What are three things the client could do right now to improve themselves and/or the organization?
Interview 4	• Simone has great leadership skills. • She has a lot of patience, doesn't get bogged down by pressure. • She is a people person; we have a diverse team here and she does well. • She is good at both technical and business, which is so rare to find. She can translate between the two. Her technical skills are impressive.	• Simone needs to organize and prioritize better, she cannot do it all, and the team cannot do it all, either, without making mistakes and being stressed and bogged down. Needs to put projects in phases or waves rather multiple deep streams concurrently, and do fewer and prioritize per business need. • What is Simone's role vis-à-vis project management versus leadership? Is a PM required at this point? • Could she be more familiar with the team?	• Prioritize and organize. Nothing; everything on the whiteboard. Pick top 3, then solve, rather than all 10 concurrently, and it's chaotic and maybe not great quality. What is the process to prioritize? What are the criteria? And learn to say "no" or "later" to customers. • Would we perhaps want to work on building team spirit? • Measure or be realistic about the capacity of the team since they are in transition, then see what we can do in terms of projects. • What are the incentives to work extra hard? Recognition programs, points, team, thanks, etc.

	What are the client's strengths?	What are the client's areas of potential opportunity, growth, and improvement?	What are three things the client could do right now to improve themselves and/or the organization?
Interview 5	• We work on different teams, but work closely together, and I appreciate how technical she is. Simone is also very intelligent in business application. Good data into solid information into good decisions. • Simone is process-oriented, and builds that structure for all of us to benefit from. Good controls, processes, and validation. • Collaborative and building relationships. • She is easy to talk with and even disagree with.	• Sometimes she makes her mind up, and cannot move off that. For example, we have new initiatives and people, so occasionally we might need to reprioritize or rethink the original directions. Get a bit more flexibility. • Simone grew up in IT, and she is collecting her next level of knowledge across the health system.	• Simone is trying to set up the way we do our analytics. We are still forming, cleaning up, and building, and at some point we need to be optimized. She is getting there, but we need to centralize the analysts. • Next level of thinking and leadership—going from leading her own team to looking across the whole organization. Decisions for the team but now for the organization. Pick up more exposure and expertise across disciplines. • She needs to accelerate the rate of change. Turn that team around; get the resources and increase momentum or people might disengage. Kyle also needs to drive the value, and they need to get some wins earlier rather than later.

Template 2-8. 360 Interview Myers-Briggs Short Assessment

Purpose: A summary of the Myers-Briggs Type Indicator. Knowing MBTI types can help illuminate where there may be conflicts between your client and some of their colleagues.

How to use: While collecting 360 interview input, it can be useful to find out the interviewees' MBTI types. You can ask the interviewees directly or attempt to determine their preferences using this shortcut.

Help your client identify their tendency in each quadrant, and then locate which of the 16 personality types they correspond with.

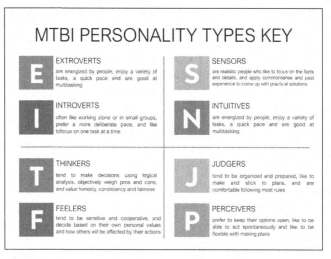

Template 2-9. Email Invitation to Complete Profiles

Purpose: An email to send to your client to begin the process of collecting their profiles.

How to use: This is an optional email template to use in whole or in part. Adapt it to your client's culture and work style. Put it in your own words and brand it to your business. Send it to your client to request that they complete the profiles you select for their assessment process.

Hello <*client name*>,

Thank you for a great conversation this evening. Here are the profiles that I mentioned for you to complete as part of the coaching program. Please let me know if you have any questions.

A few tips to remember:
- Each profile is voluntary. If you are not comfortable taking one, contact me.
- Your profile results belong to you and are entirely confidential. They will not be shared with anyone on your team or within or outside your organization unless you yourself share them.
- Take the profile in a "shoes off," relaxed frame of mind. There are no right or wrong responses, no better or worse results—only the ones that are correct for you.

You will need to complete each profile in one sitting, so plan for about <*number*> minutes of uninterrupted time. Please complete them by <*date*>, so we can review in your next coaching session.

To begin taking the profiles, please click on the following links:
- <*Add a link to each profile you have selected to use in your assessment process.*>

Thank you,
<*Your name*>

Template 3-1. IDP Form

Purpose: This is a framework for your client's development plan and the foundation of the four-step coaching model. After deciding on competencies to focus on, you should work with your client to fill out this form.

How to use: This is an optional form to use in whole or in part. Adapt it to your client's culture and work style. Put it in your own words and brand it to your business. Your client will fill out the top half during goal setting and use the bottom portion to take notes throughout implementation. Reference *FYI* and use it to define what being "skilled" in areas for growth looks like and identify practices your client will use to begin to develop these competencies.

Name: *<Client's name>*

Competencies I want to build:
1.
2.
3.

Specific behaviors I want to adopt or strengthen:
1. *<Competency from above>*
    o *<Specific behaviors that would demonstrate an increase in this competency. List two to three. Ensure they are measurable; someone else should be able to see you demonstrating this behavior.>*
    o
    o

2. *<Competency from above>*
    o
    o
    o

3. *<Competency from above>*
    o
    o
    o

Potential challenges:
1. *<Identify what challenges may get in your way while building these competencies. List two to three. What barriers do you foresee? What makes them challenges for you?>*
2.
3.

Observations During Implementation

Actions	Client Observations	Tools
<Competency> • *<What actions or experiments were attempted this week to support your development of this competency?>* • •	• *<List any observations, both your personal observations as well as those of people around you, in response to these practices and experiments.>* • •	• *<What tools do you have available to support your development? What people are around to support you? What self-care practices do you use to support your own growth and development?>*
<Competency> • • •	• •	
<Competency> • •	• •	

Template 3-2. Simone's IDP

Purpose: A sample completed IDP featuring Simone.

How to use: Use this as a sample as you begin developing your competence and confidence using the IDP template.

Simone's IDP

Name: Simone Smith

Competencies I want to build:
- Composure
- Receiving feedback
- Listening

Specific behaviors I want to adopt or strengthen:
1. Composure
   - Patience
   - Impulse control
   - Consciously make a choice about how I want to respond

2. Receiving feedback
   - Manage defensiveness, pause
   - Ask clarifying questions in a nonjudgmental answer
   - Start to choose different responses going forward

3. Listening
   - Let people finish, don't interrupt
   - Understand the feedback
   - Restate the problem in my own words to everyone's satisfaction

Potential challenges:
1. MYSELF
2. Time—rushing to the next thing rather than stepping back and taking stock
3. Working against the implicit teachings of hierarchy that medicine instills
4. Forgetting to use my new tools

Observations During Implementation

Actions	Client Observations	Tools
Composure • "Count to 10"—hold back first response (verbal or nonverbal) and regain composure after emotional response is triggered • Visual cues • Detect and control triggers	• I've noticed that counting to 10 and employing a softer tone resulted in a non-situation (which is the ideal outcome). • Even though I was internally frustrated that the tech had not reviewed the chart to understand the clinical question that prompted the workup, I was able to avoid conflict. • In other situations, rather than get irritated with technicians, I kept my composure and told myself to let it go. By taking a step back, I had time to understand the root cause, while not compromising excellent patient care.	• *FYI: For Your Improvement* • Sticky notes at my workstation reminding me to count to 10 • People giving me feedback about how I'm handling the situation • NADINE • Tom's support • Self-care
Receiving Feedback • Ask for concrete examples • Initial task at time of getting feedback is to accurately understand what people are trying to say; the decision to accept or reject criticism is made at a later point in time • Thank people for the constructive criticism • View constructive criticism as an important part of the path to cultivating a culture of excellent patient care • Start choosing different response mechanisms going forward	• I'm less defensive and more receptive to the content of constructive criticism. I'm less reactive when I hear the advice. • I ask myself more often about the "why" to constructive criticism, rather than viewing it as a criticism of my character or standards. • I viewed the feedback as support rather than criticism. • I've seen a reflection of my own defensiveness and harsh tone during recent in-person interactions with my mom and sister, both of whom I have not seen in person for years. It has been enlightening to "watch myself" in them—I now realize that I've learned some of these traits from them. I can "unlearn" this response mechanism and choose my own path.	
Listening • Don't interrupt • Ask for the "why" of their decisions to understand their viewpoint • Restate the problem in my own words to everyone's satisfaction	• After the person has finished sharing their perspective, I tell them "I hear you" and genuinely mean it. The priority is that I let them know they are heard. • I restate my understanding of the "why" to their words to make sure I have not misperceived the intention behind them. • If I catch myself in haste or not able to listen fully, I come back at a later time, apologize for not being fully present, and ask to have a more in-depth conversation.	

Template 3-3. Executive Competencies

Purpose: A summary of the most common executive competencies used in IDPs based on my work with clients for 30-plus years. This is most helpful for clients whose companies do not have an executive competency framework (such as startups or small companies).

How to use: Use this as a framework for any client.

Common Executive Competencies

Executive competencies are skills and behaviors that cultivate the best performance. Organizations using a competency-based approach to leadership are able to identify and develop leaders.

Take a look at the following competencies to assess where your strengths are, as well as where you might have room to grow.

Managing Self

- **Executive presence.** Do people instinctively look to you for answers and direction? Having executive presence means being calm, confident, and comfortable taking charge. But perhaps you avoid taking the lead or grab the lead even when it's not needed. Executive presence is a meaningful way to manage yourself.
- **Approachability.** Do people gravitate toward you? Approachability entails being warm, engaging, and gracious. It is important in your work because you need to connect with colleagues and customers. Approachability, and how you manage yourself, is also important in your personal life. Are you approachable or do people hesitate to approach you? Conversely, do you overshare and need to be liked too much?
- **Conflict management.** Do you see conflict as a way to find common ground and improve relationships? Good conflict management involves being a good listener and a creative problem solver. Perhaps you avoid conflict by accommodating everyone, or perhaps you insist on being right without regard to other solutions or people's feelings. Conflicts at work and home are inevitable, but how you handle them and manage yourself is your choice.
- **Comfort around higher leadership.** Do you understand how leaders above you think, and what they need? Being comfortable with people or boards higher up than you means knowing how to speak their language, and to create an approach that will help get the job done. Or are you nervous, mismanaging yourself or misreading the situation? Conversely, perhaps you spend too much time trying to "kiss up."
- **Interpersonal savvy.** Do you enjoy relating to all kinds of people? Find yourself talking to the bus driver as easily as your CEO? Interpersonal savvy means that you are tactful, positive, and empathetic, and can calm any kind of situation. But perhaps you don't read others well, or conversely, perhaps you spend too much time glad-handing? Building your interpersonal savvy can make the difference between being effective and not being effective.
- **Patience.** Do you wait for folks to catch up before acting? Are you sensitive to processes and people? Taking the time to understand someone's perspective and the information is vital at work and home and makes teamwork and life more enjoyable for all involved. But some people jump too soon and are irritated, while others take too much time to make decisions or act. Finding the balance of patience is tough, but necessary.

Productivity

- **Time management.** Do you focus on the most important matters first? Do you get more done in less time than others? Time management is key to productivity, and ultimately to your worth in the market, whether you work for yourself or a company. But perhaps you are disorganized and waste time. Alternatively, perhaps you are so tightly scheduled that you have no downtime?
- **Written communications.** Writing is one of the top five skills executives need to succeed. Good writing means being clear, succinct, and able to elicit the right effect in the reader. Does your writing achieve this? Or are your written communications lengthy and confusing? Or perhaps you write very well, but rely on writing instead of having a meeting or making a call? Knowing which medium to use is key to your productivity.
- **Planning.** Can you set goals, milestones, and timelines? Planning also involves assigning the right tasks to the right people. Anticipating roadblocks is important too. Perhaps your planning and productivity are hampered by a last-minute approach to work? Or conversely, maybe you are too detailed and inflexible with your plans?

Managing Teams

- **Presentation skills.** Are you able to capture your audience's attention, and convey your message in an effective way? Are you comfortable when presenting? Or perhaps you are shy and flat? Or alternatively, perhaps you oversell? Knowing how to make presentations is an important part of engaging and managing teams.
- **Hiring and staffing.** Do your hires learn quickly, over-deliver, and get promoted . . . sometimes even beyond you? Then you have the very special ability to select talent. This means being astute, listening, knowing what the business needs, and embracing people with complementary skills to round out your team. But if you have high turnover soon after employees start, or you find yourself having to fire many people, you may need to build your hiring and staffing skills and processes.
- **Building effective teams.** Do your teams accomplish their projects in a positive and cohesive way, and within a strong and diverse culture? Are you able to assemble, build, and manage the team to be its best? Or perhaps you have not been able to create a common mindset. Or, alternatively, you have created a team of similar-minded people who don't meet their goals. Organizations need effective teams for today, and for tomorrow. You are measured by your team's success, and it is your legacy.
- **Directing others.** Effective delegation means laying out a plan and purpose, then bringing out the best in people while delegating work. Do people understand your direction? Are they motivated to follow through? Or perhaps you don't get the results you intended? As you elevate in leadership positions, your success depends on others. So delegation becomes even more important.
- **Motivating others.** Do you create a culture in which people want to do their best? People who are engaged and empowered get great results. But perhaps you find folks confusing because one size does not fit all. Or perhaps no matter what you do, people don't seem to care much. Managing effective teams requires motivating others.
- **Meeting management.** Do your meetings hit each agenda item and run on time? Are all participants engaged and follow up with their tasks between meetings? Or maybe you have a hijacker who ambushes your meeting, and gets away with imposing their own agenda? Meetings can add up to costly wasted time if not managed properly.
- **Managing diversity and inclusion.** Are you able to adapt your communication style to everyone? Do you engage, hire, develop, and promote all kinds of people and styles? Being aware of your own self and culture enables you to embrace others, whether they are similar or different. Perhaps you have some conscious or unconscious preferences or biases against certain types of people? Or perhaps you are too lenient with certain groups? Being inclusive is one of the most important aspects of managing teams, because it offers a larger pool of candidates, encourages innovation, and keeps HR out of your office.

Career

- **Career ambition.** Do you know what your underlying needs are from your career? It's important to understand how to mobilize and push your development and career forward. Or perhaps you are bored in your current situation, but not sure what you would prefer? Or maybe you know exactly where you would like to be, but come across as too pushy? Ambition is a good thing; how to go about fulfilling it can be the tough part.
- **Boss relationships.** Do you find it easy to update, interest, and engage your boss? Do you also find it easy to receive feedback, guidance, and advice from your boss? When they are having a hard time, do you know how to help? Or maybe you are not comfortable with your boss, and avoid contact when possible. Or perhaps you see them more like a peer, and it's turning out to be a problem. Bosses make or break your job, and even your career. Learning how to manage them is key to advancing your career.
- **Interviewing.** Do you find that your interviewing process yields the best jobs for you? Do you take into account how to answer behavior-based questions, how to demonstrate your EQ, and what to research and observe about your potential future employer? Or maybe you just go with a gut feeling, or how the company looks on paper. Selecting your employer and manager is one of the most important things you can do for your career.
- **Self-development.** Career development depends on self-development. Are you aware of your strengths and the areas to improve to achieve the next level of your career? When was the last time you received honest, informed, and helpful feedback? But maybe you are not motivated or don't know how to develop yourself. Some folks spend a lot of time learning, but not enough time applying new skills to truly progress in their career.
- **Political savvy.** Corporate politics are a fact of life, and navigating them in an effective and discreet way will advance your career. Do you understand where the land mines are, who the power players are, and how the interpersonal relationships work? Perhaps you are unaware of these dynamics, and say or do things that have career-limiting consequences. Or perhaps you are too keenly aware of corporate politics, so much so that people do not trust you.
- **Dealing with ambiguity.** Are you able to shift gears to accommodate change? Are you comfortable with the fact that some degree of risk and uncertainty is part of the job, and that you occasionally have to make calls with insufficient or ambiguous information? Or perhaps you jump to a solution out of discomfort? Alternatively, perhaps you wait too long and gather too much data before acting? The higher you go in leadership, the fewer trodden paths there are, and the more complex business forces are. Therefore, dealing with ambiguity is an important part of career progression.
- **Negotiating.** Are you able to understand different stakeholders' underlying needs, and see the common ground to settle differences with diplomacy and tact? Are you trusted? Or perhaps you are too accommodating? Or, alternatively, maybe you're too attached to a position and forceful? Negotiations, compromises, and competing priorities across the organization are all part of the course. How you negotiate is a key component to your career progression.
- **Standing alone.** There are times when you will be the only leader willing to champion an idea or work on a tough assignment. Do people trust you and count on you? Or are you not comfortable taking the lead on a controversial issue? Alternatively, perhaps you stand alone too much. Career progression has its moments of courage and conviction. Knowing when and how is key.

Template 4-1. Agenda for Coaching Conversation

Purpose: A suggested agenda to structure your coaching conversations. You will find your own pacing and template over time.

How to use: This optional agenda should be updated based on the culture and work style of the person you are meeting with. Put it in your own words and brand it to your business. If your client needs structure and is accustomed to agendas in their business setting, use this meeting agenda to structure the time. Send it in advance and add it to all coaching calendar invitations. If you think your client will find it off-putting, feel free to use this as a guide for your conversation without sending it to your client.

Coaching Conversation Agenda

5 min.	Warm up and reconnect
15 min.	Updates on the work-life front; what's been happening since we last spoke; observations on homework
25 min.	Review IDP: competencies, experiments, observations, and feedback
10 min.	Refine or renew experiments and practices
5 min.	Top three things from today's conversation; logistics for next session (if needed); review new homework

Template 4-2. Meeting Notes Form

Purpose: A note taking form for keeping track of key points in the coaching sessions. This is for your own records and not typically shared with the client.

How to use: This is an optional form to use in whole or in part. Adapt it to your client's culture and work style. Put it in your own words and brand it to your business. Remember to keep the details high level, per the guidance in this book, to defuse any risk of revealing confidential information about your client or their company.

Client name: _____

Session Number	Date	Previous Session Highlights	Notes	Homework and Three Things

For Interoffice Use Only

Template 4-3. Sample Session Summary for Client

Purpose: A suggested format for summarizing your notes and insights to share with your client. This helps ensure clear communications and improved engagement on experiments and practices agreed to in the coaching session.

How to use: Refer to your notes from the session and provide meaningful themes, assignments, and other relevant details for your client's notes. Be aware that consistency on your part is crucial. Once you begin this report-back, your client will expect it. Be sure to adhere to any unstated promises in your behavior and do this only if you can consistently summarize the coaching session in this manner. Remember to build time into your calendar to do this soon after each session (within one business day at most).

<Date and session number>

Themes:
- Company proposed coaching to become a member of the executive team, a promotion.
- Strategic planning to identify and connect with key stakeholders now in new role—list of leaders, teams, and timelines.
- Company events are uncomfortable. How to feel comfortable at the big event (three topics she can choose from).
- How to manage the separation with current manager; how to leverage relationship going forward. Reviewed conflict profiles, knowing avoidant how to approach.
- Mother is presenting a win/lose, me/them situation with husband. What are choices? FIRO-B, and how difficult to draw line, but plan to and practice together. Happens at work in old team too, with manager.

Three things that stand out about our time today [*client POV*]:
- Helping find sustainable ways to implement changes.
- Find more balance and tone down.
- Themes and solutions are good professionally and personally too.

Homework:
- Take notes after company event and three topics.
- Start the rotation of meetings with new stakeholders.

Template 4-4. Client Session Journal Form

Purpose: A handy tool your client can use to capture notes, insights, and action items for themselves. Particularly if it's clear your client doesn't have basic note-taking systems in place or would benefit from separating work and coaching notes, this can help keep them process between sessions.

How to use: This is an optional form to use in whole or in part. Adapt it to your client's culture and work style. Put it in your own words and brand it to your business. Offer this journal template early in the implementation phase to a client who would benefit from structured notes. Remember to revisit the insights they are getting from journaling.

Goals for coaching session:
-
-
-
-

Feedback:
- Do more or continue doing:
  - ○
  - ○
  - ○
  - ○
- Improve on or change:
  - ○
  - ○
  - ○
  - ○

Lessons learned:
-
-
-
-

Next steps and actions:
-
-
-
-

Other:
-
-
-
-

Template 4-5. Pre-Session Form

Purpose: If your client will benefit from more intentional structure and support, use this form to get them thinking and processing (and completing experiments!) ahead of your coaching session.

How to use: This is an optional form to use in whole or in part. Adapt it to your client's culture and work style. Put it in your own words and brand it to your business. If you decide your client will benefit from this kind of pre-call reflection, send it to them in advance of the coaching session. You may need to feel your way into what will work best for them. Is sending it with the current session notes and assignment the right way to go? Or will it be more effective to send three to five days before the coaching session? Whatever your cadence, and perhaps the agreement you make with your client, do it consistently throughout the program. If you notice your client isn't completing this activity, inquire why and whether sending it at another time or in another way would be better for them.

Complete this form and email it to me at least 24 hours before each coaching session.

Client name: _____ **Date:** _____

1. What have I accomplished since the last coaching session?

   _____

   _____

2. What didn't I get done, and want to be held accountable for?

   _____

   _____

3. What have I learned about myself since the last coaching call?

   _____

   _____

4. Is there any good news I would like to share with my business coach on this next call?

   _____

   _____

5. What challenges have I experienced since our last coaching call?

   _____

   _____

6. What business opportunities have come my way since the last call?

_____

_____

7. Have I been able to achieve balance in my life since the last call?

_____

_____

8. What do I want to accomplish by the end of this next coaching session?

_____

_____

Template 4-6. How to Prepare for a Coaching Session Checklist

Purpose: A checklist is another way to hold your client accountable and help them prepare for a coaching session. This is most useful at the beginning of an engagement or anytime you see your client struggling to come to the coaching session fully prepared.

How to use: This is an optional form to use in whole or in part. Adapt it to your client's culture and work style. Put it in your own words and brand it to your business. If you decide your client will benefit from this kind of support, send this list to them in advance of the coaching session. I recommend reviewing it early in the coaching engagement to show them how to prepare for coaching and treat the work of coaching.

Coaching Session Prep Checklist

Use this checklist to prepare for our call each <week/month>.

- One <*Week/Month*> Prior
    - ☐ Block out time on your calendar to complete the necessary work
    - ☐ Write out your task list
- Daily
    - ☐ Work on your task list
    - ☐ Make notes about your struggles
    - ☐ Keep a list of questions for our next call
- One Day Prior
    - ☐ Complete and return your pre-call form
    - ☐ Review your struggles and questions list
    - ☐ Verify the time and day of your appointment
- Immediately After
    - ☐ Review your notes from the call
    - ☐ Expand on your plan (if necessary)

Template 4-7. Miracle Diary

Purpose: A practice for clients to record positive events and happy moments when working on deepening gratitude and appreciation. Journaling can help your client process events and emotions to support learning.

How to use: This is an optional activity to use in whole or in part. Adapt it to your client's culture and work style. Put it in your own words and brand it to your business. Assign this practice during a coaching session for clients working on deepening appreciation, gratitude, or joy.

My Miracle Diary

Starting a miracle diary where you record good luck, positive events, and happy coincidences transforms the way you see yourself in the world.

1. Start by writing down the people in your life whom you are grateful for, their positive qualities, how they have contributed to your life, and what they have done for you. Who has loved you, spent time on you, accepted you, and supported you?

2. Write down the synchronicities and coincidences. When have you experienced good luck, happy accidents, or fortunate resolutions when things looked bad, but turned out well?

3. You should also include:
    o Any happy memories from your life
    o Kindnesses you have received
    o Gifts (physical, emotional, mental, or spiritual)
    o Things you can enjoy that are free or inexpensive (the sunshine, a smile, your body, air to breathe)

4. Write about any and all forms of abundance that you can see around you.

5. Optional: Include experiences that have been painful and difficult. If you wish to transform painful experiences, ask yourself what they have taught you, or identify a positive effect you can take from them. See if you can take something positive from or find a silver lining in these events.

6. Read your miracle diary whenever you need a boost or you start doubting the process of life or the compassion of the universe.

Template 4-8. Coaching Interventions Aid

Purpose: There are many interventions for coaches to deploy when working with clients, including the ones listed in this template. You will develop your own that align to your voice and values, and add interventions you have found effective in various situations you experience as a coach.

How to use: Reference these interventions as you work with a client. Highlight any interventions you find yourself turning to the most. Add your own interventions or otherwise revise this list so that it's most useful to you. This is not for sharing with clients.

Supportive Interventions

Supportive interventions include strategies for supporting or celebrating your client to help them release a block or be seen in this moment.

Anchor New Ways

When developing a new competency, it's powerful to tie that new skill to adjoining competencies or the role the client occupies. Over time, this helps the new competency become more automatic. This is likely more helpful as you get into the middle of implementation and can help to connect the dots of the overall program and outcomes so far, as well as anchor those outcomes in new competencies.

Coach's questions or statements:
- "This competency is linked to an overall executive skill area of X. How will improvement in this area improve X overall?"

Build Trust

This is core to relationship building and sets the foundation for the entire coaching program. Show that the relationship is grounded in integrity, showing up as your full self, and being trusting and trusted. Share information about the process; inform your client of what's happening along the way and how the process will work. You're always working to build trust with your client.

Coach's questions or statements:
- "How are you experiencing our time together and work?"
- "How are you feeling just now or these days?"
- "Do you have any questions about the process or how we'll work together?"

Camera Work

This can be significant for certain competencies, such as presentation skills or improving nonverbal communications. Recording, with permission, can illustrate tremendous opportunities for continued development. Use this intervention when your client has a challenge that self-observation would be especially helpful in overcoming.

Coach's questions or statements:
- "What do you observe about your nonverbal communication?"
- "Are your words aligned in tone and intent with what your face and body are expressing?"
- "How are your employees responding to you at this moment?"

Cathartic

Help the client release tension or come to terms with emotions that are blocking their progress. If the client is afraid of risk or failure, feels incompetent, or is frustrated, helping them release these unhelpful restrictions is powerful. This is used when you notice an emotional block or hesitancy to move forward with an action or a practice.

Coach's questions or statements:
- "In your heart of hearts, what are you feeling about this topic?"
- "What is the most intense part of this situation?"
- "What are you ready to let go of?"

Celebrate

Highlight progress, insights, and positive outcomes from the experiments the client is engaging. Use at any time to celebrate small wins and big wins to keep your client in process and reinforce desired new behaviors.

Coach's questions or statements:
- "Let's take a moment to celebrate this achievement."
- "That is a huge win. How does it feel to accomplish that?"
- "What a helpful insight. What does that tell you about your growth in this area?"

Connect the Dots

Show how experiences are connected. Highlight patterns you see in your client and their circumstances. Help them see the system within which they're operating and the powerful actions they can take to improve themselves in that system.

Coach's questions or statements:
- "Do you see how this is related to X?"
- "I see a pattern here, so zooming out, where else does this show up in your life?"

Encourage Experimentation

Engage your client to try a new behavior or language to create a different outcome. Present it as experimentation, trying something new, and piloting a concept. This is used in almost every coaching session as part of reviewing the IDP's actions and observations.

Coach's questions or statements:
- "I'm inviting you to practice X in the coming weeks. How does that sound? Will you commit to that experiment?"

Engage

Build real-time rapport with the client. Define the relationship and the expectations. Use this especially in the beginning, but remember that you're always in a process of reengaging, between sessions and at the start of each session.

Coach's questions or statements:
- "What is on your mind now?"
- "What have you been working on?"
- "What has occurred to you about our engagement?"

Inform

Give information and knowledge. If you know something your client needs to know, don't wait for them to discover it. Share your knowledge to help them learn from your experiences. This can be a helpful jump start to further exploration and study on the client's behalf.

Coach's questions or statements:
- "Let me share some research with you."
- "This book/article has been helpful with other clients."
- "I have experienced this before, and here are some ideas to address this challenge."

Monitoring

Used in session and very helpful in person, monitoring is the work of coaching. It's helpful to see how the client interacts with their team or customers and their office environment and how people respond to them. This is an action that a coach takes; they may offer observations afterward that could help in the "Actions" section of the IDP.

Coach's questions or statements:
- "How are you doing on your experiments? Let's review them."

Offer Support

Used in session, this can help clarify what support the client needs to make progress. Use this when your client could use some additional help and may not know how to ask for it. Build the client's self-esteem, self-confidence, and self-respect. Demonstrate empathy for their experiences while holding the tension of development and learning. Underscore that this is a safe space for deep emotions.

Coach's questions or statements:
- "How can I help you?"
- "What would be supportive?"

Prescribe

Give instructions, advice, or recommendations. This is helpful if the client lacks confidence or is unable to direct their own learning yet.

Coach's questions or statements:
- "I see you would like to work on X. Maybe you could give Y a try."

Reframe

Help the client see a situation in a different light. Show a new way of looking at a situation, person, or conflict. This is helpful if the client seems stuck in a certain perspective or is not able to see other sides of a situation. This helps them learn perspective taking, a key skill in building self-awareness.

Coach's questions or statements:
- "Let's look at this from another perspective."
- "Can you argue the other side?"
- "If you were the other person in this dynamic, how might you be feeling or what might you be thinking?"

Rehearse or Role Play

For difficult conversations or experiments, offering to role play the other person or even your client's role can be helpful to model the interaction. This is powerful for the client to see how it can be done (role model) and then practice in their own voice and style (rehearse) with your feedback and support.

Coach's questions or statements:
- "Would you like to practice this situation so you feel better prepared when it comes up?"

Reinforce

This is a version of celebration, focused on lessons learned, insights gained, and progress made. It helps the learning to stick. The three good things practice (found later in this chapter) is an example of this reinforcement intervention. This is especially helpful if the client is having success with some new actions. Reinforce the learning and the positive outcomes they've created.

Coach's questions or statements:
- "Do you see how your improvement in X has a knock-on effect in Y?"
- "What further insights can you share from this accomplishment?"

Round Back

Take good session notes and return to topics previously discussed. Revisit the IDP and key themes from prior conversations, and reflect on what is similar to prior episodes or experiences. This is a key intervention for coaching conversations and used regularly in sessions.

Coach's questions or statements:
- "Let's review the themes from last time."
- "This seems to come up in your relationships. Let's look at a few examples from our time together."
- "How is this related to the experience you shared last time?"

Shadow

Often leveraged at the outset of a coaching engagement, the opportunity to be with your client in their day-to-day work can be illuminating. You have a chance to observe and assess them in a variety of interactions and can use those insights to continue their learning.

Coach's questions or statements:
- "I'd like to shadow your interactions during X so we can identify experiments that can help you reach your goal."

Challenging Interventions

Challenging interventions include strategies for pushing your client to do more, dig deeper, challenge their biases or assumptions, or expose the core issue.

Assess

Foundational to coaching, assessment is about continually assessing your client's thinking, approach, engagement, and commitment. This also includes self-assessment. Continually assess in coaching conversations and spend some time after each session to self-assess as well.

Coach's questions or statements:
- "Am I being a good coach?"
- "Are they overcoming obstacles?"
- "How is the health of our relationship?"

Draw Out
A regular intervention used to engage the client in sharing more information or providing more context. This is helpful if you believe the client is holding back or hasn't made time to deeply reflect.

Coach's questions or statements:
- "Let's explore X more."
- "Tell me more about Y."

Increase Insight
Help your client deepen their awareness of a particular insight. You help them draw conclusions and shed some light on a topic so they can understand themselves and the situation more. Use this when a new insight is made or you have fresh observation from an action. You can help make the learning even deeper and broader by increasing insight.

Coach's questions or statements:
- "What conclusions can you draw from that?"

Stimulate Motivation
Part of your job as a coach is to keep the client engaged in the work of coaching. Leverage the 360 process and profiles to learn what motivates your client and tie their experiments and actions to these personal desired outcomes. This is important when your client seems stuck or isn't making the progress you expect to see.

Coach's questions or statements:
- "How does this help you achieve your goal of X?"
- "How is this related to your vision for yourself as a leader?"

Wonder Out Loud
A posture of curiosity is taken in session to explore alternative approaches and different possibilities to offer a new way of thinking. This can be used when you want to open your client up to another point of view or softly challenge their thinking and assumptions.

Coach's questions or statements:
- "I wonder if you've considered X?"
- "Have you thought about Y?"
- "What would research tell us about Z?"

Directly Challenging Interventions
Directly challenging interventions more assertively confront or challenge your client. Use them when they seem stuck in a particular belief, bias, attitude, or assumption that isn't correct, complete, or helpful. Your client may be digging into a position or making conclusions based on something other

than the facts you can see in the situation. Use these interventions selectively to directly confront your client and invite them to see another perspective. These interventions help you support your client in getting underneath what drives their beliefs more directly.

Catalyst
When your client needs to make a decision, sometimes you need to be the catalyst for that decision. When you're hearing the same thing and your client seems stuck, you can challenge them to action.

Coach's questions or statements:
- "What additional piece of information do you need to decide?"
- "What is going to light a fire under this?"
- "What are you waiting for?"
- "Why are you unwilling to make a decision?"

Challenge Thinking Process
Be courageous to directly confront your client and their thinking process.

Coach's questions or statements:
- "How did you get from A to B?"
- "What information did you use to make those conclusions?"
- "Upon what beliefs is that conclusion based?"

Confront
Challenge the client's assumptions. Stimulate their awareness of their own behaviors, attitudes, or beliefs.

Coach's questions or statements:
- "Is there an underlying belief you are aware of?"
- "In your heart of hearts, what do you believe about that?"

Connect Actions to Beliefs or Values
Understand if there is a belief system or value that underpins an action or a behavior. Question the underlying belief or bias that may be in play. Some of these may be long held and unconscious.

Coach's questions or statements:
- "What belief system is driving this behavior?"
- "What value do you place in behavior X?"
- "What is important to you about this?"

Question
Challenge their logic, conclusions, and assumptions. Dig deeper into what they're truly feeling about a situation and what happened. Push back a bit.

Coach's questions or statements:
- "Can you explain your logic?"
- "What data did you use to draw that conclusion?"
- "Are you holding any assumptions that may no longer be true?"

Template 4-9. Active Listening

Purpose: An overview of listening types as a skill builder and job aid for you or your client.

How to use: This is an optional form to use in whole or in part. Adapt it to your client's culture and work style. Put it in your own words and brand it to your business. For your own skill development, use and practice the effective types of listening outlined here. You can also adapt it for clients working to improve their listening skills.

The Five Key Elements of Active Listening

1. Full Listening
Use your own body language and gestures to convey your attention.
- Look at the speaker directly. If you are on a virtual session, be sure to set your camera so you're looking at your client and not off to the side, which is highly disengaging.
- Nod occasionally.
- Smile and use other facial expressions and gestures.
- Note your posture and make sure it is open and inviting.
- Encourage the speaker with small verbal comments like "yes" and "uh-huh."

2. Deep Listening
Give the speaker your undivided attention and acknowledge the message. Recognize that nonverbal communication also "speaks" loudly.
- Put aside distracting thoughts. Don't mentally prepare a rebuttal!
- Avoid being distracted by environmental factors. Turn off your reminders and put your phone on silent. Close your email, message apps, and anything else that can distract you.
- "Listen" to the speaker's body language.
- Refrain from side conversations when listening in a group setting.

3. Reflective Listening
Our personal filters, assumptions, judgments, and beliefs can distort what we hear. As a listener, your role is to understand what is being said. This may require you to reflect on what is being said and ask questions:
- Reflect what has been said by paraphrasing: "What I'm hearing is . . ." and "Sounds like you are saying . . ." are great ways to reflect back.
- Ask questions to clarify certain points: "What do you mean when you say . . .?" or "Is this what you mean?"
- Summarize the speaker's comments periodically.
- Ask open-ended questions, not yes or no questions.

Tip: If you find yourself responding emotionally to what someone has said, say so and ask for more information: "I may not be understanding you correctly, and I find myself taking what you said personally. What I thought you just said is this; is that what you meant?"

4. Sympathetic Listening

Interrupting is a waste of time. It frustrates the speaker and limits full understanding of the message.

- Allow the speaker to finish.
- Don't interrupt with counterarguments.
- Don't judge the speaker.
- Pay close attention and express your sorrow, happiness, or whatever emotion is appropriate for their situation.

5. Facilitative Listening

This goes beyond even sympathetic listening because it implies and requires you to extend an especially helpful approach to the other person or people.

- First ask the speaker about their own ideas for how to solve their problem.
- Be kind and honest in your response.
- Assert your opinions respectfully.

Template 4-10. Conflict Overview

Purpose: An overview of conflict styles and unique strategies for responding to conflict. It's useful in coaching new ways to approach competencies in conflict management and in helping your client adapt their natural style to something more appropriate in a particular situation. It mirrors the feedback your client would receive from the Thomas-Kilmann Instrument during the assessment step.

How to use: This is an activity form to use in whole or in part. Adapt it to your client's culture and work style. Put it in your own words and brand it to your business. In working with your client, you can use this to try to uncover what's happening in a conflict situation. You give it to them as a learning aid for their own deeper study and interpretation of a challenging situation.

Learning Objectives
- Define and illustrate five decision-making styles.
- Achieve your desired negotiation outcomes through the careful analysis of interests.

Understanding Conflict
Conflicts almost always represent situations in which two people or groups disagree about what is true or what is important. These different perspectives produce different maps of the world and senses of reality. Out of this confusion, conflict emerges.

These conflicts are likely a product of miscommunication, poor negotiation, preconceived bias, or misinformation, coupled with faulty extrapolation. Regardless of the faulty basis for the conflict, it is nonetheless real and is likely to feed on itself, making for more conflict.

Definition of *conflict*: Any situation where your concerns or desires differ from another person's or group's. What are examples of conflict in your world?

Conflict can be positive and negative. Too much of the wrong type of conflict can tear an organization, a team, or a unit apart. Too little conflict leaves too much unsaid and leads to underperformance and suppressed differences that eventually erupt as a more pernicious type of conflict.

Five Types of Conflict
A useful tool in thinking about conflict is the Thomas-Kilmann conflict model, which allows for two dimensions or drivers for conflict: assertive and cooperative behavior. From this, we can derive five types of conflict:
- **Competing** is assertive and uncooperative. You try to satisfy your own concerns at the other person's expense.
- **Compromising** is intermediate in both assertiveness and cooperative. You try to find an acceptable settlement that only partially satisfies both people's concerns.
- **Accommodating** is unassertive and cooperative. You attempt to satisfy the other person's concerns at the expense of your own.
- **Avoiding** is unassertive and uncooperative. When avoiding, you sidestep the conflict without trying to satisfy either person's concerns.
- **Collaborating** is assertive and cooperative. When collaborating, you try to find a win-win solution that completely satisfies both people's concerns.

```
            Assertive   ┌──────────────┐      ┌──────────────┐
                        │              │      │              │
                        │  Competing   │      │ Collaborating│
                        │              │      │              │
                        └──────────────┘      └──────────────┘
   ▲
Assertiveness              ┌──────────────────┐
   │                       │                  │
   │                       │   Compromising   │
   │                       │                  │
   ▼                       └──────────────────┘

            Unassertive ┌──────────────┐      ┌──────────────┐
                        │              │      │              │
                        │   Avoiding   │      │ Accommodating│
                        │              │      │              │
                        └──────────────┘      └──────────────┘

              Unassertive  ◄──────────►  Cooperative

                         Assertiveness
```

Six Strategies for Responding

Effective leaders respond to conflict in a variety of ways and aim their response at making the conflict as creative as possible. This model assumes that the situation demands an approach to conflict that provides the best desired outcome.

To frame the conflict and choose the right method, we can apply six strategies to decision making and negotiation:

- How important is my relationship with the other person? Am I willing to give it up over the conflict?
- Am I certain which solution or outcome is best? Or is it just my idea? Is the best outcome some form of collaboration?
- How important is the issue to me? And is my valuation legitimate? How much do they value this?
- Do I need the other person's ongoing buy-in for something? What if I win, but really lose because I no longer have their engagement?
- How much time do we have to resolve this?
- How is power distributed, and how might that change?

Review your results. Which of the modes do you tend to use most? Which do you use infrequently?

_____

_____

_____

Role Plays

Think of a current or upcoming conflict you have to deal with. Write a description below.

_____

_____

_____

Role play that situation and note any reflections here.

_____

_____

_____

Now consider which conflict style you would normally use for this conflict. Which one should you use? Discuss with a partner.

_____

_____

_____

_____

Template 4-11. Difficult Conversation Outline

Purpose: A practice for preparing for and conducting a difficult conversation.

How to use: This is an optional form to use in whole or in part. Adapt it to your client's culture and work style. Put it in your own words and brand it to your business. Review the framework with your client and provide it as an exercise for them to complete.

Goals of the Conversation

- Aligned understanding and expectations, particularly when strong emotions are involved
- Meant for situations that can be resolved without HR or other formal disciplinary interventions
- Simplify the process to stay focused.

Overview of Framework

- Establish a positive mindset and common ground.
- Frame the goal.
- Listen intently.
- Plan next steps.

Framework in Action

- Establish a positive mindset and common ground:
    - We both care about what happens to the <*patient/staff/colleague*>.
    - I appreciate what you do.
    - This conversation is in service of doing our best."
- Frame the goal (10 percent of the conversation)
    - Start with your good intentions and the big picture of common good or goal.
    - Use a contrasting statement: "What I don't want is <*this*>; what I do want is <*this*>."
    - Be clear and succinct about the situation and what you're asking.
- Listen intently (50 to 60 percent of the conversation)
    - Listen carefully to the other person's response. Allow for an initial reaction.
    - Reflect back what you're hearing. "I want to be sure I understand." Then describe it.
    - Correct misinformation in a neutral way.
    - Review the benefits of moving forward.
- Plan next steps (30 to 40 percent of the conversation)
    - Return to the goal. Restate it and check for agreement.
    - Summarize concerns and actions to be taken regarding the topic.
    - Plan next steps with a specific timeframe for follow-up.

Template 4-12. EQ Exercise: Finding Joy

Purpose: For clients who are struggling to find happiness, joy, or freedom in their day-to-day life. If they are not experiencing joy in their life, they probably aren't their best leader either. This practice helps your client see what is already present in their life and tune into what is good and happy. If this continues as a pervasive challenge, I strongly recommend you refer your client to a professional psychotherapist for further support.

How to use: This is an optional activity to use in whole or in part. Adapt it to your client's culture and work style. Put it in your own words and brand it to your business. Offer it to a client to help increase their ability to recognize the joy, happiness, and freedom already present in their life.

At the end of each day, spend 15 minutes reflecting and responding to the following prompt:

When did I experience joy or happiness today?
- *What happened?*
- *Who was present?*
- *What was happening in my body?*
- *What was my emotional response?*
- *What was I telling myself about this situation and those in it?*

Document your reflections daily. Review your notes at the end of each week for themes and insights. Bring these insights to your next coaching session.

Template 4-13. EQ Exercise: Meditation

Purpose: For clients who could benefit from identifying their emotions in a safe setting, this meditation helps them access and feel emotions, then reflect on the experience to identify themes and trends over time.

How to use: This is an optional activity to use in whole or in part. Adapt it to your client's culture and work style. Put it in your own words and brand it to your business. I recommend you practice the first time in a coaching session, and then offer it as an exercise for your client to practice between sessions. You can also choose to record this guided meditation in your own voice and offer it as an audio file to your clients.

At the end of each day, spend time practicing this meditation exercise.

1. Take a seated position on a cushion, on the floor, or in a chair. You should be comfortable but upright. Let your shoulders relax. Close your eyes or adopt a soft downward gaze.
2. Notice your body. Where is it making contact with the floor, with your chair, or with the cushion? Where does your body end and your support begin?
3. Notice your breath. For the next four to five breaths, meter each inhale and exhale, feeling your breath flowing into and out of your body.
4. Shift your awareness to your body. Slowly scan through your body from head to toe, observing any feelings or emotions that are present in each point in your physical body.
5. You might have detected numerous feelings or emotions throughout your body. Return to one of those feelings or emotions to focus on for now.
   - Where in your body is this emotion located?
   - How big or small is the feeling?
   - Where are its edges? Are they sharp or soft?
   - Does the feeling have a color? And if so, is it changing or remaining the same?
   - Is the feeling heavy or light?
   - Is the feeling moving or still?
   - Is the feeling hard or soft? Is it rough or smooth? If I could touch this feeling with my hand, what would its texture feel like?
6. Step back from the detailed exploration of the embodiment of this feeling. Can you name this feeling or emotion?
7. Continue to get to know this emotion for another five minutes. When you think you have reached a level of comfort with and understanding of this feeling, gently open your eyes and bring your attention back to the room you are in.
8. Take a final set of cleansing breaths, using a heavy, audible exhale each time.
9. Take at least 10 minutes to document everything you can recall about the embodiment of this emotion in your journal.

Repeat this practice daily at the same time and location, if possible. Review your journal at the end of each week for themes, trends, or insights. Bring these insights to your next coaching session.

Template 4-14. EQ Exercise: Recognize Triggers

Purpose: Clients who experience being triggered by others and struggle to see their own patterns in this challenging circumstance. This practice helps them deepen their self-awareness and learn to recognize their own patterns and reactions. It deepens their agency over their emotional reactions and invites them to own their part in the situations they find upsetting or challenging.

How to use: This is an optional activity to use in whole or in part. Adapt it to your client's culture and work style. Put it in your own words and brand it to your business. Offer the practice to clients who could benefit from learning to sense and identify their own triggers.

At the end of each day, spend 15 minutes reflecting and responding to the following prompt:

What strong emotions did I feel today (e.g., frustrated, mad, stressed, disrespected)?
- *What happened?*
- *Who was present?*
- *What was happening in my body?*
- *What was my emotional response?*
- *What was I saying to myself about this situation and those in the situation?*

Document your reflections daily. Review your notes at the end of each week for themes and insights. Bring these insights to your next coaching session.

Template 4-15. Personal Evolution Worksheet

Purpose: A two-part process to guide your client through an exploration of their vision for their life, relationships, career, and so on. Offer this to a client who is working through questions of identity and vision for their life.

How to use: This is an optional activity to use in whole or in part. Adapt it to your client's culture and work style. Put it in your own words and brand it to your business. Review both parts of the worksheet in a client session, then ask them to complete part 1 as homework. Review that work in a coaching session, then assign part 2.

Which qualities would you like to have? One of the most important and profound questions is "Who do I want to be?" It is great to have goals for your relationships, career, and finances, and to plan for fun, but have you ever thought about planning to be the person you would like to become?

Part 1: Who Do I Want to Be?
1. Get a blank piece of paper and sit down somewhere comfortable and quiet.
2. Imagine someone whose qualities you admire. They can be known to you personally or not.
3. Which of their qualities do you like or admire? The love of your mother or the laughter of your father? The compassion of Mother Theresa? The courage of Nelson Mandela?
4. What appeals to you about them? What are their manners, attitudes, and traits? Try to get a really good feel for who they are and how they act. Are they kind to others? Are they confident? Are they calm under pressure?
5. Take your time and write down as many personal qualities as you can think of—list at least five. Use single words to describe them, not sentences. For example, list single word qualities like *relaxed* or *confident*, rather than a complete sentence like, *When under stress, Dad takes it easy.*
6. Remember to focus on who they are being, not what they are doing.
7. Once you have a list of qualities, ask yourself if *you* have them. For example, if you wrote *patience*, ask yourself, "When have I been patient?" If you wrote *strength*, ask yourself, "When have I demonstrated strength?"
8. If you doubt that you have these qualities, ask yourself if you have ever demonstrated them. For example, if you chose *confident* as a quality, but don't think you have confidence, ask yourself, "Have I ever been confident?"
9. Repeat this question for each of the personal qualities you would like to have.

Part 2: Who Is the Person I Want to Become?
1. When you have satisfactorily answered the question "Who is the person I want to be?" draw up a list of the three qualities that are most important to you.
2. Write these down, along with a brief explanation of what they mean to you.
3. Visualize these qualities in your mind and see, hear, and feel the person you want to be.
4. To accelerate the process of becoming who you want to be, practice visualizing these three qualities once a day.

Template 4-16. Self-Awareness Activity: Weighing Options

Purpose: A classic T-chart to help a client who is weighing a decision with two competing options or paths. This template uses an example of a client deciding whether to close a successful business now or in the future.

How to use: This is an optional activity to use in whole or in part. Adapt it to your client's culture and work style. Put it in your own words and brand it to your business. Put the decision your client is considering at the top of the T-chart with some instructions for them to follow as homework.

Find a quiet place to do this work. Take a few cleansing breaths with big, audible exhales, and sit comfortably or stand with both feet on the floor. Be sure you can work uninterrupted for at least 20 minutes.

Bring your specific situation to mind and frame it as a question. Then work through these prompts:
- What are the positive aspects of this question?
- How is this a good idea?
- What benefits does this yield for me, my health, my family, or my life?
- How is this in service to my greater vision for my life?

Really think about this question, feel in it your body, notice your emotions, and pay attention to what your mind is already saying. Take 60 seconds to sit with it before you begin capturing your reactions and responses in the chart.

What is possible if I close my business now?

Pros	Cons

When that feels complete, turn your attention to the next set of prompts. If you are feeling distracted, take a short break—take a walk or make a cup of tea—to reset and refocus.

As you think about your specific situation, work through these prompts:
- What is challenging about this question?
- What negative implications do I imagine will happen?
- What are the downsides for me, my health, my family, or my life?
- How does this limit what is possible in achieving my vision for my life?

Take 60 seconds to sit with your thoughts and then capture your reactions and responses in the chart.

What is possible if I close my business now?

Pros	Cons

Template 4-17. SWOT Analysis Worksheet

Purpose: Use the SWOT (strengths, weaknesses, opportunities, and threats) analysis for a client who needs to reflect on and identify focus areas for development. This can be helpful if they are struggling to identify competencies to develop or seem stuck with their assessment of a situation.

How to use: This is an optional form to use in whole or in part. Adapt it to your client's culture and work style. Put it in your own words and brand it to your business. Help your client identify their personal leadership strengths and weaknesses, as well as opportunities and threats in their organization or industry.

Strengths *What strengths, skills, abilities, advantages, and resources give you an advantage?*	Weaknesses *What challenges, lack of skills, obstacles, or needs put you at a disadvantage?*
Opportunities *What new skills, potential markets, business ventures, resources, and marketing channels give you an advantage?*	Threats *What potential problems do you face that put you at a disadvantage?*

Template 4-18. Time Management Quadrant

Purpose: An exercise for clients struggling with feeling overwhelmed or not being able to extract themselves from their day-to-day tasks to operate more as a leader. It includes a summary of time management concepts in a model popularized by the Covey Leadership Institute, which walks the client through how they're really spending their time and what actions they can take to invest more time in nonurgent but important matters.

How to use: This is an optional activity to use in whole or in part. Adapt it to your client's culture and work style. Put it in your own words and brand it to your business. Assign it as homework and review the results and reflections in a future coaching session.

Adapted from Covey (1989).

- **Quadrant 1: Matters that are important and urgent.** These are things such as crises, emergencies, or deadlines. Remember that business proposal you worked overtime on because it was due the next day? These are important matters of daily operations that must be addressed before they become urgent to avoid stress and conflicts. Manage this quadrant.
- **Quadrant 2: Matters that are important but not urgent.** This is where you should spend your time. It is all about planning. Addressing these matters helps you lead more effectively and deliberately. This is a quadrant of opportunities to learn, to improve yourself and your relationships with others, to focus on innovative and creative solutions to long-standing issues, and to drive results in a more thoughtful and strategic manner. Focus on this quadrant.
- **Quadrant 3: Matters that are not important but urgent.** This is where most of us sit. We tend to focus on matters that are urgent without considering their level of importance. The problem with this is we lose track of the important matters. It affects your priorities just because it's urgent. Avoid this quadrant.
- **Quadrant 4: Matters that are not important and not urgent.** Obviously, these are what they call time wasters. Thus, they're mostly matters you shouldn't spend much time on, like mindless Facebook scrolling or binge-watching movies. These matters aren't really that helpful to you. Limit this quadrant.

Directions for Self-Assessment

1. Reflect on your last two to four weeks at work. Refer to your calendar if that is helpful.
2. Capture the ways you spent your time. What meetings did you attend? Was there planning or thinking time in your calendar? How are you developing yourself and your team? Were you writing strategic proposals, preparing for a huddle, writing a presentation for your boss, or updating metrics for the team's monthly report? Capture as much as you can about how you spent your time.
3. Next, estimate the percentage of time each week you spend in each quadrant. Review everything you captured in each quadrant and estimate how much time that represents each week or on average over the span of weeks you considered. Write that percentage in the quadrant box.

Q1 Urgent and Important (Manage)	Q2 Not Urgent and Important (Focus)
Q3 Urgent and Not Important (Avoid)	Q4 Not Urgent and Not Important (Limit)

Individual Action Planning

Based on the results of my self-assessment, I plan to do the following:

1. What will I stop doing? (Q3, Q4, Q1)

   _____

   _____

2. What will I delegate? To whom and by when? (Q1)

   _____

   _____

3. What support do I need from my peers or leader to make these changes?

   _____

   _____

Template 4-19. Tolerations Worksheet

Purpose: A worksheet for your client to help identify things they've been tolerating in their life and work to prioritize and change them.

How to use: This is an optional activity to use in whole or in part. Adapt it to your client's culture and work style. Put it in your own words and brand it to your business. Review the worksheet in a coaching session and talk through an example. Then assign the remainder of the worksheet as homework. Ask your client to bring the completed worksheet to the next coaching session so you can review the results and reflections together.

What Are You Tolerating in Your Life?

The things we tolerate—broken light bulbs, home and office clutter, conversations we've been avoiding, wanting to make a change in our diet—block us from our happiness.

Use this table to list 25 things you have been tolerating in your life and your plans to remedy the issue.

	What Are You Tolerating?	Toleration Solution	Due Date
1			
2			
3			
4			
5			
6			
7			
8			
9			
10			
11			
12			
13			
14			
15			
16			
17			
18			
19			
20			
21			
22			
23			
24			
25			

Template 4-20. Trust Article and Practice Exercises

Purpose: For clients struggling to keep or build trust in an important relationship, this template includes an article about building authentic trust, followed by two practice exercises for the client complete. This also invites them to look at what they are doing to contribute to the situation and what actions they are willing to take to try to rebuild trust.

How to use: This is an optional activity to use in whole or in part. Adapt it to your client's culture and work style. Put it in your own words and brand it to your business. Review with your client in a coaching session, then assign the exercise to read the article, reflect on the current level of trust in a meaningful relationship, and complete the action plan for building trust.

Building Authentic Trust

Mutual trust forms the foundation and dynamic precondition for any positive relationship. Trust is dynamic. It's not an inert foundation—trust is part of the vitality of relationships. It's an emotional skill that involves responsibility, commitment, and choice. We build trusting relationships by being trustworthy ourselves and by trusting others—successful relationships require both of these virtues. But often it's our ability to trust, not our own trustworthiness, that's the issue. We believe that others need to earn our trust rather than adopting the perspective that trust is a choice we make and an action we take. Trust can't be taken for granted; it must be continuously cultivated through conversations, commitments, and truthfulness. Although trust involves vulnerability and risk on our part, it also opens up new and unimagined possibilities.

Authentic trust means being both reflective and honest with ourselves and others. All forms of trust involve relationships and interactions, but with authentic trust, the focus is on the relationship itself. Authentic trust requires self-trust, confidence, and optimism. In addition, it always involves vulnerability and risk. When we trust others, we count on their sense of responsibility and integrity, believing they will choose to act in a trustworthy manner.

But no matter how much we trust someone else, there is always the possibility the other person will behave or react in a way that is different than we expected. To build trust, we must think about this in a positive way. Although trust carries risk, it also opens up new and unimagined possibilities.

The Basis of Trust

Our level of trust in another person is based on the assessments we make of them in four areas:

- **Sincerity.** We make assessments based on how aligned someone's actions are with their words, values, and beliefs, and how consistent their conversations are when they speak to different people.
- **Competency.** These assessments relate to a person's level of knowledge, skills, and resources. We make competency assessments based on whether we believe they have the capacity to accomplish the task at hand, or if they have access to the resources necessary to develop this capacity.
- **Reliability.** We make assessments about someone's reliability or credibility based on what has happened in the past—how often, in our experience, they have kept or broken their commitments.
- **Caring.** We make assessments about whether the other person has our best interests in mind and if they will make decisions and take action that reflect concern about our well-being or what we hold to be important.

When you find yourself questioning the trustworthiness of another person, stop and ask, "What are my assessments about this person in the areas of sincerity, competency, reliability, and care? Are they grounded in experience, reality, or perception?" In addition, ask yourself, "Are my expectations of others aligned with my assessments of the four areas of trust?"

Build Trust by Being Trustworthy

Being trustworthy is based on the same four areas:

- **Sincerity.** In your interactions and relationships, build confidence in your sincerity by being aligned with your integrity and "walking your talk."
- **Competency.** Be clear about what you are committing to. Don't agree to do things you don't have the capability, or the resources to gain the competency, to complete.
- **Reliability.** Make and meet your commitments. The key to trust is action, and in particular, commitments—commitments made and commitments honored.
- **Care.** Build relationships with others that are based on mutual values, concerns, and commitments. Show your care for these relationships by taking action that aligns with your shared values.

The quality of your relationships and your ability to influence and lead others are often directly connected to the promises you make and your ability to manage multiple promises to different people. But many of us are not very good observers of ourselves and how we make and manage the web of commitments we live in. Because of this, we may not see the negative impact we're creating by not taking care of our commitments. Whenever a promise is made and then broken, something is diminished in the relationship and our ability to influence others. The following chart shows the aspects that are affected when we make or break commitments.

	Agreements	
Break		**Keep**
|	Trust	|
|	Relationships	|
|	Success	|
|	Self-Esteem	|

Build positive relationships and improve your ability to influence and lead others by being as good as your word. Do what you say you will do and don't do what you say you won't do. Understand what you are committing to. Are you clear about the expectations of others? Make strong promises—promises you are absolutely committed to keeping—then follow through. If you can't follow through, then manage your agreements through renegotiation and recommitment.

This article is based on Sieler (2004).

Exercise 1: Discerning Levels of Trust

1. Review the material on the four elements that form the basis of trust: sincerity, competency, reliability, and caring.
2. Bring to mind a challenging relationship where mistrust has been a factor affecting its health and productivity.
3. Assess this person on the four elements of trust using a scale of 0 to 5 (where 0 = low/not at all, 3 = mixed, 5 = high/almost always).
4. Write down your score and a few reasons for your assessment to ensure you are grounding your perspective.
5. Total your score at the bottom.

Four Elements of Trust	Score (0–5)	List a few reasons for your assessment to ensure you are grounding your perspective.
How sincere is this person?		
How competent are they, related to our shared work or purpose?		
Are they reliable or credible?		
Do they care about me, our shared work, and our relationships?		

Total score (0–20 points): _____

Evaluating the Results

- **0–7 points:** You both have some important work to do to repair this relationship. Start with the assessment's highest score to see if you can rebuild your relationship from a place of strength. Consider asking them to complete this worksheet, and have open dialogue about where you each are in trusting each other. Set a shared goal about where you want to be in terms of mutual trust.
- **8–15 points:** You have some strengths to build upon. Perhaps there is one area to improve as a focus and some areas that are mixed. These are rich domains to explore how to set goals to improve trust in a targeted way.
- **16–20 points:** You have a healthy relationship and a consistently strong level of trust to rely on. The occasional misstep is repaired quickly thanks to this strong foundation of trust.

Exercise 2: Trust Assessment and Action Plan

Bring to mind a challenging relationship in your work or personal life. Have this be someone who is important to you and your sense of success and happiness, someone you interact with regularly, and someone you consistently find yourself challenged to trust.

Review the Trust Matrix

Grounding of assessment is the evidence supporting your assessment. If you assess this person as a poor timekeeper, your grounding would be the several times they have arrived late. Your *willingness to take risks* is a statement about your personal orientation to extending trust and faith in someone else. Many factors go into your willingness to take risks, including your upbringing, cultural background, and sense of safety in the relationship or work setting.

Consider a challenging, but important, relationship that you have and your sense of trust in it. Put a mark on the trust matrix below to indicate where you stand, at this moment, with this person. Include the date next to the mark.

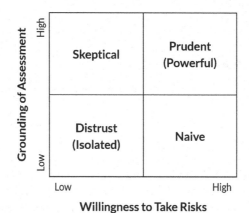

Now think about an action you can take to move toward prudent trust. How do you find resilience and confidence to take more risk with this person? How do you seek a more current or accurate grounding of your assessments, letting go of "old tape" where appropriate? Write down that action:

_____

When you take this action toward prudent trust, notice what happens. How does this person respond? How are you experiencing this new action? What comes up for you, and what do you notice about others? Make some notes for yourself.

_____

After two weeks (or more if needed) of taking this action to move toward prudent trust, reflect on the status of the relationship. Have you shifted on the trust matrix? If yes, mark and date where you are on the matrix now. If not, reflect on your assessments and willingness to take risks as key levers in moving the level of trust in this relationship. Make adjustments to one or both and repeat the process.

Template 4-21. Uncover Your Inner Wisdom Worksheet

Purpose: A directed journaling exercise for clients who need to tap into their inner wisdom to make an important decision or decide to move forward.

How to use: This is an optional activity to use in whole or in part. Adapt it to your client's culture and work style. Put it in your own words and brand it to your business. Offer this reflection tool to help a client move on from anything significant or gain insight into where they are.

Write a letter that no one will read to help reveal your heart's messages and wisdom.

1. Put the question you want answered at the top of the page.
2. Write down all the things you wish you could say and get it all out. Free-write—don't edit or analyze. Don't stop until your heart feels free.
3. Include all your memories, positive and negative.
4. Try not to analyze what you are writing; just write without judgment and let it flow from the heart.
5. When you have finished, walk away for a few hours before reading it, or better yet, sleep on it.
6. As you read over what you have written, highlight or underline anything that strikes you as interesting, unusual, or significant. These are the messages and the wisdom your heart is bringing through to you. Think about these messages and what wisdom your heart is revealing to you.
7. When the time is right, ask yourself what you would like to do with the letter. For example, you could put it in a keepsake box, place it in a bottle and throw it in the ocean, burn it, bury it, or even send it.

Template 4-22. Vision Board Exercise

Purpose: An exercise for a client who needs help identifying what they want in work and life to serve as a road map for their development.

How to use: Review the vision board exercise with your client, then assign the exercise to complete a vision board between coaching sessions. Ask your client to bring their completed board to the next coaching session and share their experience creating it.

Create a vision board to manifest your intentions for your work and life. This visual representation of your goals can include artwork, photography, illustrations, graphic elements, quotes, and phrases. A vision board helps you picture what you want in your life and is an engaging way to capture images and words that remind you of that vision. It helps you set a direction and serves as a regular reminder of your goals.

There are many ways to create a vision board—some people like to use a large poster board; others use a smaller wrapped canvas frame. All that matters is creating something that's meaningful to you.

1. Consider what matters most to you. Take some time to reflect on the areas of your life where you want to manifest change. These should be the parts of your world that hold the most meaning and where improvement will hold the most satisfaction.
2. Find inspiring images related to these areas of focus. Gather some of your favorite magazines, head to your favorite online graphic or photography store, or create your own art.
3. Choose some words or phrases that hold power and inspiration for you. Use short phrases or single words so they fit on your board.
4. Get your glue stick out and make a visually interesting collage with the images, graphics, and words. There are no rules—feel free to overlap images, stack words, and decorate the edges. Make it something you want to look at every day.
5. Find the place in your office or home where you will see this at least once a day. Put your vision board on display to motivate you and keep you focused on manifesting your goals.

Nadine's vision board is included here as an example.

Template 4-23. Wheel of Life Exercise

Purpose: This aid directs you through an assessment of your client's life and a short practice to evaluate balance in each area of importance. Use with a client who seems out of balance or generally dissatisfied with their life.

How to use: This is an optional activity to use in whole or in part. Adapt it to your client's culture and work style. Put it in your own words and brand it to your business. Work with your client to fill in the wheel during a session and then assign as homework reflection on the completed wheel. You can also assign this as an activity as homework to complete between coaching sessions.

Each section in the wheel of life represents balance between the different aspects of your life.

1. Change, split, or rename any category in the figure so that it's meaningful and represents a balanced life for you.
2. Rank your level of satisfaction in each area of the diagram from 1 to 10 (where 1 = very unsatisfied and 10 = very satisfied).
3. Draw a straight or curved line based on your ranking to create a new outer edge for the wheel. The new perimeter of the circle represents your current wheel of life. What story does it tell? Where do you want to adjust?

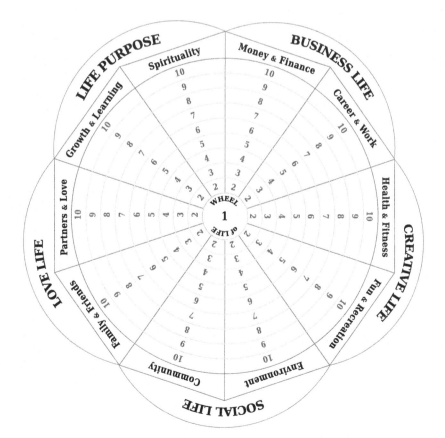

Template 4-24. Three Good Things Gratitude Exercise

Purpose: A process that a client can use anytime they need more gratitude. I use this process to close every coaching session, which helps ensure that we end on a high note and reflect the client's positive outcomes from the session.

How to use: This is an optional activity to use in whole or in part. Adapt it to your client's culture and work style. Put it in your own words and brand it to your business. Assign it to clients who are working to increase their gratitude and grace, or use it at the end of each coaching session.

1. Get grounded. Put your feet on the floor and feel all edges of each foot making contact with the surface. You can do this sitting or standing.
2. Take a few cleansing breaths. Practice metered breathing: Breathe in for five seconds, hold for five seconds, breathe out for five seconds. Repeat three times.
3. Reflect on the previous hour (or day):
    o What three good things came out of the last hour?
    o What made these outcomes possible?
    o Why were they meaningful?
    o How can you create more of this in the rest of your day?
4. Capture your insights in a journal or workbook.

Review your entries at the end of the week. What themes emerge for you? What insights can you gain? What impact has this practice had on your mood?

Template 4-25. One Door Closes, Another Door Opens Exercise

Purpose: A self-awareness exercise for any client who is struggling to let go of something that has ended or to find the good in what is ahead. Examples include a job change, a relationship ending, a change in their family structure, or a reset of an important work relationship.

How to use: This is an optional activity to use in whole or in part. Adapt it to your client's culture and work style. Put it in your own words and brand it to your business. You can use this in a coaching session or assign it as an exercise to complete between sessions. Ask your client to bring their insights and reflections to the next coaching session to discuss together.

Find a quiet place where you won't be disturbed for at least an hour. Have a notepad or journal nearby and remove any distractions.

1. Take a few moments to bring yourself to this space. Put your feet on the floor. Feel the full edges of your feet and toes touching the floor. Take a few breaths to center and bring your attention to this task.
2. Picture what is changing or finishing. Make sure you have a good image of it in your mind. Do you notice any changes in your emotions, mood, or body as you think about this change?
3. When you have a full sense of this change, write down what is changing or finishing in your journal. Include whatever shifts you noticed in your emotions, mood, or body as you thought about this change. Write to completion; leave no details out.
4. Come back to a full mental picture of the thing that is changing or finishing and imagine placing it on the other side of a door. (If possible, take your journal and physically place it on the other side of a door.)
5. Close the door.
6. Recenter yourself. Put your feet on the floor. Feel the full edges of your feet and toes touching the floor. Take a few breaths to center and bring your attention to this moment.
7. Picture a door in your mind. Open it and walk through it in your mind. What is on the other side of this change?
    ○ What is there?
    ○ What could be there?
    ○ Who is there?
    ○ What is possible in this change?
    ○ What is there for you in this new beginning?
8. Write down what you see, feel, and hear now that you're on the other side of the door. What is happening in your body? What mood or emotions are you experiencing? What are you saying to yourself about this change and new beginning? Write to completion; leave no details out.

Review your journal for key themes or insights about how you are processing this change and what will help you move to a new beginning. Bring this assignment to your next coaching session to review and discuss.

Template 4-26. Coping-Strategies Wheel Exercise

Purpose: Use this with a client who needs reminders about their calming and self-care tactics. Note that this creative process may not be a good fit for every client.

How to use: This is an optional activity to use in whole or in part. Adapt it to your client's culture and work style. Put it in your own words and brand it to your business. Help the client brainstorm tools they have for self-care or things they want more of in their life. Invite them to search online for inspiration. Assign this exercise for them to complete as homework before the next coaching session.

Think about all the calming and self-care tools you have at your disposal. Some examples include yoga, rest, hydration, getting outside, playing with your dog, calling a friend, mindfulness practice, adult coloring books, listening to music, measured breathing, or a favorite cup of tea.

1. What are your top eight skills or tools. What practices help fill up your cup? List them here:
   o
   o
   o
   o
   o
   o
   o
   o
2. Create a coping-strategies wheel using a paper plate or large paper circle divided into eight wedges. Write one skill or tool in each wedge. You can color it or use artwork of your own creation or from the internet to make it visually fun and interesting.
3. When you find yourself at your wits' end, spin the wheel and use the coping skill or tool that lands at the top.

Template 4-27. Using Strength in a New Way Exercise

Purpose: A practice for any client looking to expand their effectiveness through new uses of existing strengths, as well as any client struggling to remember their own capabilities. Building on strengths has been proven to develop higher levels of happiness and help lower levels of depression.

How to use: This is an optional activity to use in whole or in part. Adapt it to your client's culture and work style. Put it in your own words and brand it to your business. Walk through this exercise with your client, using one strength as an example. Help them identify new ways to express that strength and build a plan for showing it in new ways in the coming weeks. Invite them to complete this process for other strengths they have to continue expanding their expression of current strengths.

Identify your strengths by taking an assessment or through your own sense of your life and leading. Remember that a strength is something that is core to who you are, easy to use, and gives you energy.

1. Select one of your greatest strengths.
2. Consider a new way to express that strength each day. Identify up to three areas of your life that could benefit from it.
3. Express the strength in a new way each day for at least one week.
4. Record your experiences using the strength in a new way in your journal. What did it help create? What did you learn? Was it difficult or easy to use your strength in this way?

Before your next coaching session, review these journal entries for themes or broader insights.

Template 4-28. First 90 Days Agenda

Purpose: A helpful checklist for a client who has experienced a job change and needs to navigate and assimilate quickly into a new role or organization. This will help them learn the critical information they'll need to know to be successful in their new role.

How to use: This is an optional activity to use in whole or in part. Adapt it to your client's culture and work style. Put it in your own words and brand it to your business. Walk through this worksheet during a coaching session, then assign it as an exercise to complete before your next coaching session.

Questions to Ask

- ☐ Who are my stakeholders, and what are their agendas?
- ☐ Who are the formal and informal leaders? How do I bond and align with them?
- ☐ How do my boss and other stakeholders like to communicate?
- ☐ What are my key projects and goals within the first 30 to 90 days?
- ☐ How does my department support the other areas of the organization?
- ☐ How is my department positioned to contribute to the company's goals and strategy?
- ☐ What are my department's key successes?
- ☐ How does my role support my department's and organization's short- and long-term strategy?
- ☐ What will enable me to quickly demonstrate my value to the organization?
- ☐ Where are the biggest areas of ineffectiveness or the cultural pitfalls? What is my approach to them, in my department and in departments affecting mine?

Actions to Take

- ☐ Take the time to find out why things are done the way they are before you begin offering solutions for a complete overhaul.
- ☐ Review and start to test out business and department goals and objectives.
- ☐ Schedule standing meetings with key colleagues, with an identified personal strategy.
- ☐ Learn organization-wide processes and systems.
- ☐ Determine when to hold ongoing touch-base sessions with your direct and indirect managers.
- ☐ Actively seek feedback on processes and ways to contribute.

What I'll Know by the End of My First 90 Days

- ☐ Company and department strategy, mission, goals, and key initiatives
- ☐ The beginnings of your own department strategy, mission, goals, and key initiatives
- ☐ Funding or budget
- ☐ Whom you've met and how you'll interact with them
- ☐ How you'll add value
- ☐ Strategic priorities for your role
- ☐ Performance expectations, including how you and your team will be evaluated
- ☐ Short-term and long-term goals
- ☐ Your manager's assessment of your performance thus far

Template 4-29. Interview Questions for Meet-and-Greet Appointments

Purpose: A helpful guide for a client who is meeting colleagues, partners, and peers for the first time. This is a good supplement to Template 4-28.

How to use: This is an optional form to use in whole or in part. Adapt it to your client's culture and work style. Put it in your own words and brand it to your business. Walk through this interview template with your client during a coaching session and ask them to identify new colleagues, peers, partners, and even customers where it would be a useful framework for a discovery conversation. Help them put the template in their own words and build a plan to use it.

Use this as a starting point to plan your meet and greet interview questions.

The Basics
- What do you do for *<organization>*?
- When should I touch base with *<name>*?
- How do you like to communicate? (*For example email or phone to discuss issues in detail.*)
- If we were working together and you started having a problem, how would you like us to handle it? (*This is your chance to invite the interviewee to give you negative feedback directly, no matter how petty or small it seems.*)
- Can you share any dos and don'ts to working well with you? (*Think back to two people you have worked with in your career. One person worked with you in an incredibly productive manner. The other person pushed your buttons regularly.*)

Organizational Culture
- What is rewarded around here?
- Are there any written or unwritten rules I need to know about?
- What "puddles" could I accidentally step in?

Questions to Ask Key Clients
- What key challenges are you facing in your area in the coming year?
- What top-priority outputs will you need from my role or area in the coming year?
- Is there any history that I need to know about our areas to work well with you and your people?

Information About My Role
- Tell the person about yourself, including the key thrusts of your role and a few outputs you will produce in the first 18 to 24 months.
- Share a copy of your resume or CV and key contact info. (*Since peers and co-workers will likely have little knowledge of your background, this is one of the few times when it is socially acceptable to share your resume within your own organization.*)

Any other questions I didn't think to ask?

Template 4-30. Group Coaching Overview

Purpose: An overview of the pros, cons, and best practices of group coaching. This template outlines the many benefits of group coaching and helpful tips for preparation and facilitation.

How to use: This is an optional form to use in whole or in part. Adapt it to your client's culture and work style. Put it in your own words and brand it to your business. Review this when your client can benefit from some group facilitation or coaching with their team.

Many coaches prefer in-person group coaching. There are a few reasons for that, including the ability to better scale your time. When you coach a group of people at once, you spend much less time preparing for the session, and much less time conducting the sessions, because rather than conducting a dozen one-hour sessions per week or month, you are conducting a single two-hour session.

What Is In-Person Group Coaching?

Group coaching is when everyone comes together to meet at the same time. It's generally used by coaches who are working with one specific challenge so group members are better able to support one another. For example, fitness studios and alcohol and drug treatment centers use group therapy in addition to face-to-face meetings. Group coaching is also quite useful in treating mental health conditions.

Generalized life coaching is less suited to group coaching because everyone has such different issues. This makes it more difficult for the coach to give advice and support, and group members will have a harder time supporting one another effectively if they aren't focused on the same thing.

Advantages of Group Coaching

- The major advantage to coaching in a group setting is that you are setting up a support system that extends far past yourself. If everyone is working toward the same goal, then they will be supporting one another at the same time that they are working for themselves.
- Another advantage with group coaching is that you only have to prepare once. Rather than preparing for an individual session every time you meet with a client, you'll only need to prepare for the group session.
- Maximizing your time is also a major benefit. For example, consider a coach that spends 30 minutes with 15 clients per week. That's 7.5 hours just being in session (not to mention extra time spent preparing for the session, traveling, waiting for clients if they are late, or facilitating sessions that run long). Compare that with 15 clients in a two-hour group session each week.
- You'll also be able to offer clients a lower fee, but make more money overall. That's because you'll get more clients at a lower price and still be able to help them, because it is in a group setting. For example: If five one-on-one clients are paying $200/week, you'll make $1,000; if 15 group coaching clients are paying $100/week, you'll make $1,500. That's a pretty significant difference.
- Group coaching participants will gain something from the group that they'd likely never have gotten in a one-on-one session: advice and encouragement from people who are walking the same path. They will also benefit from hearing the advice and guidance you give others, and thus grow exponentially faster.

Disadvantages of In-Person Group Coaching

- The biggest disadvantage of being in a group setting is that you don't have one-on-one time with a client, and therefore may not be able to get to the same level of communication as in a private in-person session, depending on your niche. You might not be able to build a very close relationship, which could be just what they need. A group setting is definitely more anonymous and makes it harder to get to know people.
- You'll also lose clients who are not comfortable in a group session or really need privacy in their coaching session. Sometimes you will have clients who are embarrassed about whatever life problem they are trying to overcome and are not able to do group coaching.
- You'll have to charge less for group mentoring than you would for personal sessions. While you're probably going to make more money overall, you might not, and you may have trouble charging your one-on-one rate in the future if people know group sessions cost less.

How to Set Up In-Person Group Coaching

1. Decide which part of your expertise you are going to coach people on. Choose a specific topic like prepping to run a marathon, success at work, or improving confidence. You can run different groups if you want to expand into other topics.
2. Make sure you do introductions. Your group members are going to be a source of support and encouragement for one another, so take some time, perhaps even an entire session, to allow them to get to know one another. This will not only help them learn from one another, but also make people less likely to leave the group halfway through. Start with asking each group member to say their name and what they want to get from the group. Write this down.
3. Make sure that everyone in the group has the chance to speak. Some people are going to be very talkative and outgoing, and others are going to be quite shy. Make sure that you are calling on the shy ones to ensure they get to benefit from the group session as well.
4. Be aware that it will take time before the group begins to trust you as their mentor and begins to trust one another. This will probably mean a few uncomfortable sessions at first, but eventually there will be a more comfortable atmosphere in which people feel OK sharing their successes and failures.
5. Make sure you have rules and everyone knows what they are. Set rules about showing up on time, confidentiality, boundaries, and how to respond after someone has shared (and when), and anything else you think is appropriate.
6. If someone has an issue that isn't for group sharing, you can meet with them privately for a few minutes and offer options for private sessions. It is too difficult to deal with issues like these in a group setting.
7. Make sure to follow up with your clients a few weeks after the sessions have ended. Think of something personal about each of them, such as whether they have children, and mention it. Not only will this motivate you, because you'll see that your coaching actually helped them; they will appreciate the follow-up and will be much more inclined to do a future coaching session or recommend you to their friends.

Remember your role in the group setting. You are there to listen to the people in the group, reflect their statements back to them in a way that is easy for them to understand, and advise them on finding solutions to their problems, while also holding everyone accountable for reaching their goals.

Template 4-31. Team Assessment Questionnaire

Purpose: An assessment of team health and trust that can be used in team coaching and facilitation.

How to use: This is an optional form to use in whole or in part. Adapt it to your client's culture and work style. Put it in your own words and brand it to your business. You can use this to assess a team during your interactions or give it to the team to complete as prework before or during a workshop. The combined assessment can be insightful and illuminate gaps and opportunities for the team. You could also use it in an individual coaching session for a leader to assess their team's trust level and build an action plan.

In his book *The Five Dysfunctions of a Team*, Patrick Lencioni identifies five dysfunctions of a team: absence of trust, fear of conflict, lack of commitment, avoidance of accountability, and inattention to results. This assessment is designed to assess a team's health based on these five dysfunctions.

Rate each statement using a three-point scale (where 3 = as a general rule, 2 = occasionally, and 1 = infrequently). Then use the scoring rubric to determine your score.

Statement	Rating		
	1	2	3
1. Team members are passionate and unguarded in their discussion of issues.			
2. Team members call out one another's deficiencies or unproductive behaviors.			
3. Team members know what their peers are working on and how they contribute to the collective good of the team.			
4. Team members quickly and genuinely apologize to one another when they say or do something inappropriate or damaging to the team.			
5. Team members willingly make sacrifices (such as in budget, turf, or head count) in their departments or areas of expertise for the good of the team.			
6. Team members openly admit their weaknesses and mistakes.			
7. Team meetings are compelling, not boring.			
8. Team members leave meetings confident that their peers are completely committed to the decisions that were agreed on, even if there was initial disagreement.			
9. Morale is significantly affected by the failure to achieve team goals.			
10. During team meetings, the most important—and difficult—issues are put on the table to be resolved.			
11. Team members are deeply concerned about the prospect of letting down their peers.			
12. Team members know about one another's personal lives and are comfortable discussing them.			
13. Team members end discussions with clear and specific resolutions and calls to action.			
14. Team members challenge one another on their plans and approaches.			
15. Team members are slow to seek credit for their own contributions, but quick to point out those of others.			

Adapted from Lencioni (2002).

Scoring

Use this table to combine your ratings and calculate a score for each of the five dysfunctions.

Dysfunction 1: Absence of Trust	Dysfunction 2: Fear of Conflict	Dysfunction 3: Lack of Commitment	Dysfunction 4: Avoidance of Accountability	Dysfunction 5: Inattention to Results
#4_____	#1_____	#3_____	#2_____	#5_____
#6_____	#7_____	#8_____	#11 _____	#9_____
#12 _____	#10 _____	#13 _____	#14 _____	#15 _____
Total: _____	Total: _____	Total: _____	Total: _____	Total: _____

Point Total

- 8 or 9 points: This dysfunction is not a problem for the team.
- 6 or 7 points: This dysfunction could be a problem for the team.
- 3 to 5 points: This dysfunction needs to be addressed.

Regardless of your scores, it is important to keep in mind that every team needs constant work, because without it, even the best ones can deviate toward dysfunction.

List two ways you can enhance your team's effectiveness based on these results:

1. _____

_____

_____

2. _____

_____

_____

Template 4-32. Icebreaker Activities

Purpose: Several easy-to-implement icebreaker activities for use in a group setting. A good icebreaker brings people into the room and helps them shift focus from whatever they just left so they can be fully present with the team. They'll help participants center on a shared activity and give them a sense of what the workshop will entail.

How to use: These are optional activities to use in whole or in part. Adapt them to your client's culture and work style. Put them in your own words and brand them to your business. When you are working with a group, it's helpful to choose an icebreaker activity that, well, breaks the ice. Find activities that fit you and your brand of facilitation

Two Truths and a Lie

Each participant offers three statements about themselves: two that are true and one that is a lie. The group needs to identify which one is not true. This usually results in some fun sharing and storytelling.

For example, one female participant in a group offered:
- I worked for the San Francisco 49ers.
- I've traveled to 15 countries.
- I am a yoga instructor.

You can see that these are three interesting statements and create great openings for a shared story or experience (sports, travel, yoga). This person had been to only 10 countries in their travels, so that was the lie.

My Favorite Food Growing Up

This activity invites people to share something safe from their childhood: a favorite food or treat. This simple sharing can reveal great insights about a family structure, a culture, parental roles, and sibling memories. It's a simple activity that can create some great openings for further connection and community within the team. One team I worked with took this to the next level and hosted a potluck of their favorite foods for the next team gathering.

My Dream Job

Sharing a dream can be vulnerable for people. Offer this for teams that are working on their strengths or starting a project together. This helps reveal what someone really cares about, what they are good at, and where they want to contribute their talents. This can be a powerful way to align work with strengths, positioning each person to contribute their absolute best to the work at hand.

Lunch With a Famous Person, Dead or Alive

This activity is a fun way to understand what is important to each group member. Often you will learn that someone is interested in art, travel, history, or other topics from which to build further relationships. Sometimes a participant will describe a desire to have lunch with a parent or family member who is no longer with us as their famous person, offering a chance to build trust and support within the team.

A Few of My Favorite Things

This is a great way to get to know some interesting new things about the people on the team.

Provide a list of no more than five prompts; for example:

- My favorite song or band
- My favorite food
- My favorite book
- My favorite magazine
- My favorite vacation (taken or planned)
- My favorite movie
- My favorite hobby
- My favorite guilty pleasure (keep it PG)

After each person writes down their answers on an index card or piece of paper, tell everyone to fold their paper and put it in a bag or hat. Then each member of the group picks a paper and takes turns reading the favorite things while the rest of the group tries to guess the person.

Template 4-33. Team Charter Template

Purpose: A template to help the team develop a vision, values, and processes for team effectiveness.

How to use: This is an optional form to use in whole or in part. Adapt it to your client's culture and work style. Put it in your own words and brand it to your business. Use this as a framework when working with teams or to facilitate important conversations about the foundations of team effectiveness.

Document your team's answers and update them as necessary.

Vision and Values
- What is the purpose of this team? Why does it exist? Why is it worth investing this time and effort?
- What shared values are needed to guide how we approach our work and how we work with one another?
- What would we see that would indicate we have been successful?

Team Processes
- How will we organize to accomplish the work? What is the best structure? What roles are needed?
- What planning and problem-solving process are we going to use?
- How will we make decisions?

Goals
- What are the deliverables?
- How will we measure success?
- What are the timeframes?

Communication and Coordination
- What information needs to be shared?
- When will we meet, how frequently, where, and so on?
- How will we keep up to date on the team's progress? How will we communicate between meetings? How often?

Authority and Accountability
- To whom is the team accountable?
- What is the team's decision-making authority? Do any decisions require outside approval? If so, how will approval be obtained?
- Which decisions can be made by subgroups, and which need to be made by the whole team?
- How will we track and report progress on commitments and action items?

Individual Communication Styles
- Complete, compare, and discuss <*DiSC or another profile*>.

Template 4-34. Feedback Survey for Team Retreat

Purpose: A starting place to create a thoughtful evaluation to distribute to participants of any team retreat you facilitate.

How to use: This is an optional form to use in whole or in part. Adapt it to your client's culture and work style. Put it in your own words and brand it to your business. Update the questions to reflect the key components of the retreat to gather feedback from each participant. Be sure to include the sponsor's goals for the retreat so the team can provide input on those as well.

Using a five-point scale, please rate the event
(1 = very dissatisfied and 5 = very satisfied).

		Rating				
1.	Please rate the concepts covered at this retreat	1	2	3	4	5
2.	Please rate the presenters	1	2	3	4	5
3.	Please rate the activities	1	2	3	4	5
4.	Please rate the facilitator	1	2	3	4	5
5.	Please rate your enjoyment of the event	1	2	3	4	5
6.	Please rate the environment (e.g., room, temperature, food)	1	2	3	4	5
7.	Please rate your level of learning	1	2	3	4	5
8.	What would you do differently, now that you have participated in the retreat?					
9.	What were your most significant insights?					
10.	How could this event be improved?					
11.	What related events would be helpful?					
12.	Do you have any final comments?					

Thank you for your feedback!!

Name (optional): _____

Template 5-1. Email Invitation to Second 360 Interviewees

Purpose: A suggested email to use for reconnecting with the client's 360 interviewees and initiating a second interview.

How to use: This is an optional email template to use in whole or in part. Adapt it to your client's culture and work style. Put it in your own words and brand it to your business. Use this email template to initiate a second 360 with your interviewees.

Hello <*name*>,

Thank you for your input on <*client name*>'s coaching program. We are nearing completion of the program, and I wanted to check back in with you to see what you've noticed.

Please select three of the dates and times below that can work for you. If you have an administrative assistant whom you'd prefer I work with, please copy them into this email thread so we can get this meeting booked.

<*Insert several dates and one-hour blocks of time that are available in your calendar. Provide up to twice the number of slots you will book. For example, if you have five people to interview, offer 10 slots, and ask the interviewee to pick three. That way, if anyone chooses the same slot you have back-up options and can minimize the number of back-and-forth emails required to book the time.*>

I look forward to seeing you again and learning what shifts you have seen <*client*> making. As a reminder, your input will be anonymized and confidential. We will talk more about how it will be used when we meet. Please reach out if you have any questions or concerns in the meantime.

Sincerely,
<*Your name*>

Template 5-2. Second 360 Interview Meeting Invitation and Agenda

Purpose: A suggested meeting invitation and agenda for the second 360 interview to set the meeting date and time, as well as to communicate the interview's structure.

How to use: This is an optional email template to use in whole or in part. Adapt it to your client's culture and work style. Put it in your own words and brand it to your business. Send this with the calendar invitation and include the video-conference link, meeting location, or telephone instructions, as appropriate. If the interviewee prefers to book their own meetings on their calendar, you can send this as an email confirming the time and logistics.

Hello <*name*>,

In advance of our meeting, please find the agenda below.

Agenda

5 min.	Reconnect and review the purpose of this conversation
30 min.	Your feedback: • What shifts you have seen them make relative to your initial input on strengths, areas for improvement or growth, and highest leverage actions to take to improve the team, organization overall, or company? • What areas remain as opportunities for continued growth and development?
5 min.	Questions and clarifications
5 min.	Next steps, thank you, and close

We are nearing the end of the coaching program, and this is the time to review what changes, if any, you have observed in <*client name*>. Thank you for your candid input in support of your colleague's growth as a leader.

To recap our agreement on confidentiality: All input is anonymized and confidential. The feedback is reviewed in summary, without attribution, to provide <*client*> with specific feedback on where shifts have happened and what work remains to become even more effective as a leader.

Sincerely,
<*Your name*>

Template 5-3. Second 360 Notes Form

Purpose: A note-taking form to capture feedback from the 360 inputs during the second interview.

How to use: This is an optional form to use in whole or in part. Adapt it to your client's culture and work style. Put it in your own words and brand it to your business. Use it to take notes during the interview, and remember to mix up the columns and rows to anonymize the feedback per your agreement with 360 interviewees.

	What positive shifts or improvements have you seen relative to your initial input?	What areas for growth or development remain that should be built into their leadership IDP?	Do you have any helpful comments for this person to hear related to the coaching program?
Coaching client			N/A
Interview 1 / role			
Interview 2 / role			
Interview 3 / role			
Interview 4 / role			
Interview 5 / role			
Interview 6 / role			

Template 5-4. Post-Coaching Results Example

Purpose: This is an example of how you could summarize the post-coaching feedback and results. In keeping with the confidentiality commitment, these results are the client's to share with their leader, teams, or colleagues.

How to use: This is an optional form to use in whole or in part. Adapt it to your client's culture and work style. Put it in your own words and brand it to your business. Use this template to synthesize the post-coaching 360 input from your client's interviewees. List the competencies the client focused on at the top and summarize the feedback for your client to review and build into their ongoing development.

	Understand what Suneel and team do	Mentoring of team	Less intense or more approachable	Not interjecting unsolicited advice	More sharing credit for progress	More ownership in shared projects	Effective
Competency	Business acumen	Building strong teams	Executive presence	Political savvy and interpersonal skills	Humility and continuous improvement	Accountability	Quality work
Direct Report	Yes	Yes	Little	Yes	Yes	Yes	Yes High detail, service, and standards
Direct Report	Yes	Yes Cares and develops us	Yes Wasn't an issue before	Yes He still researches beforehand— very informed	Yes Shares with our clients and with his team	Yes	Yes Dashboard, internet site, project list per pillars and strategic goals
Direct Report	Yes	Yes Includes and helps me	Yes Always been approachable	Yes Never an issue	Yes	Yes	Yes Perfect work
Manager	Yes	Yes	Yes	Yes	Yes	Yes	Yes High quality, high capacity
Team	Little	Yes Obvious shadowing and helping	Yes Very much	Yes	Yes	Yes	Yes Always was before
Team	Yes	Don't know	Yes	N/A	Yes	N/A	N/A
Team	Yes	Yes	Yes	Yes	Yes	Yes	Yes Always was before
Other	Don't know	Yes	Yes Always was well directed and appropriate	N/A	Yes	Yes	Yes Always was before
Other	Little	Little	Yes Very much	Yes Very much	Don't know	Yes	Yes Gemba time?
Other	Don't know	Don't know	Don't know	Little	Don't know	Don't know	Don't know

What else did you notice?

- Suneel seems to be a lot more humble. I knew he wanted the best for the organization, but somehow it used to come off all wrong. However, now he is clearly humble, eager, and happy to be here. A very dramatic change occurred in Suneel.
- Wow, lots of things. Some small, some big. He now includes me in his communications and other things, so I feel included and considered. Now he says, "It is our observation" or "In my experience." He always managed the projects very well, but now we see it more and appreciate it more.
- Some other people need coaching.
- Still happy to work with Suneel and his team. Great resource, and he was so great to work on his part from what I can see. Even when things are teed up to take a shot, he doesn't and is gracious. Carry on! Good work. Perhaps others could benefit from this kind of thing too.
- He is so happy and helpful. His team seems to enjoy working with him—not like they are waiting to go into the principal's office. Instead they look forward to it, and I hear them discussing it.
- I am pleasantly surprised by his sense of humor now. Who knew?
- Suneel is a powerful leader. There is a lot that people don't realize in terms of his projects, and how he is developing the function and his team members. I noticed that he is starting to be asked and share what he and his team are doing, and it is all excellent work and vital to the business.
- Partners more. Clarifies more; helps and intervenes politely when needed. Biggest change is intensity. When you get to know him, he is really down to earth and not stuck up at all. Now everybody can see that, now that he is showing his real side more.
- He cares. He doesn't give up.
- Better scope and more role definition. No conflict anymore. More ownership and relationship building. Shows more caring when looped in, and looped back when something didn't go as planned.

What else might Suneel consider working on?

- Closer relationship with one person (but can the other person change?)
- Being nit-picky here . . . don't go overboard now and over-promote others.
- This is not in his direct control, but others need to move on too—just like he has—and let the past be in the past. Our team is not cohesive in other ways. Other teams and organizations have retreats, and planning and social time together. We have proposed this before.
- What is being done to retain him to get a career path for him. I hope he doesn't leave us as he continues to grow.
- Maybe Suneel can present at the directors' department meeting and the CLC. Present his team and his projects—and have a waiting list if the presentations create more demand than can be handled.

Template 5-5. Final Meeting Agenda With Sponsor or Direct Leader

Purpose: An agenda for the final meeting with your client's direct manager, sponsor, or program manager—the person who initiated coaching, if not your client. This agenda allows you to maximize time with the leader while continuing to build a relationship and increase your understanding of your client.

How to use: This optional agenda should be updated based on the culture and work style of the person you are meeting with. Send the agenda as an email or calendar invitation, depending on the arrangement you made with the sponsor in the initial meeting. Be sure to include your client in all conversations related to the specifics of their development. You may want to attach Template 1-1 as a reminder of the coaching process.

Final Sponsor Meeting Agenda

5 min.	Salutations and reconnection
3 min.	Purpose of this meeting and desired outcomes from our conversation
5 min.	Review four steps of coaching program, noting where it currently sits in the overall phases
20 min.	Discuss feedback on *<client>*'s progress: • What shifts do you see in this person relative to your initial feedback and goals for coaching? • What are remaining areas for growth or development? • How will you support this person in their ongoing development needs? *(If talking with a direct manager)*
5 min.	Questions, concerns, and other topics to cover
2 min.	Close and next steps

Attachment: Overview of the Coaching Process

Template 5-6. Agenda for Final Coaching Conversation

Purpose: An agenda for your final coaching session to ensure you cover all the important topics required for a healthy ending. Caring for this ending with great intention is essential. You have been on a lengthy and vulnerable journey with your client. This is where you bring all this work to a healthy and positive conclusion.

How to use: This optional agenda should be updated based on the culture and work style of the person you are meeting with. Send this agenda out in advance so your client can come with their input.

Final Coaching Conversation Agenda

3 min.	Purpose of this final coaching session
5 min.	Reflect on the entire journey, from initiation through the four phases to this point
20 min.	*<Client>* shares important moments from this experience: • What stands out for you in this overall journey? • What is one key thing you are taking away from this coaching engagement? • Where do you see opportunities for continued development or growth? • How will you support yourself with the practices, exercises, and experiments you have engaged throughout coaching?
20 min.	Share the second 360 inputs (if you haven't already)
10 min.	Coach's thoughts and feedback
2 min.	Three things gratitude exercise and close

Template 6-1. Are You Built to Be an Executive Coach?

Purpose: A self-assessment to help you evaluate your readiness for entrepreneurship. Use your answers to build a development plan and strengthen your resolve.

How to use: Take this assessment during the early stage of exploring entrepreneurship to evaluate your strengths and where you should focus in terms of developing your entrepreneurial skill set.

As you take serious steps toward becoming a business owner, it's helpful to have some insight into your strengths as an entrepreneur and areas you may need to pay special attention to in order to become or remain successful.

Be brutally honest with yourself when rating each of these assessment questions. Use a five-point scale (where 1= none or low; 3 = some or mixed; and 5 = extensive or high). Then total your results and interpret them.

Questions	Rating (1–5)
1. How many years have you been an executive or a leader in the area where you want to coach others?	
2. What is your training, education, or experience in human psychology or motivation?	
3. Are you able to apply and articulate a clear coaching method?	
4. What is your level of self-discipline and organization?	
5. What is your level of self-motivation?	
6. How skilled are you to have difficult conversations with clients, even if it means risking the relationship at times?	
7. What is your level of capability in administrative tasks to set up and run the business?	
8. Do you have skills in business development and sales?	
9. Are you able to apply strong marketing skills to promote your services?	
10. Do you have strong financial skills, both in forecasting budgets and in managing the day-to-day operations of a business?	
Total	

Interpret Your Results
- **0–20 points:** You may not be ready to be an entrepreneur. Examine where you scored low (1 or 2) and build your skills in these areas. Build your own IDP to help you grow in the areas more critical to setting up and running your business.
- **21–30 points:** You have some strengths to build upon and other areas to further develop before you're fully ready. Examine the areas where you scored lower and determine if this is something you can quickly develop. Consider the option to outsource this area as you're getting started, and build that into your budget and plan.
- **31–50 points:** You are on your way! You already have several strengths as an entrepreneur. Consider shoring up your skills in any areas that aren't as strong in the early months of entrepreneurship.

Template 6-2. Weekly Planner

Purpose: A template to help you make progress toward your top priorities and wellness throughout the week.

How to use: Use this worksheet to set your focus for your top goals each week and maintain a connection and commitment to your own self-care.

Weekly planner for the week of: _____

Top Five Goals This Week	Quick Hits or Tasks
1.	•
2.	•
3.	•
4.	•
5.	•

	Monday	Tuesday	Wednesday	Thursday	Friday	Saturday	Sunday
My wellness goals:							
Tracker:	☺☻☹	☺☻☹	☺☻☹	☺☻☹	☺☻☹	☺☻☹	☺☻☹

Pick list: meditation, journaling, reading, yoga, Qigong, cardio walk, weights

Reminders for next week:

Template 6-3. Time Management Worksheet

Purpose: A worksheet to help you evaluate where you spend your time in the main buckets of entrepreneurial work.

How to use: Use this template to track your time for two weeks. How many hours are you spending in each category? Compare that against the ideal for the phase your business is in and make any necessary adjustments.

Do the Work
- Coach
- Consult
- Continuous development
- Collaborate

Business Operations
- Budget
- Invoicing
- IT
- Goal setting

Build the Pipeline
- Client meetings
- Proposals
- Networking
- Follow-ups

Do the Work	Business Operations	Build the Pipeline

Early-Stage Business Building		
20%	30–40%	40–50%

Thriving Business		
70–80%	10%	10–20%

Template 7-1. Business Feasibility Worksheet

Purpose: A method to fill out your vision for your business—what makes you unique in the market and how you can be a viable operation—through inquiry and reflection.

How to use: Use this template to help you think through the definition of your business.

Early in the ideation of your business, it's helpful to take a step back to test the logic of your thinking and the feasibility of the business you are mapping out. Use this worksheet to determine whether your business idea is feasible according to these two phases of business creation: Does my idea make sense? Is my idea feasible?

Phase 1: Does My Business Idea Make Sense?

Write out your ideas for your service offering. Do your coaching service ideas make sense? Most of your original ideas will be sharpened in this phase of evaluation.

- Do I intend to:
  - Serve a new or underserved market?
  - Provide a new product or service?
  - Offer a better value compared with competitive solutions?
- Do I differentiate myself by offering:
  - A more elegant approach?
  - Better performance?
  - Greater convenience?
  - Greater value?
  - Easier access?
  - Better customer service?
- Do I have the resources necessary to be excellent in my service offering?
  - Do I have the necessary technology and equipment?
  - Where will I operate my business?
  - Do I have the required expertise?
  - Will clients need to access my business location? Or can I do all my coaching off-site with my clients?
- There is always competition. Do I know who or what that is?
  - How and where can I compete?
  - How do I compare myself with the competition where it's relevant?
  - What would be the most important distinction between me and my competition in the minds of my customers?
- Can I define who my customers are?
  - Who are my executives?
  - Who are my customers other than end clients? Sponsors? Any other stakeholders?
  - Is there anyone else who would buy or sell my service?

Phase 2: Is My Idea Feasible?

Once you have honed your service offerings through these basic pressure tests, take another step back to assess the feasibility of your idea. In this phase, you'll research the industry; products, services, and competition; markets and customers; and financial questions. You'll use this research to inform your business plan as you look for ways to improve your value, conduct your business, begin forecasting sales, figure out costs, and so on.

Primary Research

Talk to other business owners! Speak with potential customers.

Secondary Research

Consult your library's business section and review information from trade associations, suppliers, small business associations, and so on.

- Industry:
  - How is business conducted in this industry?
  - Am I able to participate?
  - Do I have a network that will support me in building my client base?
- Products, services, and competition:
  - What solutions are already available?
  - Who provides solutions, and what's done well or poorly?
  - Where can I compete?
  - Where am I unable to compete?
- Markets and customers:
  - What is the size and segment of each potential market?
  - Where are they located?
  - What are their demographics?
  - What are their psychographics?
  - How do I reach them?
- How can I price my service to ensure a profit?
  - Think Economics 101: marginal revenue, earning power, and so forth.
  - What will be the perceptions of quality, value, and so on?
  - What is my break-even point and scalability?
- What are my capital requirements?
  - Startup capital
  - Capital to sustain me through negative cash flow.
- Sales and cost estimates (units and money)
  - Estimate sales and cost estimates for the first three years
  - When will sales revenue "consistently" exceed costs?

Template 7-2. Dr. Nadine's Suite of Services

Purpose: An example of how to define your work to potential clients. Perhaps your long-term vision is to do more than coaching. This gives you a way to think about that progression of services.

How to use: Use this template as inspiration for how to define your suite of services. You'll include this information in your website copy, promotional materials, building your business plan, or coaching bio.

Executive Coaching

Using a four-step process, Dr. Nadine provides executive coaching to VP, C-level, and board clients to develop and reach leadership and organizational goals and to build on key leadership competencies.

The Four-Step Executive Coaching Process

1. Assessment
   - Self-assessment
   - Surveys and profiles (including MBTI, Strong Career, FIRO-B, TKI, and 16PF)
   - 360 feedback
   - Other sources
2. Goal setting
   - Individual development plan
   - Areas of opportunity
   - Obstacles and challenges
3. Implementation
   - One-on-one coaching sessions
   - Homework and practice
   - Experimentation
4. Feedback
   - Review and wrap-up
   - Follow-up 360 feedback
   - Review and recommend
   - Close and monitor

The Relationship

The coach-client relationship is integral to the success of the Dr. Nadine executive coaching program, so you can count on her to demonstrate customer focus, patience, commitment, integrity, perspective, and humor.

Confidentiality and Discretion

Everything we discuss is confidential.

Unique and challenging situations are welcome.

Team Coaching and Retreats

Team coaching and retreats are most effective when colleagues are engaged in the process. The Dr. Nadine method ensures engagement by using preplanning processes for coaching and retreat agendas. This strengthens the effectiveness because participants can help shape the agenda.

Dr. Nadine will:
- Use formats for preplanning, which may include surveys, interviews, consultation, preparation, and expectations management.
- Review notes with key stakeholders.
- Work with leaders to build an agenda that maximizes targeted results and engagement.
- Facilitate team coaching and retreat, as well as provide follow-up notes and action items.

Executive Coaching Program Design and Implementation

Dr. Nadine creates in-house executive coaching programs that strengthen participants' leadership and enhance both the bench strength and the culture of the organization.

These services consist of:
- Building and running coaching programs that support leadership academies, talent review, succession planning, and leadership and management training.
- Training and supervision programs to enhance coach effectiveness.

Career Coaching

Dr. Nadine works with clients to determine what careers they were built for and to devise a plan and support to get there. This includes administering profiles to assess their areas of passion, skills, work values, interests, interpersonal needs, and areas of motivation. Uncompromising in her commitment to supporting her clients to achieve career success, whether in existing roles or in new challenges, Dr. Nadine has a very high success rate.

Dr. Nadine also assists clients to further develop each client's career management skills, personal leadership, and opportunity awareness. The approach includes:
- An in-depth personality and career review, including profile administration and analysis and identification of key jobs and professional fields that match the client's passions, skills, and values.
- Identifying key skills gaps that might be barriers to entry into the target job or profession.
- Providing career strategy development and planning.
- Assisting with resume, personal brand, online image, marketing, and interview preparation and practice—this is the famous Red Chevy method!
- Helping with the negotiation process once an offer is made.

Template 7-3. ROI of Coaching Worksheet

Purpose: A guide to help you think through the financial benefits you have to offer a client or company based on four ROI measures.

How to use: This is an optional form to use in whole or in part. Put it in your own words and brand it to your business. Review the material in this book and in this template to fully understand the four measures of ROI that are important for executive coaches to communicate. The results of your self-assessment indicate areas to continue to develop as an executive coach.

The table shows what organizations want from coaching. How do you measure, from poor to excellent, in each of the four categories?

	Poor	Good	Excellent	Comments
Employee life cycle				
Money				
Competencies				
You				

1. ROI by Employee Life Cycle

This is the life cycle of an employee, from onboarding (step 1) to offboarding (step 9). The value of coaching varies based on when the coach is engaged.

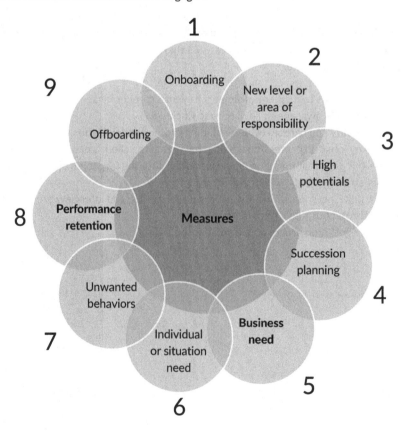

2. Money: The Cost of Not Hiring an Executive Coach

A top-performing account executive at a large technology firm had recently been promoted to vice president of sales for the North American division. The executive had consistently exceeded his sales quota by 200 percent and had landed key marquee Fortune 500 customers in his previous role. However, he was underperforming in his new position. His direct reports were struggling to hit their individual quotas, the overall team morale had declined sharply, and engagement levels were plummeting.

Consequently, the CEO was considering replacing him. As a last attempt to rectify the situation, the CEO urged the VP to partake in executive coaching, to which he grudgingly agreed. After four months of twice-weekly intensive coaching sessions (at a total cost of $30,000), his performance increased markedly. Team members felt a much clearer sense of purpose. The VP had learned to be less prescriptive in his directions, affording team members a greater sense of authority and the ability to foster more genuine and authentic relationships with customers. After reviewing recent 360 assessments and performance metrics, the CEO was confident that a replacement would no longer be needed.

You can calculate the ROI of executive coaching using the formula:

$$\%ROI = \frac{(\text{Benefits Achieved} - \text{Executive Coaching Costs})}{\text{Executive Coaching Costs}} \times 100$$

Calculate the benefits achieved by determining the costs incurred as a result of failing to hire an executive coach:

Purpose	Calculation	Cost
Cost of an external executive search agency	25% of $177,000 (annual compensation rate)	$44,250
Costs assumed by the internal recruiting team	50 hours in aggregate among five team members at $60/hour (annual rate)	$3,000
Opportunity costs assumed by internal C-suite stakeholders as a result of participating in candidate debrief meetings	40 hours in aggregate among eight team members at $200/hour (annual rate)	$8,000
Lost two-year productivity as a result of external (versus internal) hire	25% productivity loss over two years at $177,000 (annual compensation rate)	$88,500
Lost productivity during four-month search process as a result of underperforming VP	0.33 (4/12 months) at $150,000 (annual compensation rate) multiplied by a 50% productivity loss	$25,000
Additional salary required to hire external candidate (18% over two years)	$150,000 (VP annual compensation rate) multiplied by 0.18 over two years	$54,000
	Total	$311,250

Considering only these costs, the organization has achieved an ROI of 938 percent:

$$938\% \text{ ROI} = \frac{(\$311,250 - \$30,000)}{\$30,000} \times 100$$

This analysis only scratches the surface because it does not include other tangible and intangible benefits associated with coaching, including avoiding productivity loss among direct reports, increased rates of turnover, and strained customer relations.

The Society for Human Resource Management (SHRM) reported that it costs a company, on average, six to nine months of an employee's salary to replace them. For an employee making $60,000 per year, that comes out to $30,000 to $45,000 in recruiting and training costs.

3. Competencies

There's nothing like cold, hard numbers to drive home the impact of executive coaching. To effectively calculate the ROI associated with investments in executive coaching, it's important to clearly outline its the objectives. The following table delineates the top 10 competencies of C-level leaders that executive coaching can address. Identify the highest-priority objectives, determine the associated costs, and assign a monetary value to each.

Competency	Negative Impact	Positive Impact to Executive and Employees	Positive Impact to Business
Self-awareness	Distorted sense of self	Increased awareness of blind spots, enhanced leadership abilities	Increased ability to meet objectives, increased business performance
Interpersonal relationships, listening skills, and empathy	Inability to build and foster a collaborative work environment	Improved relationships with leadership, co-workers, and stakeholders	Increased employee satisfaction, increased retention rates
Influence	Inability to effect positive change	Increased levels of motivation, inspiration	Increased business performance
Leading during times of change	Lack of adaptability in times of transition, "change fatigue"	Increased sense of involvement, decreased sense of uncertainty	Increased competitive positioning, increased global positioning, increased financial performance
Communication skills	Confusion, unclear direction	Increased business transparency, reduced conflict	Improved brand image, improved internal and external communication
Motivation and engagement, leading with vision and purpose	Low levels of productivity	Increased felt responsibility, increased engagement levels, increased sense of purpose	Increased productivity
Building effective teams	Misaligned strategy, missed deadlines	Increased opportunities for career advancement, improved workplace culture	Improved product or service quality, shorter time to market

Competency	Negative Impact	Positive Impact to Executive and Employees	Positive Impact to Business
Strategy and strategic thinking	Short-term focus, inconsistent business results	Increased sense of pride	Enhanced long-term planning efforts, more consistent ability to deliver business results that meet or exceed forecasts
Working with uncertainty and ambiguity, decision skills	Low levels of engagement	Decreased levels of absenteeism, decreased stress levels, improved workplace culture	Improved innovation processes, improved risk management
Mentoring relationships, listening skills, empathy	Lack of leadership development opportunities, strained internal and external relations	Increased opportunities for personal and professional growth	Increased customer loyalty, increased customer service, improved diversity and inclusion efforts

4. You

Lastly, how do you offer return on investment as a coach? How are your capabilities across all these metrics of influencing, industry knowledge, and customer service?

- Influencing skills:
    - Research in influencing: The relationship is the only reliable predictor.
    - Do you share success? Do you refer to coaching only for resources?
- The message is the messenger:
    - Are you credible? What is your political and social capital?
    - Do you understand the business?
    - Do you understand the motivations and priorities of the approver?
    - Are you negotiating with the decision maker?
    - Are you using L&D, OD, and HR lingo?
    - Are you a great leader yourself, and how is your team?
    - Do you have an executive coach? What's your story?
- Are you trying to "sell":
    - Do you think you are right (and they are wrong)?
    - Are you providing decision support?
    - Are you trying to remove obstacles and solve problems?

Template 7-4. Business and Personal Budget Worksheet

Purpose: A worksheet to help you determine how much money you'd need to earn to satisfy your personal budget.

How to use: Review the income and expenses categories, as well as the savings tracker. Update the template with your own information to manage the profit and loss (P&L) of your business. Be sure to keep it up to date to reflect your total expenses. Note that business expenses should be tracked separately and paid for by the business.

% of Income Spent	Summary
44% 56%	Total Monthly Income $15,250
	Total Monthly Expenses $6,775
	Total Monthly Savings $550
	Cash Balance $7,925

Monthly Income	
Item	**Amount**
Income source 1	$7,000.00
Income source 2	$8,000.00
Other	$250.00

Monthly Personal and Business Expenses	
Item	**Amount**
Rent/mortgage	$2,800.00
Electric, gas	$320.00
Car payment	$120.00
Cell phone	$45.00
Groceries	$2,000.00
Business subscriptions (billing, accounting)	$600.00
Business insurance	$250.00
Licenses, certifications	$100.00
Marketing, website	$120.00
Entertainment, meals	$220.00
Miscellaneous	$200.00

Monthly Savings	
Date	**Amount**
[Date]	$200.00
[Date]	$250.00
[Date]	$100.00

Template 8-1. Coaching Contract Checklist

Purpose: A handy checklist to make sure you have the key elements of a contractual agreement in your client contracts.

How to use: This is an optional template to use in whole or in part. Add your own terms as needed. When you're drafting a coaching agreement, refer to this template to make sure all your bases are covered.

Contract term	Included?	If no, why not?
Your approach to coaching.		
The purpose and goals of the coaching relationship. Be specific.		
The level of support you offer as a coach.		
Expectations for coach and client (e.g., what the client should expect from the coach in terms of communications, techniques, methods, and expertise).		
Opportunities and limits of the coaching process (e.g., what your coaching can and can't do; amount of progress the client should realistically expect).		
A success disclaimer (e.g., the client is responsible for the outcomes of the coaching journey, and success will depend on how they implement the advice and guidance of the coach).		
What the client is responsible for (e.g., reminders that clients need to be accountable; they are responsible for being available, staying engaged, sharing pertinent information, and so on).		

Contract term	Included?	If no, why not?
A general disclaimer that coaching is not a replacement or substitute for therapy and that coaches will not diagnose or treat disorders.		
Scheduling and cancellation policies (e.g., clear rules for scheduling, rescheduling, and canceling sessions).		
Confidentiality of the coaching sessions and data protection (e.g., how you will store and use their personal information, and how you will protect it).		
The coaching process (e.g., where and how coaching takes place, the expected timeframe, time between sessions, communication, and support between sessions).		
Terms for ending the coaching relationship (e.g., how it will end, when it will end, and what each party is responsible for).		
Payment details (e.g., how much, how often, and how to pay).		
Refund policy (e.g., whether the coach offers refunds; if so, how and when?).		
Contact data for you and your client (e.g., phone number, email address, or physical address).		
Approval to be listed as a client on marketing materials.		

Template 9-1. Marketing Plan Worksheet

Purpose: A checklist for you to build out your marketing tactics and keep track of the deliverables for your marketing plan.

How to use: Use this template to help structure your marketing plan. Consider staging the tactics so you don't get too overwhelmed and can get the critical few things done first. Focus on the first few things and build from there.

Getting Started Thought Provokers!

As you build your marketing plan, reference the material and components in this book. Use this worksheet to begin building out the elements of your marketing plan.

Marketing Element	Description	Needed?	Done?
Executive summary	In about five simple sentences, what is your business, whom does it serve, and why is it necessary in today's market?		
Target customer	Who is going to buy your service? How are you going to reach them? What is going to compel them to engage you and your services?		
Unique selling (or value) proposition	What is unique about what you have to offer? How do you differ from others in the market?		
Pricing and positioning strategy	How will you price your offering? How does that fit in the overall landscape of your service segment? How will you position yourself within this landscape?		
Your offers	What lines of service are you offering? Will you have different packages to offer? How will you bundle your services?		
Marketing materials	What platforms or mediums will you use to promote your brand (e.g., website, LinkedIn, Instagram, TikTok, or Pinterest)?		
Promotions strategy	With what messaging will you reach your target consumer? When, how, and how often? Will you have a blog? Will you host a podcast? Do you have a network that can help you get started?		

Now take your thoughts and ideas and begin to bring them to life through your branding and marketing and communications assets. I've put this in phases so you can focus on the highest-priority items first.

Phase 1
These are the items most essential to establishing a business presence for yourself:
- Company name
- Company logo
- Color palette
- Business stationery set (e.g., templates for documents, presentations, and business card)
- LinkedIn presence
- Executive headshot
- Coaching sales sheet

That's a lot! Remember to use your network and pull in people who are highly skilled at the things you are not as strong or experienced in. You can connect with a local small business association to get referrals for graphic designers, website developers, and LinkedIn experts.

Phase 2
These are also important items but can wait a bit. They will take more time, effort, resources, and thought to complete.
- **Company website:** This will include a company overview and information about your values, who you are, what you do, programs you offer, and special promotions. Much of how you talk about your business will manifest on this website. A calendar tool is a great feature to have, so people can book consultations right from your website.
- **Expand your social media:** Consider your target customer. Where do they spend their time online? If you have a few clients already, ask them where see or encounter professional services. Ask your friends if they would respond to a promotion for executive coaching on Instagram, Facebook, Snapchat, or other platform. Start small, try target advertising, track results, and build from there.
- **Blog or podcast:** It's a crowded field, so consider carefully what you have to offer and if your target client is likely to engage your offer via a blog or podcast. Make sure this is something you can commit to and stay consistent with. Monitor your metrics and adjust based on what is resonating most with your audience.
- **Webinars:** When you have a more in-depth piece of content or mini training to share, a webinar can be a powerful lead-generation tool.
- **Email campaign:** As you build your customer database, think through an ongoing email outreach that will be meaningful and helpful to your clients. This is a way to stay connected with them and keep you (and your interesting and relevant content) top of mind!
- **Collateral:** Use your company stationery to build a few marketing pieces. Consider using the four-step model with your own brand as a professional marketing asset. Create brochures, product sheets, sales promotions, and so on.
- **Network marketing:** Remember your community. Who can help introduce you to new clients? Reach out to three people a week to build your network and get introductory meetings set with potential clients.

Phase 3: Full Marketing Plan Outline

For those of you who have an aptitude for marketing or have a strong desire to grow your skills in this space, this more full and complete marketing plan is offered as a framework for you. I have completed all of these marketing components over my career. I encourage you to start small and focused and build from there. As they say, Rome was not built in a day!

- Background
  - Company or personal brand
  - Logo
  - Value proposition
  - Specific offerings (services, events, and so on)
  - Economic drivers (macroeconomic drivers that affect your business)
  - SWOT analysis (strengths and weaknesses of your business; opportunities and threats in the competitive landscape)
- Market analysis
  - Market sizing
  - Market segmentation
  - Customer identification (including demographics)
  - Channels of distribution (how will you reach your clients?)
  - Sales process (including full sales cycle)
- Market research
  - Primary research (surveys, interviews, focus groups)
  - Secondary research (internet, associations, publications)
  - Syndicated research (analyst reports, research or consulting firms, other)
  - Competitors
  - Market share
  - Branding and positioning
  - Key marketing initiatives
  - Intelligence
- Objectives (quantify)
  - Sales (revenue, volume, margin)
  - Market share
  - Other measures (ROI, payback, break even)
- Strategies (how to achieve objectives, not specific tactics)
  - New products
  - New markets
  - Promotions
  - New programs
  - Customer initiatives
- Advertising
  - Businesses, gyms and workout studios, houses of worship
  - Yelp or another relevant review platform
  - Media (research, planning, placement, traffic)
  - Online (banners, directories, Google AdWords)
  - Broadcast (TV, radio)

- Publicity
  - Articles
  - Blogs
  - News releases
  - Press list
  - Press kit
  - Events
  - Media relations
  - Distribution (internet, wire service)
  - Word-of-mouth marketing (friends, family, community)
  - Search engine optimization and search engine marketing (talk to your web designer about this)
- Sales promotion
  - Programs
  - Training
  - Retreats
  - Contests, coupons, sweepstakes
- Collateral
  - Brochures, product sheets, flyers
  - Catalogs, manuals, instructions, installations
  - Educational pieces (whitepapers, guides, how-tos)
- Trade shows and events
  - Exhibit design
  - Booth graphics
  - Preshow promotion
  - Webinars
- Channel marketing
  - Dealer or distributor programs
  - Promotions
  - Merchandising support, POP, packaging
  - Training programs
  - Launch kits
  - MDF and co-op programs
- Direct marketing
  - Direct mail
  - Email
  - List procurement
  - Telemarketing

Template 9-2. Sample Coach Bio

Purpose: Sample coach bios for promoting your business.

How to use: Use your company stationary as inspiration to design your coach bio in your own voice and look. Use your coach bio to get new business or as a credibility builder with your clients, 360 interviewees, and sponsors.

Executive Coach

Is a leader in your organization assuming more responsibilities? Are you preparing key talent for new jobs? Perhaps your internal training programs don't hit the mark, or aren't confidential enough. Or perhaps you are looking to accelerate your own career?

Executive coaching accelerates business results by boosting the performance of key people.

Approach

Dr. Nadine's successful coaching approach is active, interactive, supportive, and goals-focused. Her substantial client list, particularly her repeat business client list, speaks for itself. Her mantra is "Together, we can do it!"

Services

- **Executive coaching**: Any level of management, including unusual or challenging cases. Excellent success with building high performers, developing high-potential individuals, preparing those with high visibility. Or helping people with behaviors.
- **Change management coaching**: Individual, project, or organizational. This includes individual preparation for new role, enterprise-wide implementation of project, or new markets or merger or acquisition.

Preparation

Dr. Nadine Greiner's success rate is 100%, and her coaching clients are able to exceed their goals at a very quick clip. Because she first served as a CEO at the age of 38, she understands leaders' experience first-hand so her clients don't have to spend time cluing her in.

Dr. Nadine is the best of the best: She coaches and trains other consultants, and teaches in master's and doctoral programs.

Nadine Greiner offers her clients the expertise that comes along with 30 years of consulting success, and a dual PhD in organization development and clinical psychology.

Personal

Dr. Nadine is fluent in French, and has multicultural experience from working internationally. She is an avid Zumba dancer and volunteer for local animal shelters.

Key Clients

Nadine Greiner, PhD
www.DrNadine.com • DrNadine@DrNadine.com • 415.861.8383

Studying With Dr. Nadine

Take your executive coaching practice to the next level.

Services

Evaluation
Dr. Nadine will conduct a thorough evaluation of your existing executive coaching practice, including your methodology, tools, business, and marketing.

Resources
You will have access to a wide range of restricted assessments only available this way to PhDs. This sets you apart from other coaches.

Access
At least twice a month you will meet with Dr. Nadine to review current challenges, answer questions, and discuss direction. She will also be available, as needed, for consultation.

Referrals
Dr. Nadine is in high demand and unable to provide coaching for every client. After working together, you will be added to her referral list.

Consultation
Rest assured, knowing that you always have Dr. Nadine to consult with about challenging cases, and blind spots.

Approach
Dr. Nadine's approach is dynamic, interactive, methodical, and solution oriented.

Preparation
To qualify, the executive coach needs:
- At least five years serving in an executive role.
- Have an education in human psychology, such as an undergraduate or graduate degree in psychology, sociology, or similar.
- Be willing to adopt the Dr. Nadine methodology, as outlined in *The Art of Executive Coaching*.

Cost
The cost is $2,000 per month, and clients can stop at any time.

Key Clients

Nadine Greiner, PhD
www.DrNadine.com • DrNadine@DrNadine.com • 415.861.8383

Human Resources and Organization Consultant

A complete portfolio of human resources and organization development products to meet the needs of executives and businesses.

Services

Human Resources
Hiring • Total rewards •
Mediation • Employee
relations • Investigations •
Workplace planning • Talent
review • Succession •
Interim CHRO (SPHR)

Organization
- DEI
- Strategic planning
- Board of directors
- M&A readiness
- Change management
- Special projects

Executive Coaching
Preparedness for future job
• New position or team
leadership development •
Performance or behavior
issues • 360 acculturation

Executive Assessments
Candidate • Individual • Leadership • Career •
Culture • M&A • VC place executives

Teams
Workshops and training • Speaking •
Culture change • Engagement • Interim CEO

Approach
Dr. Nadine's approach is dynamic, interactive, methodical, and solution oriented.

Preparation
Nadine Greiner offers her clients the expertise that comes along with 30 years of consulting success, and a dual PhD in organization development and clinical psychology. As a change agent and leader herself, Dr. Nadine has indeed walked a mile in your shoes: She served as vice president, then chief executive officer of a healthcare company at 38 years of age, which increases understanding and accelerates results.

She also coaches other consultants, and lectures in graduate and postgraduate programs.

Personal
Dr. Nadine is an avid Zumba dancer and volunteer for local animal shelters.

Key Clients

Nadine Greiner, PhD
www.DrNadine.com • DrNadine@DrNadine.com • 415.861.8383

Template 9-3. Speaker Information Brochure

Purpose: A sample marketing piece used in pitching for speaking slots at company meetings, conferences, or other venues where potential clients gather.

How to use: Create your own speaker information brochure for use in promoting your keynote speakerships. Use your company stationary as the inspiration to design in your own look and voice.

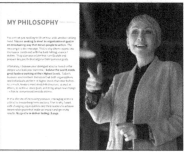

Template 9-4. Chemistry Call With Potential Client

Purpose: A sample 30-minute agenda for an introductory call with a potential client, which helps pitch your services in an engaging way.

How to use: Tailor this agenda as best you can to meet the needs of the prospective client.

Welcome and purpose of call (3 min.)	This is a short call to get to know each other. Establish this outline for the meeting: • Learn more about the client and why they are interested in exploring coaching. • Give a brief overview of the four-step coaching model (Template 1-1) and answer any questions they may have. • Provide details on process, schedule, and rates so they can make an informed decision.
Introductions (5 min.)	Have a short but compelling introduction that gives your potential client a perspective on your experience, what you'll offer them in coaching, and your "why" for coaching: *After 30 years in corporate America, I decided to pivot my career to spend more time and energy on what I really loved about my work: investing in others' growth, helping leaders be their best, and helping teams become high performing. Now, I am an executive coach, a facilitator, and an author. I'm certified in a number of assessments (including DiSC, Hogan Leadership Assessment, Driving Forces, Motivation, Enneagram, and MBTI) that help uncover superpowers and challenges for leaders, and I help people see where they can adapt their styles to be even more effective. My overarching goal is to help people experience more joy in their work and life. I have personally benefited from working with a coach off and on for more than 25 years. It was an early investment I made in myself and my capability as a leader that had a tremendously positive impact on how I live my life, engage in my marriage, and parent. I am incredibly humbled and extremely excited to be able to help others in a similar way.*
Questions about the potential client (12 min.)	• What brings you to exploring coaching for yourself? • Tell me a little bit about your background (work, life, and hobbies). • What would success look like for you after a six-month program? • What are you looking for in a coach?

Introduce the coaching process (5 min.)	• Share a high-level overview:
	  ○ Intake session, plus 10 coaching sessions, plus a closing session for a total of 12 meetings
	  ○ six-month period
	  ○ Micropractices and exercises assigned between meetings
	• Mention any current specials, referral discounts, or other pricing incentives.
	• Ask: "Do you have any questions at this point?"

Next steps (5 min.)	• Send the following materials:
	  ○ Overview of the four-step coaching model (Template 1-1)
	  ○ A contract (including any payment details you discussed)
	• Review and make a commitment for a decision timeframe (within a week).
	• Ask: "Any final questions?"

Template 9-5. Chemistry Call Follow-Up Email

Purpose: A recommended follow-up from your introductory call with a potential client.

How to use: This is an optional email template to use in whole or in part. Adapt it to your client's culture and work style. Put it in your own words and brand it to your business. Follow up the chemistry call with a personalized email to your prospective client.

Subject: Follow-Up From Our Intro Meeting

Hi *<client>*,

Thank you so much for our recent discovery call. I truly enjoyed learning more about you and your business, as well as your plans for the future.

As you mentioned, your biggest frustration comes from *<the reason your potential client isn't succeeding>*, and I think together we can tackle this and any other issues you're having.

I have extensive experience with other clients just like you who have faced similar blocks. I've successfully helped many people grow their businesses and you can read about some of their experiences here: *<URL for testimonials page>*

My *<name of coaching package>* is the most popular choice for new clients, and it's where I recommend we start. If you have any questions, let me know. If you're ready to get started, you can register at this link: *<URL>*

Thank you again for your time. I look forward to working with you to help grow your business.

Warmly,
<Your name>

Template 9-6. How to Select the Right Executive Coach for You

Purpose: A fillable form that helps a future client consider what is important to them in a coach.

How to use: This is an optional form to use in whole or in part. Put it in your own words and brand it to your business. Give this to prospective clients to help them build confidence in their choice to hire you as a coach.

The process of selecting the right executive coach can be daunting. Coaches run the full spectrum in terms of their qualifications, credentials, experience, skills, and areas of expertise. So here is a quick assessment to help guide your selection process.

Use a five-point scale to rate each factor in the table below according to how important it is to you. (0 = *not important and* 5 = *very important*)

Factors	Rating (0–5)	Notes
Coaching credentials and education		
Coach's own leadership experience		
Coach's values and culture		
Coach's reviews on LinkedIn, Yelp, etc.		
Reference checks		
Coach was reachable		
Coach answered my questions		
Coach asked me good questions		
I felt comfortable		
Coach has social media		
Coach has articles or a book		
Coach was recommended by a friend or colleague		
Total		

Scoring
- **0–36 points:** This coach may be inexperienced and may not be beneficial to you and your business. The coach might be uncertain about what you and your business need, and may struggle to move you along on the path of change and growth. I recommend looking for another coach.
- **37–48 points:** This coach may have an understanding of what you are looking for and what your business lacks as of now. They may not be well known, but likely have the skills and experience to help you in the short term. After a while, you will probably want a higher-level executive coach. I recommend continuing your search to find the very best executive coach you can find. You and your business deserve it. However, if you cannot find the perfect match, this coach might do for now.
- **49–60 points:** This coach knows exactly what you want and need. This coach is probably the best in their field, is known, and has proven results. They have a solid understanding of your immediate needs and how to meet them. They also set the stage for long-term, sustainable results. This executive coach will quickly identify blind spots and make an immediate impact, while preparing you and your business to meet your full potential!

Step 1: Evaluate Credentials

Prior to engaging an executive coach, many people look for credentials. However, don't merely look for coaches who are "certified" as some of these organizations can be marketing schemes, and many don't even require a high school degree (and besides who certifies them?). Instead, try looking for certifications that are tied to colleges and universities. And as another marker of continued preparation, look for specific licenses, certifications, and other credentials. I, for example, am certified in Myers-Briggs (MBTI), 16PF, CPI, FIRO-B, TKI, Strong Interest Inventory, and the Culture Accelerator.

Credentials, however, don't reveal the full picture. Ideally, coaches have "walked the walk" and have held executive leadership positions. According to research by *Harvard Business Review*, most executive coaches believe that prior experience in a role similar to that assumed by their coachees is a very important factor in the selection process. Executive coaches with prior industry experience tend to be more business savvy, and more effectively and quickly understand the organizational politics and dynamics at play. Finally, research shows that executive coaches should have extensive preparation in psychology or psychiatry. According to studies conducted by the University of Sydney, between 25 and 50 percent of those seeking executive coaching exhibit clinically significant levels of anxiety, stress, or depression. Executive coaches must be able to tackle and address these issues.

Step 2: Ensure Alignment of Values and Culture

It's dangerous to engage an executive coach on the sole bases of reputation and experience. Executive coaching is a partnership that lasts an average of four to six months. It's essential for executive coaches to take the time to understand your organizational culture, values, and mission. You and your employees will only fully embrace executive coaching if strong mutual understanding and cultural alignment exist. If a coach is distracted or more focused on selling additional services as opposed to investing time to understand you and your organization, this should raise a red flag.

Step 3: Conduct Reference Checks

Before signing on the dotted line, it's critical to do reference checks. Research by the Center for Creative Leadership found that 50 percent of executive coaches believe quality personal references are very important factors in their clients' executive coaching selection process. Ideally, executive coaches have worked with similar firms or industries. The research revealed that the most important factor underlying the executive coaching selection process was experiencing coaching in similar settings. To be fully successful, executive coaches must be aware of the intricacies associated with different types of companies. A professional services firm operates very differently than a biotechnology firm, for example, and faces different recruiting challenges, competitive dynamics, and regulatory requirements.

A few years ago, I was impressed by a potential coaching client who asked me the following questions to ascertain if we would be a good fit:

- What types of clients do you typically work with?
- What type of training and certification do you have?
- Do you have credentials in psychology?
- Do you have relevant business expertise?
- How will you help me achieve my goals?
- How do you measure progress and success?
- What makes for a successful coaching relationship?
- How are you the same or different than other executive coaches?
- Can I speak with some of your past clients?

By doing your due diligence and homework, you'll be able to benefit from an executive coaching process that will enrich you, your career, and your life.

Template 9-7. Using Email to Engage Former Clients

Purpose: An example of an email you could send to a former client on your email list. You can use these emails to share articles with easy-to-digest tidbits relevant to an executive's development. This also helps keep your partnership productive, even though your engagement is formally over.

How to use: This is an optional tactic to use in whole or in part. Put it in your own words and brand it to your business. You could automate the email with a mail service and develop a whole campaign of emails that keeps the thread of development going long after the contract period is over.

Subject: Three Fail-Safe Ways to Beat Feeling Overwhelmed at Work

As an executive, you're swimming (drowning, perhaps) in distractions and information overload. It's a steep uphill battle to regain focus after you've been subjected to distractions or other sources of overload. According to research, it takes an average of 23 minutes and 15 seconds to get back to the task you were attending to prior to an unruly disruption. As an executive, your success hinges on your ability to quell distractions and manage overload.

1. Check Email in Batches

Email is one of the most potent sources of information overload in the workplace. Research by McKinsey found that 28 percent of a person's workday is consumed by checking email. One of the most effective means of minimizing email overload is to check your email in chunks several times a day. A University of British Columbia study found that individuals who limit their email checking to 3 times per day are able to reduce stress levels and distractions by 47 percent. Chances are high that you're inundated with a flood of emails each day. Resist the temptation to read and/or respond to each message as it strikes your inbox. Your levels of productivity are likely to profit.

2. Consider Walks and Walking Meetings

Most of us spend the majority of our workdays tethered to our desks. The lackluster environment causes us to be more susceptible to distractions and other sources of overload. Switching up your environment by going on a walk or walking meeting can prove very effective in helping you combat overload. Walking meetings have the added benefit of enhancing your relationships with co-workers. The fact that you are walking side-by-side means the conversation is more peer-to-peer than when you are in your office and they are across a desk, which reinforces the organizational hierarchy.

3. Schedule Office Hours

Another harmful source of overwhelm manifests in the form of impromptu meetings. If your day is riddled with people walking over to meet with you at their convenience . . . get the friendly word out that you're setting up designated office hours for walk-ins. Daniel Goleman, author of the *New York Times* bestseller *Emotional Intelligence*, once stated, "One way to boost our willpower and focus is to manage our distractions instead of letting them manage us." Try to manage your distractions. Try to take control of overload in the workplace. When workplace distractions are reduced, workers are more productive, more motivated, and happier. As Tim Cook once said, "You can focus on things that are barriers or you can focus on scaling the wall."

Template 10-1. My Entrepreneurial Development Plan

Purpose: A handy template for creating an annual entrepreneurial development plan. It's important to continue to invest in yourself and your capabilities, both in the coaching practice and as an entrepreneur.

How to use: This is an optional template to use in whole or in part. Add your own sections as needed. Choose your favorite suggestions from this book (and add your own) and make a development plan for yourself. It may work better for you to focus more near term at the beginning, so adjust this to a quarterly plan with monthly goals.

My Development Plan

My goal for development is:
(What does success look like at the end of this annual plan?)

_____

_____

_____

Date of plan creation: _____

When will I review my results? *(at least quarterly)* _____

Capabilities to Develop	Q1	Q2	Q3	Q4
Growing my coaching capabilities				
Strengthening my entrepreneurial skills				
Broadening my industry or business knowledge				

Template 10-2. Wellness Self-Assessment Worksheet

Purpose: A summary of the self-assessments offered in chapter 10. Use this tool for ongoing evaluation and consideration of your well-being related to the five areas outlined in the book.

How to use: Add your own sections to this self-assessment as needed. Follow the instructions to score your wellness in each category.

Wellness Self-Assessments

Complete these self-assessments to get a sense of where you are experiencing the most stress in your day-to-day life. Then, mark your totals in the space provided in Template 10-3.

Cognitive Wellness	Yes or No
Do you forget meetings or other important commitments at work?	
Are you easily upset about work during your weekends?	
Is it hard for you to forget about working during your time off?	
Do you struggle to track projects?	
Yes Total	

Emotional Wellness	Yes or No
It's difficult for me to recognize my emotions.	
People say I act before I think.	
When I'm mad, people around me know it.	
When I'm frustrated, I don't know how to calm myself down.	
Yes Total	

Interpersonal Wellness	Yes or No
I only have one or two important relationships in my work and life.	
When I'm busy, people around me know not to bother me.	
I can go weeks or months without talking to my close friends.	
I have experienced broken friendships because of my busy life.	
Yes Total	

Physical Wellness	Yes or No
I regularly enjoy physical exercise that gets my heart beating.	
I eat a healthy diet that is balanced in nutrients and vitamins.	
I sleep at least seven hours, uninterrupted, every night.	
I drink enough water for my weight, physique, and geography.	
No Total	

Spiritual Wellness	Yes or No
I believe that miracles happen.	
Being in nature gives me joy and a sense of the bigness of our world.	
I practice meditation, mindfulness, or prayer daily.	
I would enjoy a silent retreat.	
Yes Total	

Template 10-3. Stress Status Worksheet

Purpose: Visually represent your wellness related to the five areas outlined in the book. Use the action plan to help you practice your way into healthier behavior.

How to use: Use the results of your self-assessments to complete this action plan.

Transfer your scores from Template 10-2 into the chart below. Then color in the corresponding segments in the stress status wheel. For example, if you scored a 4 in the emotional domain, you would completely color in segments 1, 2, 3, and 4.

	Score
Cognitive Wellness	
Emotional Wellness	
Interpersonal Wellness	
Physical Wellness	
Spiritual Wellness	

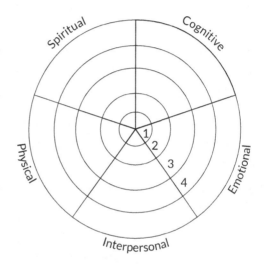

My Stress Status Summary

1. I completed the wellness self-assessment on:

2. According to this assessment, I am experiencing the most stress in these areas:
    - ☐ Cognitive
    - ☐ Emotional
    - ☐ Interpersonal
    - ☐ Physical
    - ☐ Spiritual

3. I will practice the following two actions step in these areas:

    _____

    _____

4. I will take action on these exercises by doing the following: *(Be specific about the date, time, duration, and other details that are helpful in following through with these action items.)*

    _____

    _____

5. Who can be an accountability partner for me in these practices? Whom can I share this with and ask for support in checking in with me on how my practices are going? Can someone give me feedback?

    _____

    _____

References

Caramela, S. 2023. "Startup Costs: How Much Cash Will You Need?" Business News Daily, March. www.businessnewsdaily.com/5-small-business-start-up-costs-options.html.

Cherry, K. 2022. "Erikson's Stages of Development: A Closer Look at the Eight Psychosocial Stages." VeryWellMind, August. www.verywellmind.com/erik-eriksons-stages-of -psychosocial-development-2795740.

Ciampa, D. 2017. "The More Senior Your Job Title, the More You Need to Keep a Journal." *Harvard Business Review*, July. hbr.org/2017/07/the-more-senior-your-job-title-the -more-you-need-to-keep-a-journal.

Clutterbuck, D., and S. Schneider. 1998. "Executive Mentoring." *Croner's Executive Companion Bulletin*, October.

DeAngelis, T. 2019. "Better Relationships With Patients Lead to Better Outcomes." American Psychological Association CE Corner, November 1. www.apa.org/monitor /2019/11/ce-corner-relationships.

Development Dimensions Inc. (DDI). 2023. *Global Leadership Forecast 2023*. ddiworld.com/glf.

Emmons, R.A., and M.E. McCullough. 2003. "Counting Blessings Versus Burdens: An Experimental Investigation of Gratitude and Subjective Well-Being in Daily Life." *Journal of Personality and Social Psychology* 84(2): 377–89. greatergood.berkeley.edu /pdfs/GratitudePDFs/6Emmons-BlessingsBurdens.pdf.

Eurich, T. 2018. *Insight: The Surprising Truth About How Others See Us, How We See Ourselves, and Why the Answers Matter More Than We Think.* New York: Currency.

Goldsmith, M. 2022. "Meet Marshall." marshallgoldsmith.com/meet-marshall.

International Coaching Federation (ICF). 2020. *2020 ICF Global Coaching Study: Executive Summary.* coachingfederation.org/app/uploads/2020/09/FINAL_ICF_GCS2020 _ExecutiveSummary.pdf.

Hudson, F. 2016. "A Primer on Coaching." Institute for Professional Excellence in Coaching (iPEC) blog, December 22. Ipeccoaching.com/blog/a-primer-on-coaching/1482443175219 -29c587c8-ce2c.

iPEC Coaching. n.d. "What Is Coaching?" www.ipeccoaching.com/hubfs/What%20is%20 Coaching%20-%20iPEC%20Coach%20Training.pdf.

Korn Ferry. 2015. "Korn Ferry Study Identifies Leadership Challenges Being Coached Most Often." www.kornferry.com/about-us//press/korn-ferry-study-identifies-leadership -challenges-being-coached-most-often.

Lombardo, M.M. 2014. *FYI: For Your Improvement.* Edited by H. Barnfield. New York: Korn Ferry.

Luft, J. 1961. "The Johari Window: A Graphic Model of Awareness in Interpersonal Relations." *Human Relations* 5:6–7. static1.1.sqspcdn.com/static/f/1124858/28387950 /1617395004320/THE+JOHARI+WINDOW.pdf.

McSpadden, K. 2015. "You Now Have a Shorter Attention Span Than a Goldfish." *Time,* May 14. time.com/3858309/attention-spans-goldfish.

Norcross, J.C., B.E. Zimmerman, R.P. Greenberg, and J.K. Swift. 2017. "Do All Therapists Do That When Saying Goodbye? A Study of Commonalities in Termination Behaviors." *Psychotherapy* 54(1): 66–75. doi.org/10.1037/pst0000097.

Positive Psychology Center. n.d. "PERMA™ Theory of Well-Being and PERMA™ Workshops." Penn Arts & Sciences. ppc.sas.upenn.edu/learn-more/perma-theory-well-being-and -perma-workshops.

Rashid, T. 2015. "Positive Psychotherapy: A Strength-Based Approach." *Journal of Positive Psychology* 10(1): 25–40.

Seligman, M.E.P., T.A. Steen, N. Park, and C. Peterson. 2005. "Positive Psychology Progress: Empirical Validation of Interventions." *American Psychologist* 60:410–421. 10.1037/0003-066X.60.5.410.

Seppälä, E. 2016. "The Surprising Health Benefits of Spirituality." *Psychology Today,* August. www.psychologytoday.com/us/blog/feeling-it/201608/the-surprising -health-benefits-spirituality.

Sinek, S. 2009. "Start With Why—How Great Leaders Inspire Actions." TEDx Talk, September 28. www.youtube.com/watch?v=u4ZoJKF_VuA.

Skinner, E., and M.J. Zimmer-Gembeck. 2007. "The Development of Coping." *Annual Review of Psychology* 58(1): 119–144.

Training Industry. n.d. "The 70-20-10 Model for Learning and Development." trainingindustry.com/wiki/content-development/the-702010-model-for -learning-and-development.

Wood, A.M., P.A. Linley, J. Maltby, and T.B. Kashdan. 2010. "Using Personal and Psychological Strengths Leads to Increases in Well-Being Over Time: A Longitudinal Study and the Development of the Strengths Use Questionnaire." *Personality and Individual Differences* 50(1).

Index

Page numbers followed by *f* and *t* refer to figures and tables, respectively.

About the Authors

Nadine Greiner, PhD, is an executive coach with a dual doctorate in organization development and clinical psychology. She has helped more than 1,000 executives and coaches become more effective and fulfilled at work, which has positively rippled out to thousands of their colleagues and transformed their businesses. Recognized for her immense success rate, Nadine has more than 30 years of experience in the field of executive coaching in San Francisco and globally.

In addition to her advanced academic preparation, Nadine has held several high-level positions in privately held and publicly traded companies and served as CEO at the age of 38. This unique combination of psychology, business, and executive leadership makes her a unique and effective coach who produces excellent results for her clients. Nadine speaks and lectures in postgraduate programs globally.

On a personal note, Nadine is dedicated to animal welfare and has fostered, rehabilitated, and trained thousands of cats and dogs. Twenty percent of all her profits go to animals. Nadine stays fit by running after them and by joining the dance party with her friends at Zumba.

All of Nadine's proceeds from this book, and from her previous two books, go to the protection and love of animals.

Becky Davis, MA, is an executive coach, a team facilitator, and a leadership trainer. She has held senior positions in human resources and marketing over her 30-year career, operating at the executive level for market-leading technology and healthcare companies. Her company, Insight Leadership, works with leaders and their teams to achieve excellence individually and in their shared work.

Becky has a master's in business administration with an emphasis in management and organization development and an undergraduate degree in organizational and leadership communications. She is a certified senior professional career coach and integral coach. She is also certified in the Hogan Leadership, DiSC, Myers-Briggs, and Enneagram assessments.

With insight and global experience from more than 30 years in leadership roles, Becky consults on team effectiveness, talent management, organizational change, and strategy. She coaches executives and senior leaders, partnering to explore new possibilities to create more of the outcomes they desire, personally and professionally. She has a long history of leading through kindness and compassion, investing personally in others, and creating community.

To support the greater Sacramento community, Becky will donate proceeds from the sale of this book to nonprofits addressing food and housing insecurity, two issues Becky is personally passionate about improving.

About ATD

The Association for Talent Development (ATD) is the world's largest association dedicated to those who develop talent in organizations. Serving a global community of members, customers, and international business partners in more than 100 countries, ATD champions the importance of learning and training by setting standards for the talent development profession.

Our customers and members work in public and private organizations in every industry sector. Since ATD was founded in 1943, the talent development field has expanded significantly to meet the needs of global businesses and emerging industries. Through the Talent Development Capability Model, education courses, certifications and credentials, memberships, industry-leading events, research, and publications, we help talent development professionals build their personal, professional, and organizational capabilities to meet new business demands with maximum impact and effectiveness.

One of the cornerstones of ATD's intellectual foundation, ATD Press offers insightful and practical information on talent development, training, and professional growth. ATD Press publications are written by industry thought leaders and offer anyone who works with adult learners the best practices, academic theory, and guidance necessary to move the profession forward.

We invite you to join our community. Learn more at **TD.org**